Economic Analysis of International Law

Economic Analysis of International Law

Edited by

Eugene Kontorovich

Professor of Law, Northwestern Pritzker Law School, USA

Francesco Parisi

Oppenheimer Wolff and Donnelly Professor of Law, University of Minnesota Law School, USA and Professor of Economics, University of Bologna, Italy

Edward Elgar PUBLISHING

Cheltenham, UK • Northampton, MA, USA

Published by
Edward Elgar Publishing Limited
The Lypiatts
15 Lansdown Road
Cheltenham
Glos GL50 2JA
UK

Edward Elgar Publishing, Inc.
William Pratt House
9 Dewey Court
Northampton
Massachusetts 01060
USA

A catalogue record for this book
is available from the British Library

Library of Congress Control Number: 2016932476

This book is available electronically in the **Elgar**online
Law subject collection
DOI 10.4337/9780857930163

MIX
Paper from responsible sources
FSC® C013056
FSC www.fsc.org

ISBN 978 0 85793 015 6 (cased)
ISBN 978 0 85793 016 3 (eBook)

Typeset by Columns Design XML Ltd, Reading
Printed and bound in Great Britain by TJ International Ltd, Padstow

Contents

PART IV APPLICATIONS AND EXTENSIONS

Contributors

Anne van Aaken is Full Professor for Law and Economics, Legal Theory, Public International Law and European Law, University of St. Gallen (Switzerland)

Abraham Bell is Professor, Bar-Ian University Faculty of Law (Israel), and University of San Diego Law School (United States of America)

Tomer Broude is Vice-Dean, Sylvan M. Cohen Chair in Law, Faculty of Law and Department of International Relations, Hebrew University of Jerusalem (Israel)

Bridget L. Coggins is Assistant Professor, Political Science, University of California, Santa Barbara (United States of America). Her chapter was written with Ishita Kala, B.A., Dartmouth College, 2013

Tom Ginsburg is Deputy Dean, Leo Spitz Professor of International Law, Ludwig and Hilde Wolf Research Scholar, and Professor of Political Science, University of Chicago (United States of America)

Andrew T. Guzman is Dean and Carl Mason Franklin Chair in Law, and Professor of Law and Political Science, University of Southern California (United States of America)

Ishita Kala is a third year J.D. candidate at Harvard Law School studying international law and development (United States of America)

Eugene Kontorovich is Professor of Law at Northwestern University Pritzker School of Law

Timothy Meyer is Professor of Law and Enterprise Scholar, Vanderbilt University Law School (United States of America)

James D. Morrow is A.F.K. Organski Collegiate Professor of World Politics, University of Michigan (United States of America)

Francesco Parisi is Oppenheimer Wolff and Donnelly Professor of Law, University of Minnesota Law School (United States of America) and Professor of Economics, University of Bologna (Italy)

Daniel Pi is Erasmus Mundus Fellow, European Doctorate in Law and Economics Program, University of Bologna (Italy)

Enrico Spolaore is Professor of Economics at Tufts, Research Associate at National Bureau of Economic Research (United States of America)

Paul B. Stephan is John C. Jeffries, Jr., Distinguished Professor of Law and Director Graduate Studies Program, University of Virginia School of Law (United States of America)

Introduction

Eugene Kontorovich and Francesco Parisi*

The contributions to this volume provide a birds-eye view on some fundamental elements of international law from the perspective of economics. International law lagged behind compared to other areas of law in benefiting from the influence of economic analysis of law. As Parisi and Pi (Chapter 4) point out, one possible explanation for the delayed attention of law and economics scholars to international law is given by the fact that international law was perceived to be governed by informal rules and enforcement mechanisms that resisted formal economic analysis. This volume will hopefully reveal that, contrary to this perception, economics can also successfully illuminate the understanding of informal mechanisms such as those of international law. In this vein, this volume aims at providing a pathfinder through the recent literature and, in pushing the economic understanding of international law, identifying new areas and issues for research in international law and economics.

This volume is organized into four main parts, beginning with the building blocks of the nation state, and continuing with the sources and the enforcement of international law, and various applications and extensions. What follows is a brief review and presentation of these contributions.

I. BUILDING BLOCKS

The chapters contained in Part I of this volume review some approaches to international treaty law from an economic perspective, focusing on the 'building blocks' of international order and exploring how and why, from an economic perspective, states form, determine their boundaries and collapse.

* The authors would like to acknowledge the valuable contribution of Bill Coberly in drafting this Introduction.

First, Enrico Spolaore lays out the relationship between economies of scale and heterogeneity costs derived from heterogeneous preferences for public policy, which are themselves derived from ethnic, religious, socio-linguistic or other cultural differences of different populations, which are more likely to be subsumed into a polity as the polity increases in size. Spolaore examines border creation through four approaches: pure efficient border-creation, border-creation via democratic process, border-creation as a byproduct of a world of rent-seeking leviathans, and border-creation as a result of war/conflict. He ends his contribution with formal explications of these.

In Chapter 2, Bridget L. Coggins and Ishita Kala advance the value of a 'rational choice' approach to questions of the creation and dissolution of polities. They prefer the less-popular 'constitutive' theory of state-recognition to the 'declaratory' theory. They then move to examine what incentives motivate the recognition of new states and the 'posthumous' recognition of failed states, focusing particularly on Kosovo and Somalia.

In Chapter 3, Abraham Bell examines the role of economic analyses in questions of territorial sovereignty. He repeatedly analogizes sovereignty issues to questions of property law, and explains how economic analyses in property law may be helpful to sovereignty questions. Nevertheless, he clearly states that sovereignty is a fundamentally different question from property, and thus proposes a continuum of property/sovereignty, starting with questions of pure private property on one end, moving through state-owned property, and then examining questions of pure sovereignty at the other end.

II. SOURCES OF INTERNATIONAL LAW

The contributions in Part II of this volume consider the sources of international law, providing an explanation and an economic analysis of the mechanisms through which international actors create international legal rules and obligations, namely treaties, customary rules and other accords that lack formal authority, often referred to as soft law.

The focus on sources of law is fully warranted in international law. From a theoretical point of view, international legal rules are unique and difficult to analogize to conventional sources of law in national legal systems. A critical feature of international legal rules is their consensual nature. The formation of both treaty law and customary law is governed by principles of consent. Unlike conventional sources of law, such as legislation or judge-made law that bind all subjects, whether or not they agreed to the creation of the rule in question, treaty law and customary law are binding only on states that either affirmatively (by entering a treaty agreement) or implicitly (by not opposing an emerging custom) agreed to be bound by it.

Treaties are agreements between states and/or international organizations. In Chapter 4, Francesco Parisi and Daniel Pi further develop Goldsmith and Posner's (2003) explanation of international agreements with reference to rational self-interest rather than vague, quasi-moral universal norms. They examine incentives to either form or accede to treaties as opposed to other agreements (primarily as a form of signaling, since, without an international enforcement authority, treaties may not be terribly 'binding' in a traditional sense). They further examine game-theoretical concerns regarding who will attempt to form or accede to a treaty, and how to manage high-cost/low-benefit scenarios, particularly in cases where mutual reservations are possible. Finally, they analyze the evolution of treaty law over time, giving particular attention to issues of ratification and fragmentation.

In Chapter 5, Andrew Guzman and Timothy Meyer examine states' incentives to invest in 'soft law', that is, international accords which lack binding authority. After clarifying some of the confusion surrounding the definition of the term, Guzman and Meyer move to a discussion of the role of soft law in the international legal order. States may be incentivized to use soft law over 'hard' law because it is generally less costly to develop soft law and also less costly to violate it or change it. Further, it is a helpful way to maintain flexibility in the face of uncertainty, and is also helpful as a way to solve coordination games. It may also be a way to handle domestic political complexity surrounding international agreements – a soft law choice may be a helpful compromise between two domestic parties, one of which wants hard law, the other of which wants no law at all. In the case of countries like the United States, where hard law requires the involvement of the legislature, the executive branch may choose to invest in soft law so as to avoid entangling the legislature. Finally, they analyze the incentives for states to create soft law through intergovernmental institutions, which can create a form of 'international common law' by applying non-binding gloss to existing hard law requirements. Guzman and Meyer argue that states will deploy this international common law as a way of sending costly (and therefore sincere) signals to each other about what they believe to be required by the hard law.

In Chapter 6, Parisi and Pi examine the emergence and evolution of international customary law. Legal theorists define customary law as a practice that emerges prior to the recognition of binding legal obligations and constraints. The process of formation of customary law is quite unique and different from the process of formation of the other sources of domestic law. The legal system eventually adopts and enforces practices that international actors have followed outside of legal constraints, out of a sense of obligation. The process of custom formation has been described by Parisi and Fon (2008) as a form of 'direct legislation through action'. The resulting rules emerge gradually through the spontaneous and voluntary adherence of the international community rather than through political deliberation or adjudication. Parisi and Pi summarize the 'traditional' account of customary law, examine Goldsmith and Posner's contributions to the topic, and then provide a formal model of incentives in customary international law. Traditionally, customary practice is distinguished from mere habitual or coincidental practice by '*opinio juris*', an intention to be bound by the customary law. Goldsmith and Posner, however, developed a game theoretic model which suggests that parties accept customary law less out of a belief that it is binding and more for reasons of rational self-interest. Parisi and Pi provide formal models explicating Goldsmith and Posner's theory, examining the emergence, evolution and exceptions to customary law from the perspective of incentives. They finally conclude that, with the exception of coordination games, customary law may be less likely to generate efficient rules than treaty law due to the various ways in which parties' heterogeneous incentives impede the formation of efficient customary law.

III. ENFORCEMENT OF INTERNATIONAL LAW

Legal scholars have often identified enforcement as the most puzzling and intellectually challenging characteristic of international law: what binds states to fulfill obligations undertaken toward other sovereign states or toward the international community at large is very much unlike the set of remedies that render obligations enforceable in a domestic legal system. Yet the absence of typical enforcement mechanisms is no impediment to the functioning of international law. Explanations of this characteristic abound. Scholars have argued that the absence of compensatory or injunctive remedies for unfulfilled international legal obligations is replaced by normative and moral factors that create incentives and constraints that differ in nature from those created by formal legal remedies. In the literature, Goldsmith and Posner (2003) have further argued that international agreements are closer to letters of intent than to proper contracts. This led to theories explaining the workings of international law in terms of cooperation, coordination, and signaling. Law and economics scholarship unsurprisingly starts from the assumption that international actors undertake choices motivated by self-interest, and that obligations undertaken in international law should be viewed as instruments for the pursuit of those interests.

The contributions collected in Part III of this volume address the issue of enforcement, explaining how states are incentivized to enforce international law against one another and how international law and international courts interact with domestic institutions. In Chapter 7, Paul B. Stephan examines recent scholarly treatment of several questions related to the enforcement of treaties. He finds it important to distinguish between actions taken to pursue a state's interest versus those taken to enforce legal entitlements derived from treaties, emphasizing the reputational methods of treaty enforcement, although these reputational sanctions are not unique to treaties. He finds both benefits and problems associated with 'preference for cooperation' theory when applied to states with regard to treaties. He analogizes to 'non-contractable terms' to evaluate why states might prefer informal enforcement of treaties, while asking for further research about whether treaties, by formalizing obligations, allow 'informal' enforcement to be more effective. He is hesitant to draw a sharp line between treaties and soft law. He further analyzes the nature of third party dispute resolution under treaties, pointing out that while some tribunals have sanctioning authority, others do not. Finally, after talking about differences in domestic enforcement of treaty provisions, he theorizes about the effects of varying levels of enforcement on domestic welfare. The nature of regional jurisdiction for such things may disincentivize parties to do business in states that heavily enforce these treaty obligations.

In Chapter 8, Tom Ginsburg focuses on economic analysis of the interaction between domestic and international law, treating states not as unitary actors, but rather considering both the international and domestic legal levels in the same framework. He begins by modeling the interaction between domestic and international law as a series of 'nested jurisdictions', which vary in terms of scope and depth. Power is allocated amongst these nested jurisdictions in order to produce public goods, resolve commitment problems, and reduce agency costs. He then explores several characterizations of this interplay, primarily examining the adoption of international law as a substitution for domestic legal change, as a complement to domestic systems, and as duplicative signal-sending. Finally, he examines the ways in which the availability of international devices affects the internal balance of power within a state's constitutional system. For instance, the ability of many executive branches to bind states to international agreements without the agreement of the other branches shifts the balance of power in the executive's favor.

IV. APPLICATIONS AND EXTENSIONS

Part IV focuses on applications and extensions, examining how theories in law and economics can lead us to a better understanding of the use of atrocities and war, and how behavioral economics may serve as a more helpful model for international law than pure rational choice theory.

In Chapter 9, James D. Morrow seeks to analyze when and why warring states and militaries engage in 'atrocities', that is, acts which violate international agreements, and further analyzes how developments in international law can influence parties away from such atrocities. He begins with an analysis of inter-state wars, first looking at a series of non-legal explanations for why states do or do not turn to atrocities. He suggests that ratification of treaties serves signaling and screening functions, and clearly delineates what sorts of conduct will constitute a 'violation' of international law. He then analyzes how and why democracies kill enemy civilians, which several studies suggest they are more willing to do than autocratic regimes, though they attempt to hide this behavior from their own citizens via rhetorical means, and while offering at least a flimsy legal justification.

Morrow then moves to a discussion of civil wars, which tend to be much less regular than inter-state wars and thus often feature proportionally more atrocities, particularly 'mass killings' perpetrated by the government against rebel-allied civilians. After thoroughly explaining the characteristics of both guerrilla and 'conventional' civil wars, Morrow examines why atrocities take place and who is most likely to commit them, focusing in particular on the 'war for information' in guerrilla civil wars. The evidence seems to suggest that a more 'restrained' (that is, less violent to civilians) approach to guerrilla war is generally (though not always) more effective. Morrow concludes by suggesting that although international treaties do not play much of a role in conduct in civil wars, a state's willingness to adopt the Rome Statute serves as a commitment device to reduce the likelihood of a civil war continuing or starting in the first place.

Finally, in Chapter 10, Anne van Aaken and Tomer Broude focus on the use of behavioral economics in the study of international law. Although most law and economics approaches to international law have centered around rational choice theory, van Aaken and Broude propose that the tools of behavioral economics can add much to the discussion. Rational-choice-based understandings of international law assume that collective actors such as states maximize their utility from a stable set of preferences and accumulate an optimal amount of information. van

Aaken and Broude instead propose a form of behavioral economics which includes lessons learned in cognitive psychology, and which suggests individual humans (and thus collective actors) have 'bounded' rationality, subject to various biases and heuristics. After briefly pointing out the frequent use of rational choice theory in international relations scholarship, they move to a discussion of various challenges and methodologies for the application of behavioral economics. They first suggest that states are probably even less perfectly rational than individuals, thereby making behavioral economics even more appropriate. Second, they suggest that although there are difficulties inherent in behavioral study of international action, this is just as true of any other empirical theory. Finally, they move through an analysis of treaty design using behavioralist terms, explaining why states may be hesitant to embrace new treaties even if the new treaty would be fully within their rational self-interest.

REFERENCES

Goldsmith, Jack L. and Eric A. Posner, 'International Agreements: A Rational Approach', 44 *Virginia Journal of International Law* 113–41 (2003).

Parisi, Franceso and Vincy Fon, *The Economics of Lawmaking* (Oxford: Oxford University Press, 2008).

PART I

The Building Blocks of International Order

1. The economics of political borders

Enrico Spolaore

1. INTRODUCTION

What determines the formation and breakup of sovereign states? This question has been at the center of historical, philosophical and political analyses for centuries.[1] In recent decades, a dramatic increase in the number of independent states and the spreading of separatism have renewed interest in the redrawing of borders. The United Nations now count 193 members, up from 51 in 1946. Since 1990, over twenty new states have become independent following the breakups of the Soviet Union, Czechoslovakia, and Yugoslavia, and separations from Ethiopia (Eritrea), South Africa (Namibia), Indonesia (Timor Leste), and Sudan (South Sudan). Vocal demands for autonomy or independence have spread all over the world, from the Basque Countries and Catalonia to Quebec, from Ireland and Scotland to Belgium, Corsica and Italy, and from the Middle East to Kashmir, Thailand, and Indonesia. According to Gurr's (2000) *Minorities at Risk* dataset, secessionist movements were present in at least 52 countries. These events have motivated a growing literature on political borders. Students of these issues include not only historians and political scientists but also, more recently, economists.

The new economic literature on political integration and disintegration has provided analyses where the borders of national states are not taken as given (exogenous), but are the endogenous outcomes of decisions by agents who interact with each other while pursuing their goals under constraints.[2] In other words, these studies recognize that borders are not a fixed, given feature of the geographical landscape, but human-made institutions, affected by decisions and interactions of individuals and

---

[1] For instance, see Dahl and Tufte (1973); Anderson (1983); Gellner (1983); and Tilly (1975; 1990) among many others.

[2] In economic analysis it is common to distinguish between endogenous variables, determined within the model, and exogenous variables, determined outside the model.

groups, and can be analyzed as part of the growing field of political economy. In general, contemporary political economy studies the interaction between economic and political variables: how economic forces affect political processes, and how political institutions, conversely, affect economic outcomes. While the interplay between economic forces and political institutions has been at the core of political economy for a long time, the focus in more recent years has shifted towards the deeper determinants of economic outcomes and political institutions – that is, the emphasis is now on the historical and cultural roots of institutions.[3] Sovereign states continue to be the world's most powerful political institutions. The economic literature on endogenous borders, which studies the interactions of economic and non-economic (political, ethnic, cultural) variables in the formation and breakup of states, is therefore part of the broader research agenda on the deep determinants of political-economy outcomes. Contributions to the economic literature on national borders and secessions include Alesina and Spolaore (1997; 2005; 2006); Alesina, Spolaore and Wacziarg (2000); Bolton and Roland (1997); Bordignon and Brusco (2001); Ellingsen (1998); Findlay (1996); Friedman (1977); Goyal and Staal (2004); Le Breton and Weber (2003); Spolaore (2008; 2012); and Wittman (2000) among others.[4] General discussions are provided in Alesina and Spolaore (2003); Bolton, Roland and Spolaore (1996); and Spolaore (2006; 2012).

Questions addressed in economic literature on borders are: Why do countries break up? What are the costs and benefits of secessions? Do these costs and benefits depend on international openness? Are secessions efficient or inefficient from an economic perspective? Is political disintegration related to democratization? Do decentralization and federalism reduce or increase the incentives to secede? How are the number and size of nations affected by conflict and wars? These are complex questions, and economic analysis alone is no substitute for careful historical and political investigations of specific case studies and events. Rather, the economics approach to political borders is complementary to more traditional methods. Economists, by using tools and methods that are relatively simplified and abstract but also powerful and general, can

---

[3] For a recent discussion of culture and institutions by a prominent political economist see, for instance, Tabellini (2008). A general discussion of long-term historical determinants of economic and political outcomes is provided by Spolaore and Wacziarg (2013).

[4] A closely related literature focuses on the endogenous formation of supranational unions, such as the European Union. For recent discussions, see for instance Spolaore (2013; 2015).

provide novel insights on these difficult and important questions. In a way, the economic analysis of political borders is a bold application of the two steps of economics according to Ed Leamer (2012: 2), who borrowed them from Matt Miller's description of journalism: 'simplify and exaggerate.' In this chapter we review how some concepts and results from economic analysis ('simplifications' and 'exaggerations') can shed light on the formation and breakup of nations. Section 2 discusses the key trade-off between economies of scale in the provision of public goods and political costs from heterogeneity of preferences. Section 3 presents four economic perspectives on the formation of political borders: efficient borders, borders as democratic outcomes, borders in a world of rent-seeking Leviathans, and borders as outcomes of conflict and wars. Section 4 provides an analytical illustration of the basic ideas within a simplified framework.

2. ECONOMIES OF SCALE AND HETEROGENEITY COSTS

Governments supply public goods to their citizens: a legal and judicial system, general administration and policy coordination, foreign policy, defense and security, police and crime prevention, a monetary and financial system, infrastructure for communications, public health, and so on. Providing public goods comes with economies of scale: bigger is cheaper. This is because public goods, unlike private goods, are typically non-rival in consumption. This means that each citizen can benefit from them without reducing the benefits for other citizens. Even when total costs of publicly provided services increase with the size of the population, typically their average cost is still decreasing in size because of large fixed costs that must be borne independently of population's size. Therefore, public goods tend to be cheaper per person when more taxpayers pay for them. In the data, government spending as a share of gross domestic product is indeed decreasing in population: smaller countries tend to have proportionally larger governments (see Alesina and Wacziarg 1998 and Alesina and Spolaore 2003: ch 10). Significant economies of scale have also been found for public goods provided at the subnational level – for instance, Hayashi, Nishikawa and Weese (2011) find large economies of scale in the provision of local public goods by Japanese municipalities. Larger political jurisdictions can also internalize cross-regional externalities – an issue extensively studied in the literature on decentralization and fiscal federalism (for example, Oates 1999). A special role in the literature on endogenous borders has been played by national defense and security, which are historically among the most important public goods provided by governments. In principle, by taking advantage of economies of scale, larger states can provide cheaper and more effective security to their citizens. Empirically, the relation between defense spending and state size is complex for several reasons, such as the existence of international alliances and the fact that some larger states (for example, the United States) provide defense for smaller states.[5] At the same time, larger, more powerful states may obtain additional economic and political benefits from their leading position.[6] In sum, the provision of public goods – including defense and foreign policy – is associated with actual or potential benefits from a larger size.

If economies of scale were the only factor in the formation of jurisdictions, larger polities would always be more efficient than smaller ones, and overall efficiency would be maximized with one world government. However, the economic literature on borders has stressed that a larger size may come with significant costs as well as benefits. As jurisdictions become larger, administrative costs and congestion may overcome some of the scale benefits. Moreover, an expansion of national borders is likely to bring about more diversity of preferences for public policies and types of governments across different groups of citizens.

In general, societal heterogeneity is associated with both costs and benefits. Higher heterogeneity may generate direct benefits through learning, specialization, and exchange of ideas, and societies can benefit economically and culturally when people have different preferences and characteristics. For example, diversity of preferences over *private goods* can be beneficial because it may allow a better use of resources. However, diverse preferences over *public goods* are much harder to reconcile, exactly because public goods are non-rival: all citizens of a sovereign state must share that state's government, laws, and public policies, whether they like them or not. As national borders include more diverse populations – with different values, norms, habits, cultures, languages, ethnicities, religions – disagreements over the fundamental characteristics of the state (legal system, official language, foreign policy) are more likely to emerge. In a nutshell, being part of the same country implies sharing jointly supplied public goods and policies in ways that cannot always satisfy everybody's preferences. Successful

---

5 The classic reference here is Olson and Zeckhauser (1966). For a recent discussion of conflict, defense, and national size see Spolaore (2012).

6 A further complication arises if the returns to foreign aggression are increasing in a state's size – as in Thomson's (1976) classic analysis of optimal defense spending and taxation.

societies manage to minimize the political costs of heterogeneity while maximizing the benefits from a diverse pool of preferences, skills, and endowments. Nonetheless, all other things being equal, heterogeneity and political costs tend to increase as states become larger and expand their borders. Therefore, on balance, there is a trade-off between economies of scale and heterogeneity of preferences over public policies. This trade-off has played a central role in the economics literature on endogenous borders (for example, in Alesina and Spolaore 1997; 2003; Le Breton and Weber 2003; Wittman 2000). When economies of scale become more prominent compared to heterogeneity costs, larger political systems tend to emerge. In contrast, a decrease in the benefits from size or an increase in heterogeneity costs can bring about political disintegration.

The association between heterogeneity costs and size does *not* imply that all small countries in the world are necessarily more homogeneous and must face lower political costs while all large countries in the world are necessarily more heterogenous and face higher political costs. The economic approach to borders predicts that size responds endogenously to heterogeneity costs. Consequently, there may be no empirical relation between size and heterogeneity after borders have adjusted. In some circumstances, we may even observe relatively *smaller* states in regions of the world with relatively higher heterogeneity, because people will have formed smaller polities exactly in order to reduce those high heterogeneity costs. In contrast, regions where populations are on average more homogeneous can 'afford' larger political jurisdictions. The prediction is not about an empirical relation between average size and average heterogeneity, but about the effects of a larger size on heterogeneity costs *at the margin*. No matter what the level of heterogeneity is in a given country within a given region of the world, increasing the size of that country by including additional, more diverse regions will tend to raise that country's heterogeneity at the margin. A useful analogy is the relationship between temperature and size of dwellings in preindustrial societies (without modern heating and air conditioning systems). If we assume that a larger dwelling is colder and more expensive to heat, on average we would observe smaller dwellings in colder climates and larger dwellings in warmer climates. But those smaller dwellings in colder climates may very well be *colder* on average than the larger dwellings built in warmer climates. This does not mean that there is no marginal relation between size and internal temperature: those small dwellings in cold climates would be even colder if they were larger.

The political costs associated with larger, more heterogeneous polities have been debated since classical times. Concerns about the costs of size informed, for instance, the classical Greek view that polities should not be larger than a size where everybody knows everybody else, as argued by Aristotle, who wrote in *The Politics* (350 BCE) 'experience has shown that it is difficult, if not impossible, for a populous state to be run by good laws.' In contrast, Aristotle's most famous pupil, Alexander the Great, created one of the largest, most heterogenous empires in history, showing how limited is a teacher's influence on one's students![7] The political costs of large states were also stressed by modern philosophers, such as Montesquieu (1748), who wrote: 'In a large republic, the common good is sacrificed to a thousand considerations. It is subordinated to various exceptions. It depends on accidents. In a small republic, the public good is more strongly felt, better known, and closer to each citizen,' and Cesare Beccaria (1764), who wrote:

> To the extent that society increases, each member becomes a smaller part of the whole, and the republican sentiment becomes proportionally smaller, if the laws do not take care to reinforce it. Societies, like human bodies, have their circumscribed limits, and if they grow beyond them their economy is necessarily disturbed. The size of a state must necessarily be inversely proportional to the sensitivity ['sensibilità'] of those who comprise it.

During the Constitutional Convention in 1787 the Antifederalists referred directly to such views when they contended that 'a republic with such a large territory inhabited by such a heterogeneous population was an absurdity, and contrary to the whole experience of mankind' (cited in Dahl and Tufte 1973: 9–10). To this criticism James Madison (1787), in *Federalist Paper no. 10*, opposed the famous counterargument that in a larger, more heterogeneous community it would be more difficult for a majority to impose its will on the minority.[8]

The nature, extent and implications of the political costs associated with more heterogeneous jurisdictions remain very important and controversial issues today. While there exists an important and growing empirical literature on the relation between ethnic/cultural heterogeneity and political/economic outcomes, the empirical study of the relations between measures of heterogeneity, political institutions, and the formation of national borders is still in its infancy. A difficult task is to define and measure relevant heterogeneity of preferences and characteristics across individuals, groups, and regions. Valuable information is provided by measures of ethnolinguistic fractionalization (an earlier use of these

---

[7] More seriously, Alexander's creation of a large empire is consistent with the 'Leviathan's view' of state formation which we discuss in Sections 3 and 4.

[8] For a critical discussion of these arguments, see Alesina and Spolaore 2003: 5–6.

measures in the economic literature is found in Mauro 1995). Studies at the microeconomic level connect ethnic heterogeneity to underprovision of local public goods (Alesina and La Ferrara 2005), and there is macroeconomic evidence of negative correlations between ethnolinguistic fractionalization and public outcomes, even though causality and robustness are not clear-cut (Alesina et al. 2003). Montalvo and Reynal-Querol (2005) and Esteban, Mayoral and Ray (2012) show that ethnic polarization is associated with civil conflict. However, variables such as ethnic fractionalization and polarization proxy only imperfectly for the extent and intensity of preference heterogeneity that affect the determination of national borders. More recent economic contributions have considered measures of long-term historical differences across populations, including measures of genetic, linguistic and religious distance, that have been shown to act as barriers to the diffusion of innovations and development across societies (Spolaore and Wacziarg 2009; 2012; 2013). Desmet, Ortuño-Ortín and Wacziarg (2012) show that linguistic distances between major linguistic families predict civil conflict, while even finer distinctions between languages have a negative impact on public goods provision. Arbatli, Ashraf and Galor (2015) find that deep measures of heterogeneity within populations – such as genetic diversity – are associated with more civil and ethnic conflict. Spolaore and Wacziarg (2014) study the effects of historical relatedness (measured by genetic distance) on international conflicts and wars. An interesting analysis that directly connects genetic, linguistic and cultural distances to the stability of national borders in Europe is provided by Desmet, Le Breton, Ortuño-Ortíz and Weber (2011), who find that those distances shed light on the timing and patterns of secession in former Yugoslavia and on other aspects of European borders.

Indirect evidence on heterogeneity costs and national borders is provided in Alesina, Easterly and Matuszeski (2011). They define artificial states as 'those in which political borders do not coincide with a division of nationalities desired by the people on the ground.' They propose two measures of the degree to which borders may be artificial: one measuring how borders split ethnic groups into two separate adjacent countries, and the other measuring the straightness of land borders, assuming that straight borders are more likely to be artificial. They show that these two measures are correlated with several indicators of political and economic success. Michalopoulos and Papaioannou (2011) consider the long-term effects of the 'scramble for Africa' by colonial powers. They find that partitioned ethnic groups have suffered significantly longer and more devastating civil wars. Overall, this evidence is consistent with substantial heterogeneity costs.

An important issue – and a challenge for both theoretical and empirical research – is that, in the long run, heterogeneity of preferences and relevant cultural cleavages and identities are themselves endogenous, and affected by economic and political forces (for a discussion from a political-science perspective, see Fearon 2006). For example, religious identities – Catholic vs. Protestant – played an important historical role in the determination of borders in the Low Countries, but became much less salient in more recent times, while cultural/linguistic dimensions – Dutch-speaking vs. French-speaking – have taken the centerfold in contemporary Belgium. Moreover, the nature and relevance of these different dimensions might respond endogenously to changes in the configuration of borders and to specific public policies.[9] A promising direction for future research is to link more closely the literature on endogenous borders to the growing literature on the economics of cultural transmission and change (for an overview of that literature, see Bisin and Verdier 2010).

While cultural and political variables crucially affect the trade-off between benefits and costs of national size, the trade-off is also dependent on the economic environment. In particular, the trade-off is a function of the degree of international economic integration (Alesina and Spolaore 1997; Alesina, Spolaore and Wacziarg 2000; 2005; Hiscox 2003; Spolaore and Wacziarg 2005; Wittman 2000). This is because international openness affects the economic impact of a country's domestic size. The literature on gains from trade and economic development stresses how the extent of the market is an important determinant of economic prosperity.[10] However, the size of the market does not necessarily coincide with the political size of a sovereign state as defined by its national borders. Larger states mean larger markets when political borders imply barriers to international exchange. In contrast, market size and political size would be uncorrelated in a world of perfect free trade in which political borders imposed no costs on international exchanges. Hence, market size depends both on political size (how large a sovereign state is) and the degree of international openness. Small states can prosper in a world of free trade and high economic integration, whereas a large political size is more important for economic success in a world of trade barriers and protectionism.

---

[9] Theoretical analyses of border formation when policymakers endogenously affect heterogeneity can be found in Alesina and Spolaore (2003: 76–78) and Alesina and Reich (2013).

[10] For a general discussion, see Alesina, Spolaore and Wacziarg (2005).

These relations are consistent with the empirical evidence from cross-country regressions. The effect of size on economic performance (measured by the level or growth of income per capita) tends to be higher for countries that are less open, and the effect of openness is much larger for smaller countries (Alesina, Spolaore and Wacziarg 2000; 2005, and Spolaore and Wacziarg 2005). This fact has important consequences for the endogenous formation and breakup of states. As international economic integration increases, the benefits of a large political size are reduced, and the formation of smaller political units becomes less costly. Consequently, the trade-off between size and heterogeneity shifts in favor of smaller and more homogeneous countries. The reverse source of causality can also play a role. Smaller countries have a particularly strong interest in maintaining free trade, because so much of their economy depends upon international markets. When both borders and international openness are endogenous, multiple equilibria can occur: a world where states are large and relatively closed, and remain large because close and close because large, and a different world where there are more numerous, smaller, and more open economies (Spolaore 2004). In sum, economic integration and political disintegration tend to go hand in hand.

3. FOUR ECONOMIC PERSPECTIVES ON ENDOGENOUS BORDERS

How do costs and benefits from size and heterogeneity affect the formation and breakup of polities? The economic literature on endogenous borders has investigated this question from four different perspectives:

(1) efficient borders;
(2) borders as democratic outcomes;
(3) borders in a world of rent-seeking Leviathans; and
(4) borders as the outcomes of conflict and wars.

We consider these four perspectives below.

3.1 Efficient Borders

From an economic perspective, a natural question to ask about 'efficient borders' is: What configuration of borders would emerge in an ideal world where the number and size of nations were determined to maximize total benefits minus total costs – that is, the 'size of the pie'? If costless transfers across individuals and groups were economically and politically feasible, everybody could in principle be made better off by moving from a world of inefficient borders to a world with efficient borders that maximize the sum of everybody's utilities. In such a world, optimal borders would be set such that the social marginal benefits from scale would be equal to the social marginal costs from heterogeneity. Formal analyses of optimal national size are provided in Alesina and Spolaore (1997; 2003) and Wittman (2000), while optimal secession rules are studied by Bordignon and Brusco (2001).

It should be stressed that analyses about optimal borders focus on hypothetical conditions in an ideal world, and are not necessarily a claim about reality. In fact, most economists who study optimal national size do *not* believe that we actually live in a Panglossian world where political borders are indeed set efficiently. Political economists, while deriving the efficiency conditions for borders as an ideal benchmark, have also forcefully stressed the numerous reasons why borders are *unlikely* to satisfy those efficiency conditions in the real world (Alesina and Spolaore 1997; 2003).[11] At the core of contemporary political economy is the realization that benevolent social planners do not exist. Actual borders are set through imperfect mechanisms, which may lead to substantial inefficiencies. The efficiency analysis of borders is a necessary step in order to assess how *far* from that ideal benchmark actual political boundaries are in reality. Empirical analyses have shown that actual borders are indeed set inefficiently, even at the subnational level – for instance, Hayashi, Nishikawa and Weese (2011) find that there are *too many* Japanese municipalities from an efficiency perspective.

If borders are not set optimally in the real world, how are they determined? Below we discuss three perspectives that focus on three – and imperfect – real-world mechanisms: voting, actions by rent-seeking governments, and wars.

3.2 Borders as Democratic Outcomes

What if borders are determined directly by voters? What configuration of political borders would emerge if people could freely and democratically decide whether to form a larger political union with their neighbors or secede from existing polities? Direct democratic voting over borders is historically exceptional, but it is becoming increasingly relevant in a

---

11 For a more optimistic view, see Wittman (2000).

world where voters in specific regions are asked to vote over independence (for example, in Quebec in 1995 or in Scotland in 2014). Even when the determination of national borders by democratic voting is not a realistic description of actual border formation, it provides a useful benchmark to compare actual outcomes, analogously to the efficient solution discussed above. More generally, an analysis of endogenous borders as democratic outcomes can shed valuable insights on the way the trade-off between economies of scale and heterogeneity costs can affect the formation and breakup of states and other jurisdictions in a world where citizens' references matter and have a direct or indirect impact on national formation and secessions.

Voters with preferences that are distant from the central government bear higher heterogeneity costs from living in a larger, more diverse country. If they perceive that such heterogeneity costs are higher than economies of scale, they may prefer to form smaller, more homogeneous political units. Those breakups may lead to a lower sum of everybody's utilities (inefficiency). In other words, democratic outcomes may lead to equilibria with excessive political fragmentation (too many countries).[12]

In general, inefficient outcomes tend to occur under the assumption that citizens contribute to the public good as a function of their income, not of their preferences for public policies – that is, people do not pay less taxes if they disagree more with the central government. An important question is whether appropriate compensations and side payments may change the voters' calculation and affect the stability of national borders. The response depends on whether transfers are preference-based or income-based.[13] Preference-based transfers are payments to regions that are distant from the central government in terms of preferences over public policies. In contrast, income-based transfers are redistributive transfers from richer regions to poorer regions, based on income differences. These two different kinds of transfers have very different effects on border stability.

In theory, preference-based transfers could compensate regions that would otherwise secede, and therefore ensure efficiency and stability. If a breakup is inefficient, the sum of everybody's utilities is lower after a breakup. Resources could be transferred from those who would lose from a secession (people closer to the central government in terms of preferences for public policies) to those who would benefit from the secession

---

12 For a formal analysis, see Alesina and Spolaore (1997).

13 For general discussions, see Alesina and Spolaore (2003: ch 4) and Spolaore (2010).

(people far from the central government). With such transfers, everybody – or at least a large enough majority – could be better off in the unified country, therefore ensuring efficiency and stability. Transfer schemes as means to prevent secessions and implement efficient borders have been studied by Alesina and Spolaore (1997; 2003); Le Breton and Weber (2003); Haimanko, Le Breton and Weber (2005), and others. For example, Le Breton and Weber (2003) show how that a non-linear transfer scheme, where individuals are compensated for the heterogeneity costs they suffer, can prevent secessions in a state of optimal size.

Are preference-based transfers observed in practice, and do they work? In some cases, border regions with different ethnic/linguistic/cultural characteristics from the rest of a country receive a relatively favorable fiscal treatment. Examples are special-status regions in Italy, northern regions in Sweden, and some provinces of Canada and Argentina. However, pure preference-based transfers seem to be relatively rare. There are several reasons why preference-based redistribution is not widespread: (1) feasibility and administrative costs, (2) political credibility, and (3) incompatibility with other social goals. Let us consider these three sets of reasons in order.

Firstly, preference-based transfers may be expensive to implement because of administrative costs and distortions. The relevant preferences are defined in terms of individuals' utility or disutility from belonging to countries with different characteristics (cultural, linguistic, religious, etc.). These costs and benefits are mostly non-pecuniary, and very hard to observe and measure objectively. And even if such heterogeneity costs could be perfectly observed or 'revealed', redistributive compensations would require an expensive administrative setup, implying high taxes and tax distortions (disincentives to work, save and invest). In summary, in most real-world cases preference-based transfers are likely to be either unfeasible or economically costly.

Secondly, the implementation of preference-based transfers is likely to face a more subtle obstacle: political credibility. Suppose that a region is enticed to remain within a larger country with the promise of a more favorable tax treatment. Once the region has accepted to remain within the country, the central government can break its promises. Borders are hard to change, whereas taxes and transfers can be changed more easily. Regions that accept to be part of a given country face the risk that transfer policies might be changed in the future, when the option of secession is no longer available, or available only at a higher cost. In order to be credible, preference-based transfers must be backed by some commitment to technology – for example, an international treaty protecting the country's minority. An example of international guarantee for a minority region is the 1971 treaty between Italy and Austria about the German-speaking Italian province of Bozen/Bolzano, following serious separatist disturbances (including some acts of terrorism) in the 1960s. The 1971 treaty stipulated that the province of Bozen/Bolzano should receive greater autonomy within Italy, including significant fiscal autonomy, and that disputes in the province would be submitted for settlement to the International Court of Justice in The Hague.

Thirdly and finally, even if preference-based transfers were perfectly feasible and credible, they could be in conflict with other social and political objectives. Since preference-based transfers, by definition, abstract from income differences, they may imply substantial transfers of resources from poorer to richer regions and individuals. This is likely to clash with goals of interpersonal equity or other social objectives and constraints, therefore making a preference-based transfer scheme difficult to implement politically. Similar issues emerge when considering efficient borders at the subnational level. For instance, Weese (2015), in his study of political mergers as coalition formation, considers an application to Japanese municipalities, and finds that the national government could increase welfare via a 'counter-intuitive policy' that would involve transfers to richer municipalities conditional on their participation in a merger.

Unlike preference-based transfers, income-based transfers are widespread and much easier to implement economically and politically. However, their efficiency properties and effects on the stability of borders are quite different from those of preference-based transfers. In general, income-based transfers do not ensure optimality or stability of borders, because there is no guarantee that poorer regions would be those farther from the central government in terms of preferences for public policies and types of government. It is at least as likely that income-based redistribution would *add* to heterogeneity costs within a country. Redistribution can henceforth generate additional sources of political conflict across regions, and provide incentives for richer regions to secede. Even in the absence of any other form of preference heterogeneity, interregional disagreements over income-based redistribution may be sufficient to induce country breakup. For instance, Bolton and Roland (1997) present a model where differences in income distributions across regions are at the roots of all differences in preferences over public policies, and can generate incentives to break up, even in the absence of other forms of heterogeneity.

In general, income-based redistribution has three effects on the incentives to secede in a given region: (1) a political effect, capturing the difference in desired fiscal policy between the region's median voter and the median voter in a unified country; (2) a tax-base effect, capturing the difference between average income in the region and in the unified country; and (3) an efficiency/economies of scale effect, capturing a reduction in average income because of country breakup.[14] Unless the regional median voter shares identical preferences with the national median voter (which is unlikely), the political effect is centrifugal: any region would prefer to breakup and implement its own favored fiscal policy, other things being equal. In contrast, the tax-base effect is centrifugal for richer regions (which, therefore, are more likely to prefer separation, other things being equal), and centripetal for poorer regions, which benefit on average from income-based redistribution. Obviously, the economies-of-scale effect is centripetal for all regions. Consequently, when the economies-of-scale effect is small, richer regions are likely to prefer separation, given effects (1) and (2), and even poorer regions may prefer separation, when effect (1) dominates effect (2). On balance, income-based redistribution tends to reduce the stability of national borders.

3.3 Borders in a World of Rent-seeking Leviathans

Even though voters' voice has become increasingly important in a more democratic world, national borders are still far from being the outcomes of democratic elections and processes, even in well-established democracies. For instance, citizens of the European Union have only occasionally been consulted directly about issues of political integration, and even in those cases their votes have often been disregarded.[15] A more realistic understanding of border formation and redrawing can be obtained by focusing on the remaining two perspectives (which are connected): borders as outcomes of the actions of rulers (not necessarily democratic), and borders as the outcomes of conflict and wars. Historically, decisions about border formation and redrawing have been in the hands of rulers – monarchs, dictators, colonial powers. Such rulers have pursued their own political and economic objectives, taking their subjects' preferences into account only up to a point, often in response to actual or potential threats to their own rule (riots and insurrections).[16] Following a tradition that

---

14 For a formal treatment and discussion of these separate effects, see Alesina and Spolaore (2003: ch 4).

15 Discussions of the political economy of European integration are provided in Spolaore (2013; 2015).

16 For an analysis of the goals and constraints of rulers from a political-survival perspective see Bueno de Mesquita et al. (2003).

goes back to Hobbes (1651), and includes Buchanan (1975) and others, we can call these rent-maximizing rulers 'Leviathans.' An earlier economic contribution on the shape and size of nations from this 'Leviathan' perspective is in Friedman (1977), who argued that, in equilibrium, borders maximize the rents of Leviathans, because territories tend to end up with the Leviathans who have more to gain from holding them – a sort of Coase theorem for Leviathans. From this perspective, border configurations are going to be efficient from the point of view of the Leviathans, not from the point of view of their subjects.

Alesina and Spolaore (1997 and 2003: ch 5) formalize the determination of the number and size of states in a world of Leviathans. They show that rent-seeking dictators, less concerned with the preferences of their subjects, may pursue expansionary policies leading to the formation of inefficiently large countries and empires. In contrast, democratization leads to secessions and formation of smaller countries. The effects of democratization on equilibrium borders operate even when citizens do not vote directly on borders. Citizens' preferences can have an effect on the decision of rent-seeking governments about policies and borders indirectly, because in a more democratic world rulers need a broader consent for their political survival. Democratically constrained Leviathans can obtain higher rents by forming smaller, more homogeneous polities – in other words, the breakup of states and empires may be in the Leviathans' self-interest, when they must become more responsive to their citizens' preferences. As a result, in more democratic (that is, less dictatorial) societies, Leviathans' rents are more strongly impacted by heterogeneity costs, because Leviathans must take those costs into account when setting policies and borders. Therefore, more democratic Leviathans have a stronger interest in reducing heterogeneity of preferences among their citizens, violently (repression) and/or peacefully (national homogenization via education and propaganda). In this context, heterogeneity becomes an endogenous variable, which can be affected, up to a point, by Leviathans' policies.[17] These effects can shed light on some actual historical developments. For instance, traditionally autocratic rulers such as the Ottomans could tolerate widely ranging heterogeneous minorities in their empires. In contrast, the process of democratization in the past two centuries has often been accompanied by attempts at

---

[17] For a simple formalization of these ideas, see Alesina and Spolaore, 2003, pp. 76–78. A more recent contribution is Alesina and Reich (2013), where Leviathans reduce heterogeneity costs not in order to maximize their rents, but to pursue their own preferences over types of public goods.

cultural, linguistic and ethnic homogenization and nation-building by relatively smaller central governments.

The analysis of borders in a world of Leviathans brings us closer to a more realistic analysis of the historical forces and mechanisms behind state formation and breakup. These processes have often involved the explicit use of violence in conflict and wars. Historically, Leviathans have often agreed to peaceful reconfigurations of borders. However, the logic of rent maximization and expansion of empires is also consistent with more bellicose processes and outcomes.[18] And even in a more democratic world, defense and security issues may continue to play a key role in border formation and redrawing. The relation between conflict and borders is the subject of our fourth and last perspective.

3.4 Borders as the Outcomes of Conflict and Wars

State formation and disintegration have always been closely linked to security concerns and wars. As the prominent historian Charles Tilly (1990: 67) remarked, 'wars made states, and vice versa.' Historians and political scientists (for example, Riker, 1964) have pointed to military threats and challenges as central factors in the formation of sovereign states and federations, including the United States, Switzerland, and Germany – whose borders, according to Otto von Bismarck (1864), were determined 'not by speeches and the decisions of majorities [...] but by iron and blood.' Foreign threats have often been viewed as a force for political union and domestic cohesion. For instance, Niccolò Machiavelli (1517) in the *Discourses on Livy* (II, 2) wrote that 'the cause of the disunion of republics is usually idleness and peace; the cause of union is fear and war.' This view is sometimes referred to as 'Sallust's Theorem' (Evrigenis 2008), after the Roman historian who argued that fear of an external enemy explained the internal cohesion of the Roman Republic before the destruction of Carthage. A more recent expression of this view was given by President Reagan (1987) in his speech to the United Nations General Assembly on September 21, 1987, when he said:

> 'Cannot swords be turned to plowshares? Can we and all nations not live in peace? In our obsession with antagonisms of the moment, we often forget how much unites all the members of humanity. Perhaps we need some

---

[18] For example, Friedman (1977) explicitly mentions wars as a possible mechanism leading to the allocation of territories to the Leviathans who obtain the highest rents from them.

> outside, universal threat to make us recognize this common bond. I occasionally think how quickly our differences worldwide would vanish if we were facing an alien threat from outside this world.'

A few contributions to the economic literature on endogenous borders have explicitly modeled the role of conflict, military spending, and wars, building on the formal literature on conflict and appropriation pioneered by Haavelmo (1954); Tullock (1980); Hirshleifer (1989; 1991); and Grossman (1991).[19] For instance, international conflict and defense are at the center of the analyses of state formation and breakup in Alesina and Spolaore (2005; 2006) and Spolaore (2004). In those contributions borders are affected by the fact that a country's military power matters in the settlement of international disputes. As we have mentioned in Section 2, defense and national power are public goods, and in principle larger countries can provide better and cheaper security for their citizens. In a more bellicose world, larger, more centralized countries have an advantage, whereas a reduction in international conflict reduces the incentives to form larger political unions. However, a decrease in the importance of military force may not reduce the total number of violent conflicts in the world. When borders are formed endogenously, a lower role for defense and security, by bringing about the formation of more numerous countries, can paradoxically increase the number of observed conflicts in the world. Even if the use of force is less likely in each specific international dispute, the higher number of countries raises the probability that some of those countries will enter into a military confrontation. Alesina and Spolaore (2006) show that a *lower* probability of having to use force in international relations increases the number of nations in equilibrium, and can lead to an increase in the number of international interactions that are resolved by force. Hence, a reduction in global conflict between larger political units may lead to an increase in more localized conflict between smaller political units. Analogously, improvements in the enforcement of national 'control rights' through a more effective rule of international law reduces the need for defense and force, and may therefore cause breakups of nations, possibly leading to more rather than less conflicts in equilibrium (Alesina and Spolaore 2005).

Some of these contributions also connect conflict to borders in a world of rent-maximizing Leviathans. For example, Alesina and Spolaore (2003: 106) find that the effect of conflict on borders is bigger when

[19] For an overview of the economics of conflict see Garfinkel and Skaperdas (2007). A discussion of the economic literature on national borders and conflict is provided in Spolaore (2012).

Leviathans are less democratic (dictators), but the effect becomes smaller when Leviathans face tighter democratic constraints.

The above-mentioned papers are explicitly about international conflict. A related line of research focuses on the relation between civil conflict and endogenous borders. Civil and ethnic conflicts have been extensively studied by sociologists and political scientists (for example, Horowitz 1985; Fearon and Laitin 2003) and, increasingly, by economists (for example, Collier 2001; Montalvo and Reynal-Querol 2005). While most of these studies consider conflict within given borders, a few have explicitly focused on the relations among ethnic conflict, border redrawing, and political partitions. For example, Sambanis (2000) finds that partitions do not seem to prevent recurrence of ethnic wars, and writes that '[e]ven if this solution reduces the incidence of internal war, it will almost certainly increase the incidence of international war,' an observation which is consistent with the predictions of the models of international conflict and national borders discussed above (for a discussion from a political-science perspective see also Fearon 2004). A few contributions focus on the interplay between civil conflict and international conflict. Theoretical analyses of the interactions between conflict within groups and across groups are provided by Garfinkel (2004a; 2004b) and Münster (2007).

A formal analysis where secessions are the direct outcome of civil conflict is provided by Spolaore (2008). In that context, the probability of secession and the resources spent on conflict are endogenous variables, which are a function of the periphery's incentives to secede and on the center's incentives to oppose a secession. Those incentives depend on heterogeneity costs, economies of scale in the provision of public goods, and the relative size of the two regions. Separatist conflict is more intense when the two regions are of roughly equal size, consistently with historical evidence (Horowitz, 1985; Collier, 2001). External threats may reduce the probability of secession – for reasons that would not have surprised Sallust and Machiavelli. However, foreign threats do not necessarily reduce the intensity of separatist conflict within a country. They reduce the incentives to secede in the smaller region, but also increase the larger region's incentives to resist the smaller region's secession, and may therefore lead to more diversion of resources towards conflict in the aggregate. Finally, the possibility that conflict about government policies may occur *after* borders have been determined reduces both the incentives to secede in the smaller region and the benefits from union in the larger region. The perspective of conflict over government policies within a unified country can even induce the center itself to prefer a country breakup.

An important question related to the issue of civil and ethnic conflict is whether federalism and decentalization lead to border stability or instability.[20] Generally, federalism has been viewed as border-stabilizing and conflict-reducing, especially in societies that are very heterogenous. For example, Lijphart (1990) stresses the benefits of regional autonomy as a 'power-sharing approach,' Weingast (1995) emphasizes the positive effects of checks on the central government associated with federalism, and Bermeo (2002) argues that federal states tend to do better than unitary states when accommodating ethnic conflict and minority discrimination. Inman and Rubinfeld (2005) analyze the benefits of federative arrangements in a diverse, multiethnic society (South Africa). Less successful cases of decentralization, however, have provided counterarguments against federalism as a stabilizing force. For example, the Civil War in the United States has been viewed by many as an instance when federalism provided the means for a costly attempt to secede. A costly case of destabilizing decentralization was the creation of a safe haven for guerrilla rebels (FARC) in Colombia in the late 1990s. It has also been suggested that power decentralization and federal arrangements greatly facilitated the breakups of Yugoslavia and the Soviet Union, with substantial costs and disruptions (Roeder 1991; Suny 1993).

Spolaore (2010) discusses the relations among federalism, redistribution and country stability, and provides a simple analytical model of the interplay between centrifugal and centripetal effects of decentralization and federalism. In that model, decentralization reduces the incentives to secede if and only if it is high enough. When decentralization is low, more decentralization may actually increase the incentives to breakup. In other words, an increase in decentralization is more likely to have a stabilizing effect in societies that are already highly decentralized, whereas it may have a centrifugal effect in more centralized societies. The threshold above which decentralization has stabilizing effects depends on the effectiveness of conflict activities. When conflict and force have less impact on outcomes, decentralization tends to ensure more stable polities. In sum, increasing decentralization is likely to have a positive effect on stability and efficiency in societies where institutions and norms ensure that conflict capabilities (weapons, violence) are *not* effective at determining national borders.

---

[20] For an extensive discussion, see Bakke and Wibbels (2007).

4. A SIMPLE ANALYTICAL ILLUSTRATION

This section provides an analytical framework to illustrate a few basic ideas from the economic literature on borders. We are not going to derive general results, but present a few simple examples. For detailed analytical derivations in more general settings, the reader is referred to the contributions cited in the previous sections.

4.1 Economies of Scale and Heterogeneity Costs

Consider three regions, North, Center and South, each with a population equal to $P>0$. The total cost of setting up an independent government in each region is

$$C_i = F + cP \tag{1.1}$$

where $F>0$ is the fixed cost of public-good provision (which does not depend on population size), cP is the variable cost, increasing in population size, and the parameter $c \geq 0$ is the marginal cost of government. If the three regions form a unified government, the total cost of public-good provision is

$$C_u = F + c(3P) \tag{1.2}$$

The cost per capita is $\frac{C_i}{P} = \frac{F}{P} + c$ when each region is independent, and $\frac{C_u}{3P} = \frac{F}{3P} + c$ in a political union.[21] To simplify notation, define $\frac{F}{P} \equiv f$. The difference between the two per-capita costs is

$$\frac{C_i}{P} - \frac{C_u}{3P} = (f+c) - \left(\frac{f}{3} + c\right) = \frac{2f}{3} \tag{1.3}$$

Therefore, $\frac{2f}{3}$ captures the economies of scale associated with the provision of public goods to a larger population.

---

[21] To simplify the exposition, and without much loss of generality, we assume that there are only two possible configurations of borders: a union of the three regions or full independence for each region. To simplify, we rule out a union of two regions, while the third is independent. Typically, the literature on endogenous borders considers models with many regions – often a continuum – which can be partitioned in several possible configurations (see Alesina and Spolaore 1997 and 2003).

We assume that people in different regions have different preferences over types of public goods.[22] When each region chooses its preferred type of government, each individual's utility from government services is

$$g_i = g^* \tag{1.4}$$

In contrast, if the Center's preferred type of government is selected in a political union, each individual in the Center gets his/her first-best utility from government services g^*, but citizens in the North and South obtain a lower utility

$$g_u = g^* - h < g_i \tag{1.5}$$

where the parameter $h > 0$ captures heterogeneity costs. If the North's preferred type of government is selected in the union, each citizen in the North gets g^*, but each citizen in the Center gets $g^* - h$, and each citizen in the South gets $g^* - 2h$. That is, we assume that the South is 'more distant' in preferences from the North than from the Center. Symmetrically, a union where the South's preferred type of government is selected would give utility g^* to everyone in the South, $g^* - h$ to those in the Center, and $g^* - 2h$ to those in the North.

Each individual has income equal to y, and taxes are proportional to income, with the tax rate denoted by τ.[23] To keep things simple, income y is given, and equal across regions. In a more realistic setting, income would endogenously respond to taxes, and, possibly, also to changes in borders if there are barriers to international trade, as discussed in Section 2. Here we ignore these effects.

Each individual j obtains overall utility from his/her disposable income $[1-\tau(j)]y$ and from government services $g(j)$

$$U(j) = [1-\tau(j)]y + g(j) \tag{1.6}$$

where $\tau(j)$ is the tax rate paid by individual j, and $g(j)$ is equal to g^* under independence, and equal to g^* or $g^* - h$ or $g^* - 2h$ in a union, depending on individual j's location (North, Center, South), and on which type of government is chosen.

---

22 For simplicity, we assume that people within each region have the same preferences. What matters, more generally, is that preferences within each region tend to differ less than preferences across regions.

23 We assume that income per capita is high enough to pay for government services per capita under independence (and, *a fortiori*, in a union): $y > f + c$.

4.2 Voting and Efficiency

Consider now a democratic world where taxes, type of government and borders are determined by majority vote. Taxes are going to be high enough to pay for government services (since everybody has the same income, there is no demand for redistribution from rich to poor). If the three regions are independent, each region must raise enough taxes to pay for $F+cP$, and therefore total taxes in each region must be

$$\tau_i yP = F + cP \tag{1.7}$$

which imply the following tax rate

$$\tau_i = \frac{f}{y} + c \tag{1.8}$$

while in a political union total taxes are

$$\tau_u 3yP = F + c3P \tag{1.9}$$

and the tax rate is

$$\tau_u = \frac{f}{3y} + c \tag{1.10}$$

Because of economies of scale in public-good provision, obviously taxes are higher in an independent state than in a union

$$\tau_i - \tau_u = \frac{2f}{3y} > 0 \tag{1.11}$$

If each region is independent, its citizens unanimously choose their preferred type of government and obtain utility $g_i = g^*$ (no heterogeneity costs). In a union, the Center's type of government is the median choice: 2/3 of the total population (Center and North) prefer the Center's type of government to the South's type, and 2/3 of the population (Center and South) prefer the Center's type to the North's type. Hence, we assume that the Center's type is going to be selected by a majority of voters (median voter's theorem). Therefore, the citizens in the Center get utility g^* from government services, but the citizens in the North and South get a lower utility $g_u = g^* - h$ (they bear heterogeneity costs).

Now, we can ask the key question: will a majority of people prefer independence or a union? Center's citizens always prefer a union, where they would enjoy their preferred type of government while also paying lower taxes because of economies of scale. But North's and South's citizens face a trade-off between economies of scale (lower taxes) and heterogeneity costs (a government farther from their preferences). They favor a political union if and only if their utility is higher in a union than with independence

$$(1 - \tau_u)y + g_u \geq (1 - \tau_i)y + g_i \tag{1.12}$$

that is, if and only if the benefits from lower taxes are higher than the heterogeneity costs

$$(\tau_i - \tau_u)y = \frac{2f}{3} \geq g_i - g_u = h \tag{1.13}$$

which holds if and only if

$$\frac{h}{f} \leq \frac{2}{3} \tag{1.14}$$

the key ratio $\frac{h}{f}$ captures the trade-off between heterogeneity costs (h) and economies of scale (f). In this simple setting, voting over borders obeys a straightforward and intuitive rule: a majority of voters (in fact, all voters) favor a political union if and only if the key ratio $\frac{h}{f}$ is smaller than a critical threshold ($\frac{2}{3}$). Otherwise, a majority of voters (2/3 of them) prefer independence.

Does majority voting lead to efficient outcomes in this setting? The sum of everybody's utilities in a union is

$$\sum_j U_u(j) = 3(1 - \tau_u)yP + 3g^*P - 2hP \tag{1.15}$$

while the sum of everybody's utilities under independence is

$$\sum_j U_i(j) = 3(1 - \tau_i)yP + 3g^*P \tag{1.16}$$

By definition, a political union is efficient if and only if

$$\sum_j U_u(j) \geq \sum_j U_i(j) \tag{1.17}$$

which holds if and only if

$$\frac{h}{f} \leq 1 \tag{1.18}$$

Again, the condition, quite intuitively, is expressed in terms of the key ratio $\frac{h}{f}$ – heterogeneity costs over economies of scale must be low enough for a political union to be efficient. However, this efficiency threshold is *higher* than the threshold which is required for the union to be an equilibrium under majority vote. This means that there exists a range of parameters ($\frac{h}{f}$ smaller than 1 but larger than $\frac{2}{3}$) for which a union is efficient but politically unstable under majority voting. Within that range, 2/3 of voters prefer to break up an efficient union. In other terms, we have an 'inefficiency range' characterized by:

$$\frac{2}{3} \leq \frac{h}{f} \leq 1 \tag{1.19}$$

The source of this inefficiency is that North and South voters do not take into account the net costs that a breakup would impose on the Center, and are willing to break up the union, even though the breakup generates costs for the Center that are larger than the net benefits to themselves. The fundamental source of inefficiency here is that people pay the same taxes but obtain different benefits in the union. Hence, the North and the South do not fully internalize the benefits from economies of scale and the Center does not internalize the political costs from heterogeneity. In contrast, everybody would fully internalize social benefits and social costs from a political union if the following tax-and-transfer scheme – unrelated to income but a function of different preferences for public goods – could be implemented. Each citizen in the Center should pay an extra tax equal to

$$t = \frac{2h}{3} \tag{1.20}$$

and each citizen in the North and the South should receive a transfer equal to

$$r = \frac{h}{3} \tag{1.21}$$

Under this tax-and-transfer scheme, everybody's utility in a union would be identical – i.e., everybody would get the average utility in the union AU_u

$$AU_u = (1 - \tau_u)y + g^* - \frac{2h}{3} \tag{1.22}$$

Now, voters would chose a union if and only if average utility AU_u is larger than utility under independence, which is $(1 - \tau_i)y + g^*$

$$AU_u = (1-\tau_u)y + g^* - \frac{2h}{3} \geq (1-\tau_i)y + g^* \qquad (1.23)$$

The above condition holds if and only if $\frac{h}{f} \leq 1$. Therefore, voters would unanimously break up a union if and only if it is inefficient – that is, such preference-based transfer scheme would align voting outcomes with efficient outcomes. However, as we have discussed in Section 3, preference-based transfers face problems of feasibility and credibility. For instance, we could have it that $(1-\tau_u)y < \frac{2h}{3}$ – meaning that disposable income (after the public good is paid for) could be insufficient to provide resources for the required optimal transfer from the Center to the peripheries. More importantly, the scheme would face a credibility problem if borders must be set *before* taxes and transfers are decided. Then, North and South voters may not believe that the Center will continue to transfer resources to them after they have agreed to form a political union.

4.3 Leviathans and Rents

Above we have compared efficient borders to borders chosen through majority voting. Now, we are going to consider how borders would be selected by a rent-maximizing Leviathan. Under a union, the Leviathan's rents would be equal to the costs of running the government $F+c3P$ minus the taxes that the government can extract from its subjects. How much can the government extract? In this extremely simplified example, where income is exogenous, and there are no deadweight losses or other costs from higher taxation, the Leviathan could extract *all* incomes as taxes, and obtain rents equal to

$$R_u = 3yP - F - 3cP = 3(y-c)P - F \qquad (1.24)$$

Clearly, those rents are higher than the sum of the rents of three Leviathans in charge of three independent states, each of size P, which are

$$3R_i = 3(yP - F - cP) = 3(y-c)P - 3F \qquad (1.25)$$

Hence, the sum of Leviathans' rents is maximized by a union, even when that union is highly inefficient from the perspective of its citizens, and would be broken up by its citizens by majority vote. In this simple example, the Leviathans can completely ignore heterogeneity costs because they face no constraints when setting taxes and borders. However, even dictators typically need the support of at least part of the population to survive in power. For instance, they may need to provide a minimum utility to at least a fraction δ of the population in order not to be overturned. In more general analyses, when these political constraints are taken into account, one can show that Leviathans continue to prefer inefficiently large countries as long as δ does not include a majority of the population ($\delta < \frac{1}{2}$).[24] In our simple setting, consider, for instance, a Leviathan who can survive in power by gathering to the needs of $\delta = 1/3$ of the population (or less). That Leviathan could obtain higher rents by forming a union, even if it is inefficient, as long as sufficient utility is provided to the Center, at the cost of high disutility for the periphery (North and South). As democratic constraints become more binding (δ increases, and becomes larger than 1/3), and the periphery regions gain political power, such Leviathan-ruled union becomes politically unstable (democratization leads to secessions).

4.4 Conflict and Breakup

In our example, when heterogeneity costs are high enough, the Center and the periphery regions (North and South) have very different views about borders. The Center benefits from a political union, while North and South prefer independence if heterogeneity costs are higher than economies of scale. So far, we have considered peaceful mechanisms through which this potential conflict can be resolved: voting, efficient transfers (if available), and the peaceful rule of Leviathans. Now, we are going to consider the case when borders are the outcomes of explicit conflict and wars. Suppose that the three regions are in a political union, but $\frac{h}{f} > \frac{2}{3}$, and no transfers and compensations are available. Consequently, the North and the South would like to secede, and form their own independent states.[25] However, the citizens of the Center resist the breakup of the union, because they do not want to lose the benefits from economies of scale. A civil war ensues, where the Center fights against

[24] For a formal derivation, see Alesina and Spolaore (1997 and 2003: ch 5).

[25] For simplicity, we assume that we are back to a world without rent-seeking Leviathans.

the joint forces of the North and the South (the Rebels).[26] If the Rebels win, there will be a breakup. If the Center wins, the union will be preserved. Let W_R denote the military capabilities (weapons) that the rebels acquire in order to fight this secessionist war. W_C are the Center's military capabilities. The probability of a breakup π is given by

$$\pi = \frac{W_R}{W_R + W_C} \tag{1.26}$$

This is a *contest success function*.[27] The probability that the Rebels win is increasing in their military capabilities (W_R) and decreasing in the Center's military capabilities (W_C). The Rebels will choose W_R in order to maximize their expected utility per capita, which is

$$EU_R = \pi[(1-\tau_i)y + g^*] + (1-\pi)[(1-\tau_u)y + g^* - h] - \frac{W_R}{2P} \tag{1.27}$$

while the Center will choose W_C to maximize

$$EU_C = \pi[(1-\tau_i)y + g^*] + (1-\pi)[(1-\tau_u)y + g^*] - \frac{W_C}{P} \tag{1.28}$$

When selecting W_R, the Rebels take the level of W_C as given and, conversely, when selecting W_C, the Center takes the level of W_R as given (Nash equilibrium). The first order conditions are

$$\frac{dEU_R}{dW_R} = \frac{d\pi}{dW_R}[h - (\tau_i - \tau_u)y] - \frac{1}{2P} = \frac{W_C}{(W_C + W_R)^2}(h - \frac{2f}{3}) - \frac{1}{2P} = 0 \tag{1.29}$$

$$\frac{dEU_C}{dW_C} = -\frac{d\pi}{dW_C}(\tau_i - \tau_u)y - \frac{1}{P} = \frac{W_R}{(W_C + W_R)^2}\frac{2f}{3} - \frac{1}{P} = 0 \tag{1.30}$$

which imply the following equilibrium levels W_R^e and W_C^e

$$W_R^e = \frac{h - \frac{f}{3}}{h - \frac{2f}{3}} P \tag{1.31}$$

[26] To simplify exposition and notation, we assume that the North and the South form a military alliance against the Center. The insights would be similar, but the analysis more complicated, if they were to fight separately.

[27] See Tullock (1980); Hirshleifer (1989; 1991); Garfinkel and Skaperdas (2007); and Spolaore (2012). Spolaore (2008) provides a discussion of different specifications of contest success functions applied to the determination of political borders.

$$W_C^e = \frac{\frac{f}{3}\left(h - \frac{f}{3}\right)}{\left(h - \frac{2f}{3}\right)^2} P \tag{1.32}$$

Therefore, the equilibrium probability of a breakup is

$$\pi^e = \frac{W_R^e}{W_R^e + W_C^e} = \frac{\frac{h}{f} - \frac{2}{3}}{\frac{h}{f} - \frac{1}{3}} \tag{1.33}$$

The probability of breakup is increasing in the key ratio $\frac{h}{f}$

$$\frac{d\pi^e}{d\left(\frac{h}{f}\right)} = \frac{1}{3\left(\frac{h}{f} - \frac{1}{3}\right)^2} > 0 \tag{1.34}$$

This is because higher heterogeneity costs and/or lower economies of scale raise the incentives for the Rebels (North and South) to fight for secession, while lower economies of scale also reduce the Center's incentives to fight to preserve the union. Therefore, this simple example confirms the paramount role of the trade-off between heterogeneity costs and economies of scale even when borders are not determined peacefully, but by 'iron and blood.'

If the costs of security and defense against external threats (i.e., from foreign states outside the three regions) are included in the overall costs of public-good provision – and, therefore, in f–, a reduction in external threats would imply a lower f, and, henceforth, a higher probability of secession. This can be viewed as an illustration of Sallust's theorem, which we mentioned in Section 3: a reduction in foreign threats decreases domestic cohesion and may bring about civil conflict and breakup.

REFERENCES

Alesina, Alberto, Arnaud Devleeschauwer, William Easterly, Sergio Kurlat and Romain Wacziarg (2003), 'Fractionalization,' *Journal of Economic Growth*, 8(2), 155–94.

Alesina, Alberto, William Easterly and Janina Matuszeski (2011), 'Artificial States,' *Journal of the European Economic Association*, 9(2), 246–277.
Alesina, Alberto and Eliana La Ferrara (2005) 'Ethnic Diversity and Economic Performance,' *Journal of Economic Literature*, 43(3), 762–800.
Alesina, Alberto and Bryony Reich (2013), 'Nation Building,' NBER Working paper 18839.
Alesina, Alberto and Enrico Spolaore (1997), 'On the Number and Size of Nations', *Quarterly Journal of Economics*, 112(4), 1027–1056.
Alesina, Alberto and Enrico Spolaore (2003), *The Size of Nations*, Cambridge, MA: MIT Press.
Alesina, Alberto and Enrico Spolaore (2005), 'War, Peace and the Size of Countries', *Journal of Public Economics*, 89(7), 1333–1354.
Alesina, Alberto and Enrico Spolaore (2006), 'Conflict, Defense Spending, and the Number of Nations', *European Economic Review*, 50(1), 91–120.
Alesina, Alberto, Enrico Spolaore and Romain Wacziarg (2000), 'Economic Integration and Political Disintegration', *American Economic Review*, 90(5), 1276–1296.
Alesina, Alberto, Enrico Spolaore and Romain Wacziarg (2005), 'Trade, Growth, and the Size of Countries' in Philippe Aghion and Steven N. Durlauf (eds.), *Handbook of Economic Growth*. Amsterdam: Elsevier, vol. 1, chapter 23, 1499–1542.
Alesina, Alberto and Romain Wacziarg (1998), 'Openness, Country Size and Government', *Journal of Public Economics*, 69(3), 305–321.
Anderson, Benedict R. O'G. (1983), *Imagined Communities: Reflections on the Origin and Spread of Nationalism*, revised edition, Verso, London
Arbatli, C. E., Q. Ashraf and O. Galor (2015), 'The Nature of Civil Conflict', NBER Working Paper No. 21079, April.
Aristotle (350 BCE), *The Politics*, Loeb Classic Library No. 264, 1932, Cambridge, MA: Harvard University Press.
Bakke, Kristin M., and Erik Wibbels (2006), 'Diversity, Disparity, and Civil Conflict in Federal States', *World Politics*, 59 (October), 1–50.
Beccaria, Cesare di (1764), *Dei delitti e delle pene* [On Crimes and Punishments], Livorno [Leghorn].
Bermeo, Nancy (2002), 'The Import of Institutions', *Journal of Democracy*, 13(2), 96–110.
Bisin, Alberto, and Thierry Verdier (2010), 'The Economics of Cultural Transmission and Socialization,' in Jess Benhabib, Alberto Bisin, and Matt Jackson (eds.), *Handbook of Social Economics*, Amsterdam: Elsevier.
Bolton, Patrick and Gérard Roland (1997), 'The Breakups of Nations: a Political Economy Analysis', *Quarterly Journal of Economics*, 112(4), 1057–89.
Bolton, Patrick, Gérard Roland and Enrico Spolaore (1996), 'Economic Theories of the Breakup and Integration of Nations', *European Economic Review*, 40, 697–705.
Bordignon, Massimo, and Sandro Brusco (2001), 'Optimal Secession Rules', *European Economic Review*, 45, 1811–34.
Buchanan, James M. (1975), *The Limits of Liberty: Between Anarchy and Leviathan*, Chicago, IL: University of Chicago Press.

Bueno de Mesquita, Bruce, Alastair Smith, Randolph M. Siverson and James D. Morrow (2003), *The Logic of Political Survival*, Cambridge, MA: MIT Press.
Collier, Paul (2001) 'The Economic Causes of Civil Conflict and Their Implications for Policy', in Chester A. Crocker, Fen O. Hampson, and Pamela R. Aall (eds.), *Turbulent Peace: The Challenges of Managing International Conflict*. Washington DC: US Institute of Peace Press, 143–162.
Dahl, Robert, and Edward Tufte (1973), *Size and Democracy*, Stanford, CA: Stanford University Press.
Desmet, Klaus, Michel Le Breton, Ignacio Ortuño Ortín, and Shlomo Weber (2011), 'The Stability and Breakup of Nations: A Quantitative Analysis,' *Journal of Economic Growth*, 16, 183–213.
Desmet, Klaus, Ignacio Ortuño-Ortín and Romain Wacziarg (2012), 'The Political Economy of Linguistic Cleavages,' *Journal of Development Economics*, 97(2), 322–38.
Ellingsen, Tore (1998), 'Externalities and Internalities: A Model of Political Integration', *Journal of Public Economics,* 68(2), 251–68.
Esteban, Joan, Laura Mayoral and Debraj Ray (2012),'Ethnicity and Conflict: An Empirical Study,' *American Economic Review*, 102(4), 1310–42.
Evrigenis, Ioannis D. (2008), *Fear of Enemies and Collective Action*. Cambridge: Cambridge University Press.
Fearon, James D. (2004), 'Separatist Wars, Partition, and World Order', Security Studies, 3(4), 394–415.
Fearon, James (2006), 'Ethnic Mobilization and Ethnic Violence,' in Barry R. Weingast and Donald A. Wittman (eds.), *Oxford Handbook of Political Economy*, Oxford: Oxford University Press, 852–68.
Fearon, James, and David Laitin (2003), 'Ethnicity, Insurgency, and Civil War', *American Political Science Review* 97(1), 75–90.
Findlay, Ronald (1996), 'Towards a Model of Territorial Expansion and the Limits of Empires' in Michelle R. Garfinkel and Stergios Skaperdas (eds.) *The Political Economy of Conflict and Appropriation*. Cambridge: Cambridge University Press.
Friedman, David (1977), 'A Theory of the Size and Shape of Nations', *Journal of Political Economy* 85, 59–77.
Garfinkel, Michelle R. (2004a), 'Global Threats and the Domestic Struggle for Power', *European Journal of Political Economy* 20, 495–508.
Garfinkel, Michelle R. (2004b), 'Stable Alliance Formation in Distributional Conflict', *European Journal of Political Economy* 20, 829–852.
Garfinkel, Michelle R., and Stergios Skaperdas (2007), 'Economics of Conflict: An Overview', in K. Hartley and T. Sandler (eds.) *Handbook of Defense Economics*, Vol. 2, Amsterdam: North Holland.
Gellner, Ernest A. (1983), *Nations and Nationalism*, Ithaca, NY: Cornell University Press.
Goyal, Sanjeev, and Klaas Staal (2004), 'The Political Economy of Regionalism', *European Economic Review,* 48, 563–593.
Grossman, Herschel I. (1991), 'A General Equilibrium Model of Insurrections', *American Economic Review,* 81, 912–21.
Gurr, Ted Robert (2000), *Peoples Versus States: Minorities at Risk in the New Century*, Washington DC: US Institute of Peace Press.

Haavelmo, Trygve (1954), *A Study in the Theory of Economic Evolution*, Amsterdam: North Holland.

Haimanko, Ori, Michel Le Breton and Shlomo Weber (2005), 'Transfers in a Polarized Society: Bridging the Gap between Efficiency and Stability', *Journal of Public Economics*, 89(7), 1277–1303.

Hayashi, Masayoshi, Masashi Nishikawa and Eric Weese (2011), 'Inefficient Municipal Boundaries,' Yale University working paper.

Hirshleifer, Jack (1989), 'Conflict and Rent-seeking Success Functions: Ratio versus Difference Models of Relative Success', *Public Choice*, 63, 101–112.

Hirshleifer, Jack (1991), 'The Technology of Conflict as an Economic Activity', *American Economic Review*, 81(2), 130–134.

Hiscox, M. (2003) 'Political Integration and Disintegration in the Global Economy' in M. Kahler and D. Lake (eds.) *Globalizing Authority*. Princeton, NJ: Princeton University Press.

Hobbes, Thomas (1651), *The Leviathan*, Reprinted 1982. New York, NY: Penguin.

Horowitz, Donald L. (1985), *Ethnic Groups in Conflict*, Berkeley, CA: University of California Press.

Inman, Robert and Daniel L. Rubinfeld (2005), 'Federalism and the Democratic Transition: Lessons from South Africa', *American Economic Review*, 95(2), 39–43.

Leamer, Edward E. (2012), *The Craft of Economics: Lessons from the Heckscher-Ohlin Framework*, Cambridge, MA: MIT Press.

Le Breton, Michel and Shlomo Weber (2003), 'The Art of Making Everybody Happy: How to Prevent a Secession', *IMF Staff Papers*, 50(3), 403–435.

Lijphart, Arend (1990), 'The Power-Sharing Approach', in Jospeh V. Montville (ed.), *Conflict and Peacemaking in Multiethnic Societies*, Lexington, MA: Lexington Books.

Madison, James (1787), 'Federalist No. 10. The Utility of the Union as a Safeguard Against Domestic Faction and Insurrection,' *Daily Advertiser* November 22 (available online at http://www.constitution.org/fed/federa10.htm).

Mauro, Paolo (1995), 'Corruption and Growth', *Quarterly Journal of Economics*, 110(3), 681–712.

Michalopoulos, Stelios, and Elias Papaioannou (2011), 'The Long-Run Effects of the Scramble for Africa', CEPR Discussion Paper 8676.

Montalvo Jose G. and Marta Reynal-Querol (2005), 'Ethnic Polarization, Potential Conflict and Civil War', *American Economic Review*, 95(3), 796–816.

Montesquieu, Charles-Louis de (1748), *The Spirit of the Laws,* Cambridge: Cambridge University Press, 1989.

Münster, Johannes (2007), 'Simultaneous Inter- and Intra-group Conflicts', *Economic Theory*, 32(2), 333–352.

Oates, Wallace (1999), 'An Essay on Fiscal Federalism', *Journal of Economic Literature*, 37, September, 1120–1149.

Olson, Mancur and Richard Zeckhauser (1966), 'An Economic Theory of Alliances', *Review of Economics and Statistics*, 48, 266–79.

Reagan, Ronald (1987), 'Address to the 42d Session of the United Nations General Assembly in New York', New York, September 21.

Riker, William H. (1964). *Federalism*. New York, NY: Little Brown.

Roeder, Philip G. (1991), 'Soviet Federalism and Ethnic Mobilization', *World Politics*, 43(2), 196–232.

Sambanis, Nicholas (2000), 'Partition as a Solution to Ethnic War. An Empirical Critique of the Theoretical Literature' *World Politics* 52(4), 437–83.

Spolaore, Enrico (2004), 'Economic Integration, International Conflict and Political Unions' *Rivista di Politica Economica,* 94, 3–50.

Spolaore (2006), 'National Borders and the Size of Nations' in Barry R. Weingast and Donald A. Wittman (eds.) *The Oxford Handbook of Political Economy*. Oxford: Oxford University Press.

Spolaore, Enrico (2008), 'Civil Conflict and Secessions', *Economics of Governance*, 9(1), 45–63.

Spolaore, Enrico (2010), 'Federalism, Regional Redistribution, and Country Stability', Chapter 13 in Núria Bosch, Marta Espasa and Albert Solé Ollé (eds.), *The Political Economy of Inter-regional Fiscal Flows. Measurement, Determinants and Effects on Country Stability*, Cheltenham, UK and Northampton, MA, USA: Edward Elgar.

Spolaore, Enrico (2012), 'National Borders, Conflict and Peace' in Michelle R. Garfinkel and Stergios Skaperdas (eds.), *Oxford Handbook of the Economics of Peace and Conflict*. Oxford: Oxford University Press 763–786.

Spolaore, Enrico (2013), 'What is European Integration Really About? A Political Guide for Economists,' *Journal of Economic Perspectives,* 27(3), 125–44.

Spolaore, Enrico (2015), 'The Political Economy of European Integration', forthcoming in the *Routledge Handbook of the Economics of European Integration* edited by H. Badinger and V. Nitsch, Routledge: London and New York; CAGE Working Paper No. 221 and NBER Working Paper No. 21250.

Spolaore, Enrico, and Romain Wacziarg (2005), 'Borders and Growth,' *Journal of Economic Growth*, 10(4), 331–386.

Spolaore, Enrico and Romain Wacziarg (2009), 'The Diffusion of Development', *Quarterly Journal of Economics*, 124(2), 469–530.

Spolaore, Enrico, and Romain Wacziarg (2012), 'Long-Term Barriers to the International Diffusion of Technologies', in Jeffrey Frankel and Christopher Pissarides (eds.), *NBER International Seminar on Macroeconomics 2011*, Chicago, IL: University of Chicago Press.

Spolaore, Enrico, and Romain Wacziarg (2013), 'How Deep Are the Roots of Economic Development?', *Journal of Economic Literature*, 51(2), 1–45.

Spolaore, Enrico, and Romain Wacziarg (2015), 'War and Relatedness'. Review of Economics and Statistics, forthcoming, available at http://www/mitpress journals.org/doi/pdf/10.1161/REST_a_oo554

Suny, Ronald G. (1993), *The Revenge of the Past: Nationalism, Revolution, and the Collapse of the Soviet Union*, Stanford, CA: Stanford University Press.

Tabellini, Guido (2008), 'Institutions and Culture', *Journal of the European Economic Association* Papers and Proceedings, Presidential Address, 6(2–3), 255–294.

Thomson, Earl A. (1976). 'Taxation and National Defense', *Journal of Political Economy* 82(4), 755–782.
Tilly, Charles (ed.) (1975), *The Formation of National States in Western Europe*. Princeton, NJ: Princeton University Press.
Tilly, Charles (1990), *Coercion, Capital and European States, AD 990–1990*. Cambridge, MA, Blackwell.
Tullock, Gordon (1980), 'Efficient Rent Seeking' in James M. Buchanan, Robert D. Tollison, and Gordon Tullock (eds.), *Toward a Theory of the Rent-Seeking Society*, College Station US: Texas A&M University Press.
von Bismarck, Otto (1864), 'Speech to the Budget Committee of the Prussian Chamber of Deputies', cited in F.B.M. Hollyday (1970), *Bismarck*, Engelwood Cliffs, NJ: Prentice-Hall.
Weese, Eric (2015), 'Political Mergers as Coalition Formation: An Analysis of the Hersei Municipal Amalgamates, *Quantitative Economics*, 6(2), 257–307.
Weingast, Barry R. (1995), 'The Economic Role of Political Institutions: Market-Preserving Federalism and Economic Growth', *Journal of Law, Economics, and Organization*, 11, 1–31.
Wittman, Donald A. (2000), 'The Wealth and Size of Nations', *Journal of Conflict Resolution*, 6, 885–895.

2. The economics of state emergence and collapse

Bridget L. Coggins with Ishita Kala

1. INTRODUCTION

Membership in the international community has always been dynamic, but it became much more so in the twentieth century as state 'dismemberment', 'fusion', and 'resurrection' increased.[1] In raw numbers, system membership quadrupled from 45 to 195 states.[2] There were 55 violent revolutions, 54 non-violent regime changes, and in the last 60 years alone 227 military coups occurred.[3] In every case, new leaders or governments replaced the regimes formerly in power. Additionally, by some metrics as many as 67 members, approximately a third of all states, can be classified as failed or failing, unable to provide effective governance.[4] In the contemporary world, states are being born, transforming and collapsing at a rapid pace.

Yet amidst this change, there is a remarkable amount of agreement and consistency within the international community when it comes to matters of statehood and state personality. That is to say, most countries agree about which actors are and are not states, and which regimes are and are

[1] Kunz 1955: 69.

[2] According to the Correlates of War System Membership Data (from 1911 through 2011) available at correlatesofwar.org.

[3] The time period surveyed for revolutions and regime changes was 1900–2006 and for military coups, 1950–2010. www.prio.no/CSCW/Datasets/; www.systemicpeace.org/polity/polity4.htm.

[4] Those states classified at an 'alert' or 'warning' level according to the Failed States Index for 2012 available at www.fundforpeace.org. Readers should note that this estimate probably errs quite high with reference to the more restrictive definition of state failure employed later in this essay.

not the rightful governments of those states, most of the time.[5] Traditionalist legal scholars might take this behavioral convergence as evidence of compliance with deeply held legal rules regarding statehood and legal personality or as a simple consequence of what is true, de facto. In contrast, a law and economics approach urges us to reconsider whether the force of legal obligation is the primary driver behind state behavior in these situations. It asserts that jurists too often neglect self-interested motives and that coordinated and cooperative, welfare improving outcomes can sometimes be achieved even when states are narrowly maximizing their own interests.[6] Perhaps the consensus regarding statehood and the rightful members of the international community rests upon a fundamentally different foundation than traditional legal scholars presume.

There is wide agreement that international law only arises from the explicit consent or commitment of states.[7] And there is further agreement that states are the only actors endowed with the ability to recognize and endow others with international personality, as states or otherwise, in international law.[8] This chapter focuses on why states grant legal personality, or international legal sovereignty, to new states and on why they might revoke it when a state has collapsed. How, and under what conditions, are new states accepted into the international community? Given the proliferation of failing states, why do so few of them die or lose legitimacy among their peers? These situations are not so common as to be routine, but they occur frequently enough that there is substantial state practice to review. Community determinations on these fundamental issues of sovereignty are also pivotally important to understanding the nature and dynamics of the international system writ large.

Law and economics has made commendable inroads on questions of customary international law (hereafter CIL) based upon the parsimonious assumptions that states are unitary, self-interested and goal-driven actors

---

[5] Clearly a riff on Louis Henkin's claim that, '[i]t is probably the case that *almost all nations observe almost all principles of international law and almost all of their obligations almost all of the time*' (1979: 47, emphasis added).

[6] Goldsmith and Posner 2005.

[7] Vienna Convention on the Law of Treaties, 1969, article 51. With the notable exception of *jus cogens* rules and (probably) customary international law (Bradley and Gulati 2010).

[8] Portmann 2010: 80. States are not the only actors endowed with legal personality in international law. Under certain circumstances, and with lesser status than states, personality has also been granted to individuals, non-state actors, and international organizations.

(usually interest maximizing, sometimes not). But scholars have, thus far, directed less attention toward the more foundational aspects of international society.[9] Given the paucity of analysis, we concentrate on developing ideas for future research. This chapter will incorporate theoretical insights from political science and law, but it will devote relatively more attention to political science because issues of state emergence and failure have generated more discussion in that field. The chapter will also limit its discussion to external legitimacy as an inter-state issue, fully appreciating that game theory and rational choice might also be useful tools for analyzing two-level bargaining between states and non-state actors on these topics. For example, concerning domestic secessionist movements, transnational advocacy networks, or multinational corporations with vested interests in failing states.[10]

In the pages that follow, we begin by presenting the important assumptions, definitions and theoretical priors guiding the rational choice approach that we employ.[11] The next two major sections are dedicated to state practice on the occasion of (1) new statehood and (2) state failure. Each section details the traditional legal view, proposes an alternative view based in rational choice and then provides an illustrative case analysis. The final substantive section considers the potential obstacles to applying a law and economics framework and the chapter concludes with our findings and recommendations for continued scholarly research.

2. THEORETICAL APPROACH AND DEFINITIONS

Our analysis is informed by Goldsmith and Posner's seminal work, *The Limits of International Law* (2005).[12] A provocative challenger to traditional accounts, Goldsmith and Posner employ the assumptions of rational choice, that states are rational, unitary, interest maximizing actors, to explain states' creation and compliance with customary international law. The authors submit that four strategic situations create

[9] Consistent with Bull (1977), we describe the state system as a nascent international society.

[10] Some examples can be found in Evans, Jacobson and Putnam 1993; Fearon 2004.

[11] While recognizing that there are distinctions between the approaches, we will use the terms 'rational choice', 'game theory', and 'law and economics' interchangeably.

[12] We also benefited from other works including Trachtman and Norman 2005; Guzman 2002; Verdier 2002; and Verdier and Voeten 2012.

convergence in state practice rather than *opinio juris*.[13] First, states unilateral interests might lead to convergence; each would act similarly regardless of their peers. Second, behavioral convergence may result when powerful states pursue their interests and coerce weaker states into following suit. Third, convergence might be a cooperative solution to an iterated prisoners' dilemma (PD), when leaders opt to cooperate in the first round.[14] Fourth, convergence in state practice might be the resolution of a coordination problem like the Stag Hunt or Battle of the Sexes. These four rationalist explanations stand in contrast to traditional accounts, where compliance with legal rules is predicated upon a sense of legal obligation, known as *opinio juris*, or a deeply held moral belief.

Attempting to distinguish between the force of legal obligation and self-interest is a complicated business. Early on, political scientists preferring rationalist explanations for state behavior often demanded that to effectively counter their arguments, critics would have to produce evidence of states routinely abiding by rules *contrary* to their own interests. And where states seemed to be abiding by rules despite their interests, that there was no heretofore unobserved evidence of powerful states manipulating their incentives (for example, that the relationship between norms and behavior was not spurious). Proponents of norm-based arguments countered that the most significant evidence of norms' persuasive force came in the 'editing phase' before the 'option selection' phase examined in most rational choice models. In other words, norms influenced whether or not a given decision-maker even considered certain options among his or her potential choices. Normative considerations could entirely foreclose illegal or unsavory options for an individual, for instance, or otherwise influence the nature of their choice or the structure of the game they faced.

Goldsmith and Posner have been criticized on similar grounds, their detractors arguing that they have not seriously tested the traditionalist argument and have claimed any evidence of self-interested behavior as a victory. Goldsmith and Posner are transparent about excluding 'an interest in compliance' from their analysis and note the complexity that would be required to endogenize the normative pull of legal obligations

---

13 Article 38(1)(b) of the Statute of the ICJ, indicates among its accepted sources of international law 'international custom, as evidence of a general practice accepted as law'. Customary law, then, is indicated by (1) the widespread and consistent practice of states and (2) practice premised upon a sense of legal obligation.

14 Convergence is most likely to be achieved in bilateral PDs; it becomes more difficult to achieve and maintain in multilateral PDs.

in their models. Still, critics are right that the authors overstate their empirical findings given the limitations of their research design.[15] On the other hand, traditional legal scholars often do precisely the same thing, assuming that behavioral conformity with CIL follows from a state's sense of legal obligation. States' motives are inferred from their behavior and alternative explanations are generally not entertained. We are not so ambitious as to attempt to resolve this controversy within the pages of this chapter. It is eminently possible that each of the motives contributes significantly; that their influence varies according to issue area; or that they are at least partially endogenous. Further, we offer no theories or tests of our own. Yet this discussion contains important considerations for any future research in rational choice and CIL.

On the topic of evidence, the illustrative cases we offer here should be taken in the spirit in which they are offered – none has been thoroughly vetted – instead, these are ideas of how economic thinking can inform theory in this area of CIL. We recognize that game theory's greatest strength as an analytical tool is not in its application to empirical cases, but in its ability to generate novel hypotheses and predictions. In this chapter, we trade in economic metaphors rather than formal models.[16]

The recognition decisions under consideration here are usually in the hands of a small number of decision-makers if not vested in a single individual. In most countries the establishment or breaking of diplomatic relations is an executive level decision. Therefore on this subject, many of the typical rational unitary actor problems confronted by scaling up from individual persons to states are happily avoided.

All of the international legal obligations that we discuss here are without a formal enforcement or sanctioning mechanism; there is no reporting or dispute resolution mechanism as there is in some treaty bodies. This is important because no one other than existing states, in an ad hoc manner, has standing to enforce these rules. In part, this is because the laws are customary, but even where they have been codified they have not included enforcement mechanisms. The practice of formal recognition is unlike many other commitments, however, because compliance is fully transparent. There is little opportunity to violate the rules without other states becoming immediately aware of it.[17]

---

15 Trachtman and Norman (2005: 11) argue persuasively, however, that models where norms are treated as exogenous may be a better route to advancing the debate between the two perspectives than endogenizing norms.

16 Snidal 1985.

17 The issue of implicit recognition could make the issue of rule violation less transparent, but state leaders are often explicit about their intentions when

Also unlike treaties, which often contain opt-out clauses for states that want to make a reservation or clarification regarding their commitments or withdraw entirely from the treaty, compliance with CIL is compulsory except for those states that persistently object prior to the rule's acceptance as legal custom.[18] The only other widely accepted means of opting out of CIL is to violate it with the intent of changing the rule, gaining supporters and usurping the law's authority with some new alternative rule. This will be an important aspect of interpreting the traditional legal explanation when a divergence from custom occurs. The fact that a state violates a rule is not in and of itself evidence that a country has transgressed against a deeply held communal belief. Custom can become outdated or oppose evolving community norms and, if that happens, the only real means of effecting change is through rule-breaking.

3. STATE EMERGENCE AND LEGAL PERSONALITY

Today, state emergence is fairly common. This has been especially true since the end of World War II as the withering of colonialism in Africa and Asia yielded dozens of new states, the collapses of the Soviet Union and Yugoslavia created nearly two dozen more, and various non-self-governing territories since then have transitioned to full independence. Though the pace of new statehood has slowed and no apparent wave of new independences waits on the horizon, states are still being born. Most recently, in 2011 the Republic of Southern Sudan successfully seceded from Sudan after decades of civil war. CIL and conventional law outline the defining characteristics of statehood and contain rules about when states may grant external recognition and enter into formal diplomatic relations with newcomers. Even skeptics of international law agree that there is widespread convergence in state behavior in line with these rules regarding legal sovereignty.[19] Further, the international community seems to be moving toward the codification of new rules regarding the succession of treaties, property, archives and debt manifested in the

---

they behave in a way that might seem inadvertently to imply diplomatic recognition. For example, witness Washington's handling of Taiwanese President Lee Teng Hui's 1995 visit to the US. The Clinton Administration made it very clear that the visit was not a formal diplomatic affair, but a private personal trip.

[18] For example, the Montevideo Convention (article 15) permits High Contracting Parties to denounce their commitments with one year's advance notice to the other signatories.

[19] Krasner 1999.

Vienna Conventions of 1978 and 1983.[20] This would create guidelines concomitant to the cession of people and territory from an old state to a new one.[21]

Because every new state entering the international community must separate – amicably or violently – from an existing member of the community, there is significant potential for self-interest to creep into decisions surrounding secession and recognition.[22] It may be helpful to imagine firms in an oligopolistic market being granted influence over who their new competitors will be and over how those new firms will affect the interests and capabilities of their existing peers.[23] Therefore law and economics might yield useful insights into a variety of issues surrounding recognition in addition to, or in spite of, the law. Given behavioral convergence, what other than law might explain it? When do states deviate from the law? If, as in succession, the codification of laws is in progress, what factors will determine whether, or the extent to which, they are widely ratified and adopted as laws?

For example, the Vienna Conventions regarding succession envision amicable breakups between home states and their successors. According to the Convention on Succession of States in respect of State Property, Archives and Debts, 'the passing of the state debt of the predecessor state to the successor state is to be settled by agreement between them'.[24] Unfortunately few transitions occur as smoothly as Czechoslovakia's 1993 'Velvet Divorce'. In those cases, and 'in the absence of such an agreement, the state debt of the predecessor state shall pass to the successor state in an equitable proportion'.[25] Who decides on the 'equitable proportion' due when a secession is opposed by the predecessor state? How do states, the World Bank and private creditors decide

---

[20] Vienna Convention on Succession of States in respect of Treaties 1978 and Vienna Convention on Succession of States in respect of State Property, Archives and Debts 1983.

[21] Matters regarding succession are also important when a change in governments takes place as in a revolution or coup. However, it is generally agreed that regime change does not produce new statehood, regardless of how dramatic the change in the content of governance from one to the next.

[22] This was not always true, but once the inhabited territories of the world had all been claimed, the situation became zero sum; in order for a new state to be born, an old state had to lose territory (or die).

[23] The oligopoly characterizes very powerful states and applies less well to other, normal states in the international community.

[24] Vienna Convention on Succession of States in respect of State Property, Archives and Debts 1983, article 34.

[25] Ibid, article 37.

whether there even *is* a successor state when a country disintegrates like the Soviet Union and Yugoslavia did?[26] And how is it decided? Does a newcomer's ability to make good on its predecessor's debts influence its acceptance as a new member? Or is the debt burden assessed upon a successor dependent upon politics rather than law? Does the fact that the Vienna Conventions neglect these issues militate against their widespread acceptance? Or are states content without formal rules where an agreement would be too difficult to reach and states would have to adjust their behavior too much in order to comply?[27]

Another interesting area, which we will pursue in greater detail now, is new statehood and external recognition. When and why do existing states recognize and enter into diplomatic relations with new states? How might rational choice help to explain why state practice demonstrates (or at least appears to demonstrate) such a high degree of compliance with customary and conventional international law?

A. Customary Law, Conventional Law and the Recognition of States[28]

In international law there are two ways of thinking about the significance of external recognition in relation to statehood, known as the declaratory and the constitutive theories. The dominant view is the declaratory theory. It argues that the external recognition of a state by the existing members of the international community is, and ought to be, a declaration of each state's intention to enter into diplomatic relations with newcomers whose statehood has already been established de facto. If domestic sovereignty has not been achieved, then recognition is considered 'premature' and without the force of law. According to this theory, external recognition is important because it influences the extent to which an actor is able to participate in international affairs, but it does not 'make the state.'

The less popular view is the constitutive theory. This perspective contends that external recognition consecrates new statehood. Without it, regardless of how effective an aspiring member's internal (or de facto) sovereignty is, it is not a state. These scholars find it somewhat absurd to

---

[26] In the former case, Russia was widely recognized as the successor to the USSR, whereas in the latter case, although Serbia claimed it was Yugoslavia's successor, it was not accepted as such. For an overview of the FRY's position on being required to apply as a new member to the UN see Jovanovic 1997–1998.

[27] Downs, Rocke and Barsoom 1996.

[28] The analysis in this section draws heavily from Coggins 2011.

argue that a state is a state regardless of its recognition by others because, even if this is true, it is of trivial practical importance; its statehood cannot be wielded to any meaningful effect in international affairs without recognition. Unrecognized states cannot participate in international life as juridical equals with other states. Political scientists who conceive of the state as a social construct within a nascent international society likely find the constitutive theory intuitively correct. But most jurists reject the constitutive view on normative grounds, finding it too subject to considerations of realpolitik. While the two theories were once considered 'the great debate' in public international law, there is now overwhelming favor for the declaratory view.[29]

Most would point to the 1933 Montevideo Convention on Rights and Duties of States as evidence of *opinio juris* regarding the legal definition of statehood and the rules of recognition (hereafter Montevideo Convention). Though it began as a formal treaty agreed to only by the members of the Organization of American States, the Montevideo Convention is widely considered CIL.[30] The treaty represents a formal codification of what had long been a customary practice among states. The Montevideo Convention says that a state 'should possess the following qualifications: a) a permanent population; b) a defined territory; c) government; and d) capacity to enter into relations with the other states'. The treaty also affirms the declaratory view of recognition stating that 'the political existence of the state is independent of recognition by the other states'.[31] Although various criteria for statehood have been suggested in addition to the effectiveness criteria enumerated in the Montevideo Convention, including democracy, civil liberties and the protection of human rights, they have not been as widely accepted. Furthermore there is some question as to whether these qualities are evidence of statehood or simply additional political hurdles raised, idiosyncratic to the particular state (or states) contemplating recognition.[32]

Despite a near consensus in the legal community regarding the nature of statehood and the seeming convergence in state behavior when it comes to recognizing new states, we submit that the constitutive theory is more empirically valid than the declaratory. External recognition is pivotally important to aspiring states. Without widespread external acceptance, an aspiring member will not be able to join prestigious international organizations like the United Nations (UN) and World Trade

29 Grant 1999.
30 Harris 2004.
31 Ibid.
32 For example, see Talmon 2005.

Organization (WTO); it will not be able to take out development loans from the International Monetary Fund (IMF) and World Bank; it will be unable to pursue legal remedies against other states in the International Court of Justice (ICJ); it is unlikely to receive much foreign investment or foreign aid; it will have trouble exploiting and selling its natural resources; and it might not even be able to legally defend itself if its predecessor attempts to invade. If one adopts the declaratory view, finding that states' recognition practices are not dictated by law may be interesting, but it would have far less dramatic consequences regarding the nature of sovereign statehood. Somewhat regardless of where one's sympathies lie regarding the 'great debate' though, it is clear that external recognition meaningfully affects an actor's exercise of the external benefits of statehood and that a clear customary norm and conventional rules exist regarding its assignation.

B. An Alternative Interpretation

An instrumental explanation for the widespread behavioral convergence regarding new statehood, as evidenced by recognition, suggests that compliance with CIL may actually be quite low. A few would-be states achieve the criteria established by the Montevideo Convention, but go unrecognized, as in present day Somaliland, while many others that fall short of the standard are nevertheless welcomed into the international community as state persons, recently including Bosnia-Herzegovina, Croatia, East Timor and South Sudan. It is apparent that there is a fair degree of agreement regarding the new members of the international system, but it is not apparent that state leaders are using the Montevideo Convention criteria to arrive at those determinations.

Our first task is establishing why self-interest might lead states to prefer mutual agreement regarding statehood – why states have an interest in coordinating their recognition. Knowing which actors are, and are not, endowed with the rights and responsibilities of states generates valuable gains in efficiency for the international community. Kontorovich notes, 'the recognition of states…as the primary and often exclusive actors in international law facilitates bargaining by reducing the number of relevant parties [and] the territorial sovereignty of states clearly defines property rights and responsibilities'.[33] To illustrate what would happen without widespread agreement over membership, witness the problems attendant to international treaties open to accession by 'states'

[33] Kontorovich 2008: 391.

versus those open to 'UN member states'; these problems occur because the group constituting the latter category is immediately apparent, while the group constituting the former is not.[34] The Montevideo Convention criteria, while not vague, are nevertheless open to interpretation. Widespread recognition serves a purpose analogous to membership within a club or institution like the UN; it is an unambiguous signal of social acceptance and belonging. There are no comparable litmus tests associated with the Montevideo Convention and efforts to further clarify the standards have not been successful.

Furthermore, because each new state is born by dividing the existing territory of one of the community's existing members, it is in all states' interests to ensure that the transition from one authority to the next occurs as smoothly as possible. When the states of the international community can coordinate their recognition, the process of succession of legal personality is relatively more stable. In contrast, imagine tens of multiple and overlapping recognized sovereignties in the years following a non-consensual break up as in the former Yugoslavia. Not only would the situation be highly unstable for the parties directly involved, it would likely foment conflict among outsiders as they attempted to engage diplomatically, strategically and economically with the competing authorities therein. All other things equal, it makes sense that, in the name of stability and efficiency, states would prefer the coordinated recognition of mutually agreeable new states.[35]

On first glance, the task of securing the unified, formal recognition of nearly 200 members for each new state seems inordinately complex, with high transaction costs. However, the strongest members of the international system, the Great Powers, are the principals when it comes to recognition. Their material power and their institutional authority give them both global interests and global influence. Great Power decisions serve as a focal point for the normal members of the system and – when they are unified in favor or against any new member – it initiates a cascade of new legitimacy or staunch adherence to the status quo.

Self-interests are a potentially important driver of Great Power preferences when it comes to recognition. Whether or not state leaders *act*

---

[34] Although the 'Vienna formula' has sometimes allowed for a more inclusive set of potential state parties, many states do not accept this implicit acknowledgement of statehood.

[35] This is not to say, however, that they seek stability alone or for its own sake.

upon their narrow self-interests depends upon the constellation of preferences among the Great Powers. Their choices are meaningfully interdependent because none of them can generate a recognition cascade alone and none of them wants to experience the reputational and other negative consequences attendant to unilateral recognition against the weight of the international community's consensus.[36] When the Great Powers' interests coincide in favor of a would-be state or against it, whether because of a harmony of interests or not, they easily coordinate their recognition.[37] When their interest-based preferences are split, the situation is more akin to a PD; unilateral recognition is attractive in the short term, but the routine defection from the norm of mutually acceptable recognition would leave all of the Powers worse off due to the system-wide instability it would create. Achieving and maintaining agreement becomes more difficult when a greater number of the Powers choose to weigh in on the recognition of a potential new member and, conversely, will be easier to maintain when there are fewer Powers involved.

If this alternative interpretation is correct, then we should expect that the recognition of new states will depend upon the alignment of powerful states' interests and whether they are able to generate mutually agreeable outcomes given the strategic situation in which they find themselves. In some cases the situation resembles a coordination problem, and in others it resembles a PD. The situation changes depending upon which actor's membership is at stake and on the Great Powers' engagement. This rationalist account helps to explain the behavioral convergence in state practice when it comes to recognition. It illustrates why states usually agree about the rightful new members of the international community even though their consensus is routinely at odds with the dictates of customary international law enshrined in the Montevideo Convention standards.[38]

---

[36] This is consistent with Guzman's (2002) explanation for compliance with CIL.

[37] Successful coordination among the Great Powers in these situations may also generate moral hazard. A new state member may be consistent with states' short-term interests, but because the issue of the new member's viability is not the primary determinant behind state preferences for recognition, these newcomers may be more likely to undermine system stability and security over the long run.

[38] Another possible explanation for the divergence from the rule is that the interests that generated the standards agreed to in the Montevideo Convention

The recent breakdown in cooperative non-recognition, principally between the United States (US) and Russia, nicely demonstrates the rational choice dynamics involved in cases of new state personality, even though it is a relatively rare example of non-coordinated Great Power recognition.

C. Case Study: Recognition for Kosovo, South Ossetia and Abkhazia 2008

A breakdown in compliance with the CIL of recognition, and a break in cooperative non-recognition among the Great Powers, occurred in 2008 when the US and many European Union (EU) members formally recognized Kosovo's independence and Russia counter-recognized the independence of Georgian exclaves Abkhazia and South Ossetia.[39] All three would-be state actors had been functionally independent of their predecessors (Serbia and Georgia) for years, but their positions were bolstered by a powerful external guarantor (the US and Russia respectively). Though these powerful benefactors did not hold *de jure* authority over the secessionist regions, they maintained significant influence over the territories, making it difficult to argue that any of the three were effectively independent or met the Montevideo Convention criteria.

Non-recognition had endured for years even though each patron state individually preferred recognition for its client(s) and preferred non-recognition for the other's client(s).[40] Neither predecessor would consent to their secessionists' independence.[41] The US and various European states were the first to change their policies, initially promoting, and then formally recognizing, Kosovo's unilateral declaration of independence in

---

have changed over time. Various factors might explain a shift in state preferences: power has shifted significantly, geopolitical alignments have changed, institutions like colonialism are now defunct, and tens of new states have entered the international community of states. Any or all of these changes might have contributed to changes in state preferences regarding the criteria for recognition. So the rules may be antiquated, but there are no readily available, mutually agreeable alternatives to Montevideo.

39 Bearce (2002), in an earlier work on Yugoslavia, explains Germany's apparent unilateral recognition of Slovenia and Croatia as a defection from Europe's cooperative non-recognition.

40 Russia opposed Kosovo's independence and the US opposed independence for South Ossetia and Abkhazia.

41 The acquiescence of the predecessor state is often cited as an additional criterion for formal recognition (as discussed above). If it is emergent CIL, the rule was not adhered to in these cases.

February 2008. When the US explained its deviation from the law and the explicit agreements it made under UN Security Council (UNSC) Resolution 1244,[42] Washington argued that the decision was necessitated by the exceptional circumstances in the Kosovo case.[43] Moscow countered that Kosovo's situation was 'not unique', threatened to follow suit and recognize the secessionists on Russia's border, and criticized the West's hypocrisy.[44] Indeed, they had recently offered a similar claim regarding exceptional circumstances regarding recognition for Bosnia-Herzegovina.

But Russia did not follow through on its saber-rattling. Instead, it chose to forgo retribution for the US and EU in the short term. That decision was short-lived. When Georgia tried to retake South Ossetia by force later that summer, the Russian military, ostensibly in the region as peacekeepers, countered the attack, defended the independence of the two breakaway enclaves and formally recognized them shortly thereafter. In response, the US and others condemned Russia's aggression, believing that Moscow had initiated the violence in order to break the stalemate. Further, they criticized recognition, arguing that there was no reasonable parallel to be drawn between the Georgian and Kosovo cases.

In the time since recognition, Kosovo has moved relatively more quickly toward widespread recognition as a legitimate member of the international community than South Ossetia or Abkhazia.[45] It has gained membership in a number of important intergovernmental organizations, has established political and economic ties with tens of other states and has generally become more embedded in the international community. South Ossetia and Abkhazia have not been widely embraced. Only a small handful of states recognize them in addition to Russia. Still, in neither case did the patrons' recognition effectively create full statehood and membership in the international community for their clients. Tellingly, none will be permitted to join the UN because both the US and Russia would almost certainly utilize their vetoes.

---

42 UNSC, Resolution 1244, June 10, 1999.

43 For a review of the arguments advanced and the legal issues at stake see Orakhelashvili 2008.

44 Kommersant 2008; Lowe 2008.

45 At the time of writing Kosovo is recognized by 111 states, 23 of which are members of the EU.

D. Analysis

The customary norm embodied in the Montevideo Convention has a more difficult time explaining the evolution of state behavior in these cases than the proposed self-interested alternative based in law and economics. On one hand, it is easy to see why non-recognition would be pursued as a policy based upon the facts of the cases. Non-recognition could be due to unlawful acts that resulted in the de facto sovereignty of the secessionists in accordance with article 41(2) of the International Law Commission's Articles on Responsibility of States of Internationally Wrongful Acts (2001). Or, in the case of Kosovo, possibly because the UNSC had reaffirmed the state's territorial integrity in Resolution 1244. The 2008 break from non-recognition is more perplexing, however, because the facts of the cases did not change substantially. Why did the states recognize when they did? Are these instances of premature, illegal recognition? It seems clear that the standard of independent governance was not met. In the Kosovo case, the government's agreement to adhere to the Ahtisaari plan, including a lengthy period of international supervision following its recognition, even formalized the regime's non-independence. In Georgia's breakaway regions, the extent of Russia's involvement, including the fact that many individuals had acquired Russian citizenship and that Russia established quasi-permanent military bases within each, provided good reason to doubt their independence from Moscow.

Also according to the traditional view, non-compliance with a customary law might result from a situation where the custom is ambiguous. But none of the formal statements from the US or Russia regarding recognition indicates that they were unclear as to what the legal and normative imperative would have been. One final possibility is that the break with CIL was born of a desire to change the customary rules regarding recognition. This interpretation is most plausible in the Kosovo case because the US frequently referred to the egregious human rights violations and crimes against humanity committed by Serbs and the Serbian government against Kosovo's Albanian Muslims. Again, however, in explaining its deviation from the law, the US emphasized that its recognition of Kosovo should not be considered a precedent-setting act, but instead, a response to a situation that was entirely *sui generis*.

A law and economics approach might alternatively describe the situation between the Great Powers as a repeated bilateral PD with a coordination problem.[46] The coordination problem arose because the two sides could not agree as to what constituted cooperation versus defection. Western states saw Russian support of the secessionists through the issuance of passports and the provision of economic and military aid as cheating. Russia saw the US/EU capacity building and later unprecedented and non-precedent setting recognition as cheating as well. This gradually whittled away at cooperative non-recognition between the two sides and helps to explain why cooperation broke down when it did.

Seen in this light, the content of the standards outlined in the Montevideo Convention do not dictate the practice of recognition. Instead, state leaders coordinate their recognition when they are able to in order to pursue their mutual interest in system stability and non-overlapping sovereignty. There is a norm regarding the process of the acceptance of new community members, the characteristics of whom change considerably, but it is not embodied in the Montevideo Convention's prerequisites nor is it complied with out of a sense of legal obligation. When powerful states preferences are aligned regarding a prospective new member, the strategic situation is pure coordination; when they are not it may resemble a PD. Rarely will there be no opportunity to cooperate whatsoever. What this process generally produces is mutually acceptable new states and widespread recognition as in most post-colonial states, the post-Soviet states, East Timor and South Sudan. Occasionally, it yields widespread non-recognition as in the South African Bantustans, Rhodesia, Manchukuo and Somaliland.

4. STATE FAILURE AND DEATH

On the opposite end of the spectrum, states rarely 'die' or wholly cease to be international legal persons. This trend coincides with the widespread acceptance of the territorial sovereignty rule prohibiting the acquisition

---

[46] Situations may, of course, be multilateral, but this situation is best characterized as a bilateral PD. Another interesting question, outside the scope of this chapter, is how the structure of this situation came to be; how the problem of recognition was constructed. Was Moscow opportunistic and disingenuous in its characterization of the two situations as analogous, linking the international status of one to the others? Or in linking South Ossetia to Abkhazia? In fact, we might also question whether the US and EU members saw the strategic situation similarly; there is evidence that they rejected Russia's linking of the cases as they repeatedly emphasized that Kosovo was *sui generis*. In that case, only examining Kosovo recognition, a multilateral PD might be more appropriate.

of territory by force.[47] CIL, formalized in the UN Charter and other documents, protects states from losing their legal personality when they are annexed or invaded by an outside force. Article 2(4) of the UN Charter expressly prohibits the aggressive use of force. When an illegal act of force results in a government's loss of effective control, it does not lose its external sovereignty even though it no longer meets the requirements for statehood.[48] The Montevideo Convention also affirms this.[49] The illegality of the violence leading to the loss of effective control invalidates the authority of the occupying force.[50] Even in cases of state dissolution, there is often a core unit that survives the departures of the other constituent parts, inheriting the legal personality of its former, larger self.[51] As a result, matters of succession have received more attention than the fundamental collapse of states in international law.

Yet issues of state death provide fertile ground for research in the law and economics tradition. For example, we might ask why the strength of the customary norm against territorial aggrandizement has achieved such a high rate of compliance. That is, why do states so infrequently die as a result of annexation and conquest?[52] Political scientists have presented a number of potential interest-based explanations for the norm including the rise of two superpowers with an anti-colonial agenda, the decreasing value of territory relative to markets and state leaders' strong preference in favor of durable boundaries for post-colonial states.

Another area regarding state death ripe for examination is the empirical paradox inherent in the widespread maintenance of recognition and legal personality for failed or collapsed states.[53] Perhaps extending the state death metaphor too far, we will refer to this as 'posthumous' recognition. In contemporary politics, when a state loses control it is

---

[47] For a review of the patterns of state death and explanations for its relative decline from a political science perspective, see Fazal 2007.

[48] Charter of the UN, 1945.

[49] Montevideo Convention, article 16.

[50] Crawford 1987: 132; Montevideo Convention.

[51] For example Russia succeeded the USSR in 1991.

[52] Trachtman and Norman (2005: 34) briefly describe compliance with the rule as a cooperative equilibrium in a repeated multilateral prisoners' dilemma.

[53] We define state failure consistent with Helman and Ratner (1992: 8) as those countries 'utterly incapable of sustaining [themselves] as [members] of the international community' and 'simply unable to function as independent entities'. Following Rotberg (2004), modern states' most fundamental functions (in order of importance) are the provision of: security, law, civil and political rights, and public welfare including healthcare, infrastructure and education. The most extreme failure lies in the inability to provide security.

more often the result of an internal challenge and institutional entropy than a foreign annexation. Why do these actors maintain posthumous international legal personality as states? Why do their peers not revoke recognition from actors incapable of reliably enforcing order and providing governance? Perhaps it is not surprising that actors who temporarily lose control would be granted deference on the expectation that they might resurrect sovereign authority. But the posthumous recognition norm becomes significantly more puzzling in cases like Somalia where the externally manufactured Transitional Federal Government (TFG) holds the country's international legal personality even though it has never exercised anything close to authoritative control or provided much by way of governance to its population. Most parts of Somalia have not been governed by or received basic public goods from the recognized authorities since at least 1991.

What makes this practice perplexing for rational choice is that we might expect states would attempt to coordinate their behavior to address the negative externalities associated with the sustained lapse of effective sovereignty.[54] States depend upon their peers to maintain internal order within their territories and to possess the capability to make good on their promises. Failed states cannot be counted on for either of these things and therefore generate a burden for others. Because failed states lack the ability to enforce order, they also cannot be coerced or persuaded via the conventional tools of diplomacy and statecraft; the externalities do not result from a lack of will.[55] Moreover, states that cannot control their territories or populations may present non-traditional threats in the form of refugees, terrorism, illegal trafficking, crime and even environmental degradation and the spread of disease. All other things being equal, community members should prefer capable states to failed states. Then why don't existing states move to reduce the inefficiency of posthumous recognition for non-viable members when no egregious violation of the

---

54 Failed states' actions may produce positive externalities for their peers, but we assume that negative externalities are more common. We define 'externality' quite broadly as: a beneficial or detrimental effect on one state as a result of the behavior of another state.

55 Identifying another state actor's 'type' is often important in determining whether cooperative agreements should be made in economic analysis. This, in part, explains why reputation is so significant in many models; states prefer to enter into agreement with those that will comply and reputation acts as a signal of a state's likely 'type'. State failure obviates the significance of type regarding the potential for cooperation. The information is not private; it is plainly apparent that a failed state cannot make good on its commitments even if its leaders have the will to do so.

territorial sovereignty rule has occurred? We examine this situation in further detail below.

A. Customary Law and Decertification

The traditional view of CIL and legal personality seems to obviate a discussion concerning the posthumous recognition of failed states. The dynamics of effectiveness, so pivotal to statehood, ought to take care of the problem. When a state ceases to meet the criteria required for statehood, it also ceases to exist as an international legal person and, according to the dominant declaratory theory, this is true regardless of external recognition to the contrary. In practice, this expectation cannot withstand scrutiny, however, because failed states simply do not die. In recent cases where the Montevideo Convention criteria were unambiguously not met for sustained periods, including Lebanon in the 1980s, Afghanistan, the Democratic Republic of Congo and Liberia in the 1990s, and Somalia in the two decades since the collapse of the Siad Barre regime, the states did not lose legal personality. They were consistently regarded as states and endowed with the rights and responsibilities of a state in international affairs. For example, the Rabbani government maintained Afghanistan's diplomatic missions abroad, and in the Somali case the international community has recognized various transitional authorities as Somalia's 'legitimate' government.

No legal doctrine specifically prescribes that sustained governmental collapse should result in decertification, or the revocation of the failed state's legal personality. Yet there is wide agreement that sustained internal anarchy does mean that the state legally ceases to exist. According to Kunz, 'International law determines … that the disappearance of one of [the four Montevideo Convention standards] has as a legal consequence the extinction of the sovereign state'.[56] He continues, 'territorial changes do not affect the identity of the state, except if they legally lead to the extinction of the state. But international law does not contain universally valid and obligatory criteria as to what must be the extent or the nature of territorial changes in order to lead to the extinction of the state.'[57] The same problem arises with the Montevideo Convention's other three criteria. Nor is a time period specified for the lapse of

[56] Kunz 1955: 71.
[57] Kunz 1955: 73.

the criteria before the state is extinct, during which it might be 'resurrected' and reclaim its international legal personality. Given the substantial ambiguity surrounding the rule's behavioral implications, Kunz determines that when states operate according to political considerations it is due to:

> the uncertainty of the law – the lack of the determination of exceptions to the general norm of identity in spite of territorial changes, and the lack of determination of the conditions under which the rule of identity works in spite of revolutionary changes, notwithstanding the extinction of the state under another norm of general international law – which is the ultimate reason for the lack of clarity and agreement in the doctrine.[58]

In short, greater specificity would induce greater compliance; current legal doctrine is an incomplete contract without apparent default rules.

Yet even without the formal codification of rules, the CIL directive in cases of state collapse seems clear according to the dominant, declaratory view of recognition. Actors without a defined territory, permanent population, government and the ability to participate in international relations, and those who remain unable to do so for an extended period, are not states and ought not be treated as such.[59] There is no option to maintain formal diplomatic relations because these actors are ineligible to participate and further, they are incapable of maintaining them. If recognition for those newborn states not yet meeting the Montevideo Convention threshold is considered 'premature' and without legal effect, then the international community has a robust norm of posthumous, and similarly illegal, recognition after states have died. The absence of a codified behavioral directive might help to explain why states would break diplomatic relations in a disorganized fashion, or why they would delay the withdrawal of personality for some time following a state's collapse. It cannot explain why, without exception, the states of the international community do not allow states to become extinct or why they allow individuals to maintain the façade of leadership and agency in international forums when they, in fact, have none.

---

[58] Kunz 1955: 76.

[59] For lack of a better descriptor, we will call these collapsed states 'actors' even though it is not clear that this suggestion of corporate, unitary character is true.

B. An Alternative View

Considering the topic of posthumous recognition and the potential cessation of legal personality from a rational choice perspective, we depart from one of Goldsmith and Posner's major claims and manipulate their concept for our own use. Goldsmith and Posner argue that, within the international community, so-called 'rogue states' have high discount rates that make them more likely to defect from compliance with international law.[60] Unfortunately, this characterization of rogue states does not conform to political reality. Leaders of rogue states are not impulsive and, therefore, unable to maintain cooperative relations with other states. In fact, they are quite predictable and quite stable. If they were not, they would likely not be able to maintain authority and control for very long. Rogue state leaders – the Kim Jong Ils, Robert Mugabes, and Slobodan Milosevics of the world – are inscrutable because the content of their preferences departs so significantly from most other members of the international community. The leaders of rogue states are bad for their people, but they are reliably, predictably bad. Normatively, disagreeing with their preferences and the rationale behind them is not equivalent to not being able to predict whether they can or will commit. Rogue states may have a reputation for a history of persistent objections to community norms and beliefs, but that is something different altogether.

Failed states, on the other hand, more precisely approximate the characteristics that Goldsmith and Posner attribute to rogues including 'unstable political systems', 'irrational or impulsive leadership' and that their 'citizens do not enjoy stable expectations'. These are the states, or at least the leaders, with high discount rates. An actor's external recognition and widespread social acceptance as a state does not make that actor capable of unitary rational action, or even boundedly rational action.[61] One could still model the behavior of an individual failed state leader, but the state cannot be considered to behave in a unitary manner. Therefore, we will not attempt to model their behavior or the strategic situation they confront.

Political science has given greater consideration to state failure and recognition than the law, so it offers greater potential insights into state interests and the strategic situation. Why were states without domestic sovereignty initially welcomed into the system and why do they continue

[60] Goldsmith and Posner 2005: 31.

[61] See Wendt (2004: 293) on the inside and outside constitution of state personhood for greater detail.

to persist without it? Decades ago, states with external legitimacy and little to no internal sovereignty were first dubbed 'quasi-states' by Robert Jackson (1987). Along with Carl Rosberg, Jackson argued that quasi-statehood came about as the imperial powers rushed to withdraw from Africa in the middle of the twentieth century.[62] Rising nationalist sentiment and increasing popular disillusionment with imperialism at home combined to encourage hasty independence for colonies that were often not effectively sovereign. Herbst argues that post-colonial African leaders, recognizing their mutual domestic vulnerability, are now opposed to accepting any changes in their inherited borders, including state death.[63] Leaders therefore collude in favor of the status quo for everyone as a means of assuring that they individually maintain their authority. Off continent, states defer to the regional authorities, not wanting to be branded neo-colonialists and acutely concerned about a potential domino effect should Africa's external sovereignty begin to unravel. Together, these theories provide a potential explanation for why states without domestic sovereignty exist and why those states that have failed continue to enjoy posthumous recognition; especially where these states had been born into the system as quasi-states, never truly having achieved de facto authority during their tenures.

Political scientists would say that the failed state's neighbors usually have the most to gain from posthumous recognition because they simultaneously preserve their own external legitimacy. But these states are also the most at risk of suffering from failure's negative externalities. Then again, as they are often weak themselves, they may have a higher threat tolerance than stronger, more secure states. If accurate, this situation can usefully be described as a PD where cooperation is continued, posthumous recognition. Individually, each state has an incentive to get rid of the collapsed state or states that menace them but, defensively, each state also wants to ensure that its peers don't have the option of getting rid of them one day. This situation is analogous to Trachtman and Norman's description of compliance with the territorial sovereignty norm except that, in this case, it explains why a formal rule has failed to emerge; why the international norm is contrary to the CIL implied by the Montevideo Convention.[64] In that model, the authors argue that either a 'grim trigger' or a 'penance' strategy would serve to

---

62 Jackson and Rosberg 1982.
63 Herbst 1996/7; 2000.
64 Trachtman and Norman 2005: 34.

maintain the cooperative equilibrium (in this case posthumous recognition). Presuming that the current situation regarding collapsed states is normatively undesirable though, we might find it more useful to determine the conditions that would increase state compliance with the CIL implied by the Montevideo Convention or the conditions under which a more formal rule of decertification might emerge.

C. Case Study: Somalia and Failed States' Legal Personality

Somalia has been without a capable central government since at least 1991 when a military dictatorship collapsed in the throes of civil war. Since then, various changes in local authority have occurred. First, a secessionist state, Somaliland, emerged within the borders of the former British Somaliland colony in the country's northwest and has governed itself peacefully and independently, albeit at a low capacity, since the mid-1990s. Two other autonomous, non-secessionist territories in the northeastern and central regions, Puntland and Galmudug, have also emerged. Finally, various coalitions, some supported by the international community, others not, have secured and lost control in the south-central region where Mogadishu, the capital city, is located. Some, like the Islamic Courts Union (ICU) have sometimes asserted durable control, while others have only achieved fleeting authority. The TFG, constituted by and supported by the international community, was the recognized government of the Somalia until recently.[65] However its control and authority are limited to small pockets in the south-central region and, even then, it is reliant upon local militias with uncertain allegiance to the authorities in Mogadishu. Contemporary Somalia is often described as the 'most failed failed state' in the world.

The Somali state's collapse, as is typical, generates negative externalities for its neighbors and states further afield. The TFG coalition's conflict with the Islamist Al Shabaab insurgency, active principally in the south-central region, has generated destabilizing refugee problems for Kenya and Ethiopia and the conflict itself has spilled over borders into neighboring states. In the north, illegal immigration and illicit weapons trafficking generate problems for Yemen and Oman. The effects of the state's collapse have adversely affected more distant states as well. The rapid increase in maritime piracy off the Somali coast beginning in 2008 generated economic costs both for those ships that were hijacked and for

---

[65] The TFG was replaced by the Federal Government of Somalia in late 2012; the discussion here focuses on the TFG period.

the shipping community writ large in the form of increased insurance and hazard pay for crews. Naval patrols in the area are also very costly. Additionally, Somali nationals and members of the Somali Diaspora have been implicated in several incidents of international terrorism.

Despite the persistent collapse of central government and the negative externalities generated by Somalia in its current form, it has persisted as an actor endowed with legal personality for the last two decades.[66] If the Somali state, embodied in the TFG, is considered a viable actor in the strategic situation, this may be a case of asymmetric cooperation wherein the international community has an interest in limiting the negative externalities of Somalia's failure, but the TFG is relatively indifferent as to whether piracy, for example, continues or stops.[67] This would resemble a so-called 'upstream-downstream' problem; so eliminating the problems attendant to state failure (cooperation) could be achieved by manipulating the TFG's incentives, perhaps through payoffs for policing its shores to ensure pirates do not take to the sea. But the TFG exercises so little actual authority that, despite its legal personality, it cannot really be considered capable of following through on any commitments it might make. There is no uncertainty, its commitments are not credible and the other members of the international community know it. Therefore the problem is more accurately cast as one among the members of the international community excluding Somalia.

D. Analysis

Is posthumous recognition for Somalia an example of a consistent violation of CIL? There is no particular rule that actors not meeting the Montevideo Convention criteria cannot have external recognition, but that is the logical implication of the widely held declaratory theory. According to the traditional approach, adopting formal rules would help to increase compliance with the customary rule. Because it is already legitimate and believed to be law, states simply need rules to better specify how they should behave in order to coordinate their behavior. But even in the most extraordinary case of contemporary state collapse, there has been little international discussion concerning the revocation of Somalia's legal personality or even discussion about allowing some of its territorial authority to devolve to its de facto successors in Somaliland,

---

[66] Chopra 1996.

[67] If UN reports are accurate, the local Puntland government in Somalia may directly or indirectly gain from maritime piracy.

Puntland or Galmudug. The international community insists that Somalia retain its external sovereignty.

Alternatively, perhaps this is an example of cooperation within a multilateral PD where rules have not developed to the detriment of most states and the effective functioning of the international community. There is significant African opposition to changing Somalia's borders, even within Ethiopia and Kenya, the neighbors most threatened by its collapse. At first, the practice of posthumous recognition is perplexing because the number of weak and failed states has proliferated and the negative externalities have, presumably, also become more acute. But perhaps the proliferation of weak states works to perpetuate cooperation. As the number of weak states increases, the number of states that would be better off with a more precise, formal rule on revocation declines. And while all states may be threatened by failed states, only weak states would seriously imperil their own future claim to sovereignty by agreeing to conditions under which they will revoke external sovereignty. Should their claims to effective control and authority remain tenuous or take a precipitous turn for the worse, they would have sown the seeds of their own demise.

If the characterization above is accurate, then rational choice offers potential insight into what might break the cooperative pattern. If, out of deference to weak states, strong states are preventing the withdrawal of recognition from failed states, then perhaps, as on the occasion of the recognition of new statehood, strong states could also instigate a change. Among strong states only, the situation no longer resembles a PD, as they are relatively invulnerable to a revocation rule.[68] Instead, the strong would all be better off if they could collectively revoke recognition from states like Somalia that are unable to control their territories or make good on their commitments; the withdrawal of recognition is a coordination problem. Again Great Power decisions could serve as a focal point for other states.

At least one strong state appeared ready, for a time, to withdraw legitimacy from a failed state. In 2002, a controversial decision by the Bush Administration included the so-called 'failed state doctrine', which asserted that the Geneva Conventions did not apply to the US conflict with Afghanistan. Although both countries were High Contracting Parties to the Conventions, Bush Administration advisors, noting that Afghanistan was a failed state, argued that members of the unrecognized Taliban

---

[68] Still, given their significant domestic challenges we would expect China and Russia to be relatively more hesitant to enact a revocation rule.

regime were, therefore, not entitled to prisoner of war (POW) status.[69] For various reasons, non-application of the Geneva Conventions was a non-starter, foremost among them that the laws apply to non-state actors as well as states, that they are CIL and that it contravened the long-standing US position on Afghanistan. Though President Bush later reversed his stance, it remains unclear whether the change was due to a repudiation of the argument that failed states should cease to exist according to the law or something else.[70] Should more occasions arise where strong states are unwilling to extend the basic privileges of community membership to collapsed states, and if they can coordinate that revocation, posthumous recognition may fall out of favor and compliance with CIL may increase.[71]

5. POTENTIAL CHALLENGES FOR THE LAW AND ECONOMICS APPROACH

Rational choice is not a panacea when it comes to understanding the dynamics of statehood in international law. Indeed, it is vulnerable to many of the same criticisms that law and economics scholars levy at more traditional legal scholarship. A rationalist framework, for example, can just as easily succumb to post hoc explanations based upon instrumentalism as traditional scholarship might succumb to explanations based in legal and normative reasoning. Still, many of these problems can be mitigated though careful attention to the nature of the problem or situation being examined and to the actors themselves; through empirical testing that examines all the relevant alternatives; and by being scrupulous and transparent about the strengths and limitations of each method and model employed.

---

[69] The position was roundly criticized within and outside the White House. According to Caron (2005: 219), a 'failed state doctrine not only removes the rights of the failed state … it removes all of the obligations of the failed state …' In cases like Afghanistan where the Taliban did exercise de facto authority, Caron suggests that the potential for a 'clean slate' as a matter of doctrine would generate moral hazard.

[70] Caron 2005: 220.

[71] Of course, there may also be other reasons why states are willing to sustain external legitimacy for collapsed states that have not been considered here.

A. Equifinality and Causality

The difficulty of inferring motivations from behavior is one of the more enduring and inescapable problems of the social sciences. So far, law and economics has challenged traditional understandings of international law by putting forward alternative, interest-based explanations. These scholars have been less successful at teasing out the causal relationships and mechanisms, however. For example, given two potential explanations for state compliance with CIL – one traditional explanation rooted in *opinio juris* and one rationalist explanation rooted in interest – the two are rarely examined simultaneously by either rational choice or traditional legal scholars.[72] Furthermore, the two motives are rarely mutually exclusive. Might normative, legal reasoning be limiting the set of choices a state considers, even if it seems not to factor into the final decision calculus? Might self-interested calculations which led to the creation of laws and institutions at time T later shape state preferences at time T+1? Even where rational choice seems to offer a more compelling explanation for state behavior, traditional explanations, including the normative motivations suggested by managerial and procedural models, are not often examined as competing hypotheses.[73] This challenge simply recommends careful and falsifiable empirical research.

B. States and Non-states as Rational Actors?

Many of the most interesting puzzles concerning the birth and deaths of states, other than those presented herein, must meaningfully incorporate non-state actors. Critics of the law and economics approach may question whether the assumptions of rational choice are appropriate for analyzing the behavior of non-state actors like secessionist movements, insurgent groups and indigenous peoples. To what extent can non-state actors be considered rational, unitary actors akin to states or state leaders? As Goldsmith and Posner note, pre-state and non-state actors are the most likely to violate the assumptions underlying rational choice and law and economics.[74] Scholars using a law and economics framework should be

---

[72] Indeed, this is the most common critique levied at Goldsmith and Posner; it is difficult to argue that *opinio juris* does not exist when one's research design explicitly excludes the possibility that it might.

[73] For example, theories of compliance offered by Chayes and Chayes (1995) and Franck (1995). Sandler (2008) is a notable exception in his analysis of treaty ratification and compliance.

[74] Goldsmith and Posner 2005: 8.

especially careful about applying rational choice assumptions to actors that will almost certainly not approximate them. It is always the case that assumptions represent a simplification and do not reflect reality. But the break between the assumption and reality is not the real issue. The problem arises because, in circumstances where the actors cannot be rational or, more precisely, are not even actors (see the discussion at section 4A above regarding failed states), the approach will not generate useful insights. However this is not a new problem, nor one that is unique to rational choice in political science.[75]

The greatest impediment to successfully utilizing a law and economics framework to analyze both state and non-state actors is the asymmetry of the situations they face. The deep structure of the international system is predicated upon the legitimate membership and juridical equality of states and the non-membership and inequality of non-state actors. Consequently, even in what ostensibly appear to be the same circumstances, the strategic situations between states and non-state actors are often fundamentally different. This is not necessarily a limitation. Indeed, careful modeling of the different incentives faced by states and non-state actors in superficially similar strategic circumstances will illuminate system dynamics that have heretofore been relatively neglected.

C. Behavioral Economics and Empirical Research

Another potential limitation has its roots in the behavioral critique of rational choice assumptions writ large. Cognitive psychologists and behavioral economists have demonstrated various systematic ways that human decision-makers violate the expectations of rational choice. Specifically, this research finds that humans are 'cognitive misers' and 'satisficers', controverting rational choice assumptions that actors are interest maximizers with fully ordered, ranked and transitive preferences over outcomes.

Empirical research has found that human information processing utilizes simplifying heuristics that, while very useful in day-to-day life, may sometimes lead to preferences and decisional outcomes contrary to rationalist models. For example, Daniel Kahneman and Amos Tversky's famous experiments on prospect theory show that humans' propensity for risk depends meaningfully upon whether a decision is framed as a

---

[75] See the forum on the 'state as person' in international relations in *Review of International Studies* 2004, 30:2.

potential loss or a potential gain.[76] Ultimately, much of the 'behavioral challenge' can be complementary to the law and economics project. By specifying the conditions under which systematic deviations from rational choice are likely, we can incorporate them into our models and generate hypotheses that are increasingly consistent with empirical reality. Some important work along these lines, including that by Jolls, Sunstein, and Thaler, provides a potential touchstone for approaching behavioral work in international law.[77]

Another technique for improving the external validity of rational choice research is to create models of greater complexity.[78] Empirical research, where the simplifying assumptions of ideal form PDs are violated – allowing communication, repeated play, etc. – often finds greater cooperation than rational choice models would suggest.[79] Since these relaxations conform more to the reality of state interactions, these sorts of empirical tests provide important insights for developing more robust models and better specifying the conditions under which CIL is more likely to emerge and improve state welfare.

6. CONCLUSION

This chapter argues that rational choice approaches have great unrealized potential regarding the most fundamental dynamics of international law, including Great Power recognition and the emergence of new states and posthumous recognition in cases of state collapse.

In this chapter we have limited our discussion to these two research areas, but there are certainly others. The law and economics approach's greatest strength is its ability to elucidate the situational incentives facing actors and to generate novel, and perhaps counterintuitive, hypotheses based upon the structure and interdependence of actors' preferences. In the cases that we have touched upon here, Goldsmith and Posner's framework has helped to show why states' recognition behavior has achieved such a high degree of convergence with rules other than – but often mistaken for – those prescribed by CIL. Rational self-interest also

---

76 Kahneman and Tversky 1979.

77 Jolls, Sunstein and Thaler 1998. Also see Van Aaken 2008 regarding international law in particular.

78 Van Aaken (2008: 53) notes correctly, however, that 'without abstraction there is … no academic knowledge'; parsimony is essential to good social science research.

79 Ostrom 2000.

helps to explain why states do not typically withdraw recognition from failed states even when they might prefer to do so for a given failed state menace. Law and economics research also has the potential to advance normative work on statehood and sovereignty. For example, as suggested by Norman and Trachtman, it can help to identify the conditions under which the continued operation or development of CIL is more normatively attractive than its formalization through treaties or other agreements, or conversely, when formalization will yield greater state compliance or more normatively desirable results than CIL. There are some hurdles to successfully utilizing a rational choice approach that are especially acute given the nature of the topics addressed here, but they are not insurmountable. Careful attention to the suitability of rational choice assumptions on a given topic, to the modeling decisions employed and to causal processes should suffice in most cases.

REFERENCES

Bearce, David H. 2002. 'Institutional Breakdown and International Cooperation: European Recognition of Croatia and Slovenia', *European Journal of International Relations* 8:4, 471–97.

Bradley, Curtis A., and Mitu Gulati. 2010. 'Withdrawing from International Custom', *The Yale Law Journal* 120:202.

Bull, Hedley. 1977. *The Anarchical Society: A Study of Order in World Politics*, New York, NY: Columbia University Press.

Caron, David D. 2005. 'If Afghanistan has Failed, Then Afghanistan is Dead: "Failed States" and the Inappropriate Substitution of Legal Conclusion for Political Description', in Karen J. Greenberg (ed.). *The Torture Debate in America*, New York, NY: Cambridge University Press, 214–22.

Chayes, Abram and Antonia Handler Chayes. 1995. *The New Sovereignty: Compliance with International Regulatory Agreements*, Cambridge, MA: Harvard University Press.

Chopra, Jarat. 1996. 'Achilles' Heel in Somalia: Learning from a Conceptual Failure', 31 *Texas International Law Journal* 31, 495.

Coggins, Bridget. 2011. 'Friends in High Places: International Politics and the Emergence of States from Secessionism', *International Organization* 65:3, 433–67.

Crawford, James A. 1978. 'The Criteria for Statehood in International Law', 48 *British Yearbook of International Law* 93.

Downs, George W., David Rocke and Peter N. Barsoom. 1996. 'Is the Good News about Compliance Good News for Cooperation?', *International Organization* 50:3, 379–406.

Evans, Peter B., Harold K. Jacobson and Robert D. Putnam (eds.). 1993. *Double-Edged Diplomacy: International Bargaining and Domestic Politics*, Berkeley, CA: University of California Press.

Fazal, Tanisha. 2007. *State Death: The Politics and Geography of Conquest, Occupation and Annexation*, Princeton, NJ: Princeton University Press.

Fearon, James D. 2004. 'Separatist Wars, Partition and World Order', *Security Studies* 13:4, 394–415.

Franck, Thomas M. 1995. *Fairness in International Law and Institutions*, Oxford: Clarendon Press.

Goldsmith, Jack L. and Eric A. Posner. 2005. *The Limits of International Law*, New York, NY: Oxford University Press.

Grant, Thomas D. 1999. *The Recognition of States: Law and Practice in Debate and Evolution*, Westport, CT: Preager.

Guzman, Andrew T. 2002. 'A Compliance-Based Theory of International Law', 90 *California Law Review* 1823.

Harris, David. 2004. *Cases and Materials on International Law*, 3rd Edition, London: Sweet and Maxwell.

Helman, Gerald B. and Steven R. Ratner. 1992. 'Saving Failed States', *Foreign Policy* 89, 3–20.

Henkin, Louis. 1979. *How Nations Behave: Law and Foreign Policy*, 2nd Edition, New York, NY: Columbia University Press.

Herbst, Jeffrey. 1996–97. 'Responding to State Failure', *International Security* 21:3 (Winter), 120–44.

Herbst, Jeffrey. 2000. *States and Power in Africa: Comparative Lessons in Political Authority and Control* Princeton, NJ: Princeton University Press.

Jackson, Robert H. 1987. 'Quasi-states, Dual Regimes and Neo-Classical Theory: International Jurisprudence and the Third World', *International Organization* 41:4, 519–49.

Jackson, Robert H. and Carl G. Rosberg. 1982. 'Why Africa's Weak States Persist: The Empirical and Juridical in Statehood'. *World Politics*. 35:1, 1–24.

Jolls, Christine, Cass Sunstein and Richard Thaler. 1998. 'A Behavioral Approach to Law and Economics', *Stanford Law Review* 50:5, 1471–1550.

Jovanovic, Vladislav. 1997–1998. 'The Status of the Federal Republic of Yugoslavia in the United Nations', 21 *Fordham International Law Journal* 1719.

Kahneman, Daniel and Amos Tversky. 1979. 'Prospect Theory: An Analysis of Decision under Risk', *Econometrica* 47:2, 263–92.

Kommersant. February 21, 2008 'Russia Says Kosovo Not Unique', available at www.kommersant.com/p-12092/r_500/Kosovo.

Kontorovich, Eugene. 2008. 'The Inefficiency of Universal Jurisdiction', *University of Illinois International Law Review* 389–418.

Krasner, Stephen. 1999. *Sovereignty: Organized Hypocrisy*, Princeton, NJ: Princeton University Press.

Kunz, Josef L. 1955. 'Identity of States under International Law', *The American Journal of International Law* 49:1, 68–76.

Lowe, Christian. March 11, 2008. 'NATO risks Georgia rebels' secession: Russia', Reuters.

Orakhelashvili, Alexander. 2008. 'Statehood, Recognition and the United Nations System: A Unilateral Declaration of Independence in Kosovo', in A. von Bogdandy and R. Wolfrum (eds.). 2008. *Max Planck Yearbook of United Nations Law* vol. 12, 1–44.

Ostrom, Elinor. 2000. 'Collective Action and the Evolution of Social Norms', *Journal of Economic Perspectives* 14:3, 137–58.

Portmann, Roland. 2010. *Legal Personality in International Law*, Cambridge: Cambridge University Press.

Rotberg, Robert I. (ed.). 2004. *When States Fail: Causes and Consequences*, Princeton, NJ: Princeton University Press.

Sandler, Todd. 2008. 'Treaties: Strategic Considerations', *University of Illinois Law Review* 155.

Snidal, Duncan. 1985. 'The Game Theory of International Politics', *World Politics* 38:1, 25–57.

Talmon, Stefan. 2005. 'The Constitutive Versus the Declaratory Doctrine of Recognition: Tertium Non Datur?', *Barristers Year Book of International Law* 101.

Trachtman, Joel P. and George Norman. 2005. 'The Customary International Law Game', *The Berkeley Electronic Press*, available at http://law.bepress.com/expresso/eps/598.

Van Aaken, Anne. 2008. 'Towards Behavioral Law and Economics: A Comment of Enriching Rational Choice Institutionalism for the Study of International Law', *University of Illinois Law Review* 47.

Verdier, Pierre-Hugues. 2002. 'Cooperative States: International Relations, State Responsibility and the Problem of Custom', *Virginia Journal of International law* 42, 839.

Verdier, Pierre-Hugues and Erik Voeten. 2014. 'Precedent, Compliance and Change in Customary International Law: An Explanatory Theory', *American Journal of International Law* 108, 389.

Wendt, Alexander. 2004. 'The State as Person in International Theory', *Review of International Studies* 30:2, 289–316.

3. Economic analysis of territorial sovereignty

Abraham Bell

INTRODUCTION

International law remains one of the few areas of law where economic analysis has made few inroads. The potential of economics to contribute to analysis of international law is particularly noticeable regarding doctrines of territorial sovereignty. The laws of territorial sovereignty are among the earliest to have been developed in modern international law, and are among the most important. Given the centrality of sovereignty to post-Westphalian international law, the territorial scope of sovereignty is naturally of overriding importance. At the same time, territorial sovereignty is often contested, and the rules of territorial sovereignty are constantly changing. All this would seem to indicate the potential attractiveness of normative economic analyses of the laws of territorial sovereignty.

Unfortunately, there is precious little scholarship on territorial sovereignty law that utilizes the insights of economic analysis.

In part, this gap can be filled by examining related fields of law. Economic analysis of property would appear to be a natural source of inspiration for the economic analysis of territorial sovereignty law. The doctrines of territorial sovereignty bear a strong resemblance to the laws of property in municipal law. Territorial sovereignty, like property, contains rules of acquisition, transfer and abandonment. It uses chains of title to evaluate claims, and adopts standard property maxims such as *nemo dat quod non habet* (one cannot transfer what one does not have).

Unfortunately, economic analysis of property law can only partially fill the gaps in analysis of territorial sovereignty. Economic analysis of property is under-developed in some areas, meaning that property law analyses cannot fully fill the need for economic analysis of territorial sovereignty. Moreover, as we shall see, many of the concerns of the law of territorial sovereignty differ from those of property, further undermining the possibility of using economic analysis of property to illuminate rules of territorial sovereignty.

This chapter offers a preliminary examination of potential areas of research in the economic analysis of territorial sovereignty. It begins by reviewing the contours of the law of territorial sovereignty and the small amount of research that has already taken place in the field. It then turns to several areas of research in the field of property law that can fruitfully be incorporated into economic analysis of territorial sovereignty. Finally, the chapter considers future potential directions for research, as well as the limitations of the analogy between property and territorial sovereignty.

TERRITORIAL SOVEREIGNTY

Territorial Sovereignty in International Law

The term sovereignty lends itself to multiple meanings. The encyclopedia definition of sovereignty is 'supreme authority within a territory' (Besson 2008) but the definition fails to distinguish among the several different doctrines of sovereignty used in international law. Krasner (1999) suggests there are four different kinds of sovereignty which variously touch upon questions such as internal power and recognition of such power by other states. While international law does not use the categories suggested by Krasner, the law does have a variety of distinct doctrines bearing the name 'sovereignty'. As a result, the term sovereignty can refer to several different doctrines related to very different phenomena.

The focus of this chapter is territorial sovereignty. For our purposes, the law of territorial sovereignty connotes the legitimate territorial scope of a state or sovereign authority. Any given territory may be under the territorial sovereignty of one sovereign or none; in the latter case, the territory is known as *terra nullius*. There are, of course, odd cases in which states may share territorial sovereignty (for instance, under some condominium or co-imperium arrangements), or in which territory is *terra nullius* but yet not available for others to take territorial sovereignty (arguably including such cases as territory designated as a mandate). But for the most part, any given piece of land in the world has one and only one territorial sovereign and only those with sovereign personality (i.e., states) may hold that territorial sovereignty.

While superficially similar in some ways, territorial sovereignty must be distinguished from other kinds of legally important sovereignty such as sovereign personality and internal sovereignty. The doctrines of sovereign personality, for instance, relate to the question of how an entity acquires legal personality by becoming a state under international law. Confusingly, an entity can only acquire sovereign personality if it has control of territory (among other conditions). This can potentially lead to confusion over the question of whether sovereignty refers to the status of an entity – a state or not a state – or it refers to the entity's relationship to territory – the entity has territorial sovereignty over the land, or lacks it.

There is a fairly well-developed set of doctrines circumscribing how states can lawfully acquire and lose territorial sovereignty. The classic list of modes of acquisition describes five methods of acquiring territorial sovereignty: occupation, cession, accretion, prescription and conquest. Occupation refers to possession of *terra nullius*; sovereignty is acquired by acts of possession amounting to effective control by the occupier. Cession refers to acquisition by treaty or agreement; title passes when the agreement becomes effective. Accretion refers to geological additions to riparian or littoral land where the border is set by the water course. Prescription denotes the acquisition of title by a lengthy continuous period of effective control over territory of another state, perhaps accompanied by acquiescence of the other state. Conquest refers to subjugation by belligerence; sovereignty is acquired by purposeful acts of annexation following subjugation. Conquest has gradually fallen into disrepute, and today conquest is either completely invalid as a means of acquiring sovereignty, or according to a minority opinion available only where the belligerence was lawful (as in self-defense) (Malanczuk 1997).

The modes of acquisition may be reversed, and thus sovereign title may be lost by cession, erosion, prescription or defeat to a conqueror, subject to the rules above. In addition, states may abandon title by relinquishing authority over territory, accompanied by an intention to abandon (Malanczuk 1997).

The doctrines of acquisition are used, in conjunction with historical events, to resolve territorial disputes. As the classic arbitral ruling in the *Island of Palmas* case (1928) explains, where states A and B both claim title to any given territory, adjudicators begin at a root of title – the last point in time where the disputants agree upon the territorial sovereign – and move forward, piecing together legally significant historical events to create a chain of title to the present day. Naturally, each historical event is relevant to the chain of title if it involved a valid means of acquiring or losing territorial sovereignty.

Some scholars have noted that alongside the classic list, one might place another list of such items as arbitration or adjudication, as well as acquiescence, recognition and estoppel (Malanczuk 1997). But the better way of viewing adjudication is as a means of determining a new root of title. A court that is empowered to establish territorial sovereignty will have to engage in the usual legal-historical analysis to determine a chain of title and award sovereignty to one of the claimants. Once the properly empowered panel or court awards sovereignty, the prior history becomes irrelevant. The ruling is itself the new root of title, and any future disputes about territorial sovereignty must proceed from that point forward.

Claimants may also resolve their dispute outside of court or arbitration by acquiescing to or recognizing the other's claim. Such acquiescence likewise erases the prior history and establishes a new root of title, at least for the agreeing claimants.

The classic list of modes of acquisition relies upon Roman property law, reflecting the close relationship between property law doctrines and international law of territorial sovereignty. Unsurprisingly, many of the modern doctrines of territorial sovereignty continue to resemble strongly those seen in the law of property. Property law also evaluates title by looking at chains of title stemming from a root of title. In territorial sovereignty, as in property law, titles can be relative rather than absolute. That is, territorial sovereignty disputes, like property disputes, are resolved by examining which of the claimants has a better legal claim, rather than by asking which of the parties has perfect legal title. As the 1933 Permanent Court of Arbitration said in the *Legal Status of Eastern Greenland* case, '[i]n most of the cases involving claims to territorial sovereignty which have come before an international tribunal, there have been two competing claims to the sovereignty, and the tribunal has had to decide which of the two is the stronger'. Because title is relative, 'in many cases the tribunal has been satisfied with very little in the way of actual exercise of sovereign rights, provided that the other State could not make out a superior claim'.

Economic Analysis of Territorial Sovereignty

The economic literature on doctrines of territorial sovereignty is limited.

The landmark economic analysis of territorial sovereignty is Alesina and Spolaore (2003), which relied on a series of papers dating back to 1997 (Alesina and Spolaore 2006; Alesina and Spolaore 1997; Alesina, Spolaore and Wacziarg 2001; Alesina and Wacziarg 1998). Notwithstanding its importance, Alesina and Spolaore's work cannot be seen as the last word in the field for the very simple reason that it pays almost no attention to legal doctrine. Alesina and Spolaore's concern is the territorial scope of states, and states' decisions in acquiring, shedding and governing territory, rather than the legal doctrines that apply to such decisions.

Alesina and Spolaore developed several models around the same basic set of insights. To the degree that states have control over their territorial scope, they use their power to optimize the trade-off between the benefits of size and the costs of heterogeneity. Simply put, a large state can provide some services more cheaply, such as national defense, and it can provide a large, stable internal market for goods and services. However, a large state may find that the cost of its size is a population with heterogeneous needs and desires. The gaps in preferences among the different population groups may become so pronounced as to make the large size of a state no longer worth the trouble. Alesina and Spolaore suggest that some basic factors will have predictable impacts on the calculus. For instance, international free trade lowers the benefits of the large internal market, and encourages the formation of smaller states. An increased likelihood of military aggression increases the benefits of national defense and encourages larger states.

Alesina and Spolaore observe that states' cost–benefit analysis is complicated by politics. In a Leviathan state, where the central ruler views the state's assets purely in terms of rents that the ruler can extract, the state will tend to aggregate a territory that is larger than the state's optimal size. Conversely, a democratized state, where benefits are diffused among the larger governed population, will tend toward territory that is smaller than the state's optimal size. This is because the democratized state shares burdens equally among its population, but geographic distance from the center of a large state necessarily means that periphery populations will enjoy fewer of the state's benefits.

If one is convinced by Alesina and Spolaore's analysis, there are some remarkable normative conclusions for international law. For instance, given the conflicting tendencies of dictatorships and democracies toward territory, one might suggest dichotomous rules of territorial acquisition, making it easier for democracies to expand their territory, while tilting the scales in favor of dictatorships shedding territory. One might imagine, for example, rules favoring democratic states in territorial disputes, relaxing the intent requirement for abandonment by dictatorial states, or relaxing the prescription period for democratic states. But while one can easily conjure up such doctrinal reforms, it is highly unlikely they will ever find their way into the corpus of international law. Sovereign equality among states is deeply rooted in international law, beginning with the Treaty of Westphalia, and proceeding all the way to the modern day, where it finds expression in article 2(1) of the Charter of the United Nations (Kokott 2011). It is difficult to foresee any international consensus developing allowing treaty or customary changes to the existing rules in favor of democracies and against dictatorships.

Benvenisti and Cohen (2012) use Alesina and Spolaore's work together with Posner (2006), to suggest a different doctrinal change. Benvenisti and Cohen argue for interpreting the principle of self-determination to include a limited right of minorities to secede from existing states. Arguably, no such right exists under current international law, but the principle of self-determination is noticeably vague as a legal doctrine, and Benvenisti and Cohen hopefully point to the Canadian case *Reference re Secession of Quebec* (1998) as a guidepost. In that case, the Supreme Court of Canada rejected a right of secession for Quebec under international law, but suggested that such a right might be available were the seceding group governed as part of a 'colonial empire', was subject to 'alien domination', or otherwise denied any 'meaningful exercise' of its right to self-determination.

Alesina and Spolaore observe that recent years have seen a proliferation of new states, and, thus, the shrinking of the territorial domain of existing states, but they take little note of the way these changes were accomplished. Borders have changed, in the main, due to war and the voluntary division of countries into multiple states. However, there have been very few cases of voluntary cession of territory from one state to another. Why are such transfers so rare?

Simmons (2005) provides a partial answer. Simmons focuses on the benefits provided to states by clear borders. 'Clear agreements over jurisdiction reduce risks to property rights and [] encourage transborder economic relations' while 'uncertainty reduces trade'. While voluntary cessions may be rare, Simmons points to the predominance of undisputed borders in the world as evidence for her thesis. While Simmons does not fully explore the implications of her argument, the best way of understanding it is to say that borders are sticky. Transacting changes in borders is costly, while a clear border, even if badly placed, creates utility through its clarity. Of course, if this argument is taken to its logical conclusion, Alesina and Spolaore's analysis is woefully incomplete. The territorial scope of states must be seen not only as a function of the benefits of size and the cost of heterogeneity, but of the costs of transacting changes in borders. Indeed, one might hypothesize that countries with relatively less costly decision-making apparatuses (such as strong dictatorships bordering strong dictatorships) would have more efficiently placed borders than countries where decision-making is more costly (such as large democracies abutting large democracies).

Simmons' analysis inadvertently provides an explanation for another puzzle of international law. In the many modern cases of fissuring of existing states, the borders of the new states have invariably reflected the borders of pre-existing sub-national polities. This practice is supported by the international law doctrine of *uti possidetis juris*, according to which newly emerging states' legal borders correspond to the borders of the pre-existing administrative/colonial unit from which they emerged, even though the old borders were not international boundaries (Shaw 1997; Nesi 2011). As noted by Ratner (1996), the doctrine of *uti possidetis juris* is highly problematic; lines that were suitable for internal administrative jurisdictions may not be appropriate at all for international borders. Nonetheless, if borders are indeed sticky, and clarity is generally more important than placement, *uti possidetis juris* provides a valuable way of reducing uncertainty.

Benvenisti (1996) focuses on sovereign rights in water resources to emphasize a different aspect of territorial sovereignty. As in municipal property law, international water rights are governed by an entirely different legal regime than are rights in land. While land rights generally involve plenary powers over the surface, subsurface and air, water rights are divided up into multiple use rights. Some areas within bodies of water (coastal sea lands, for instance), are considered territorial waters of states, giving the states near-total control. However, other waters are considered the open seas, subject to appropriation by no state, while yet other waters are subject to divided rights among claimant states and the rest of the world. For instance, in the 'contiguous zone', bordering states control the use of sea and seabed resources, but must respect other countries' freedom of navigation. In the exclusive economic zone, states' ability to control resources is even more limited. The fact that waters are not stationary leads to an additional set of concerns dealing with drawing water from watercourses. Interestingly, here international law has utterly failed to produce usable doctrine. For many years, the UN's draft Convention on the Law of Non-Navigational Uses of International Watercourses (1997) failed to gather even the 35 ratifications necessary to enter into force; today, only 36 states are party to the treaty.

Observing that some uses of water resources produce externalities, and noting that many of the conflicts regarding water resources involve only a small number of claimants, Benvenisti argues that international law ought to focus on encouraging negotiated resolutions; he justifies the vagueness of international water law as forcing cooperation.

This explanation seems inadequate; a better explanation can be found in the transaction cost literature regarding economic analysis of property. Barzel (1997) explains that the confounding feature regarding rights to draw water from watercourses is the high cost of measurement. Barzel observes that in areas where water is exceptionally scarce, states justify the measurement costs, and therefore, they more precisely delineate water rights in their municipal property laws. By contrast, Barzel observes, where water is less scarce, the measurement costs are unjustified, and the law suffices with vaguely or imprecisely defined rights. The problem with the international law of watercourses appears to be the attempt to impose precise rules in all situations, notwithstanding the fact that water scarcity is a localized problem, and only acute in a small set of situations.

PROPERTY AND TERRITORIAL SOVEREIGNTY

While we have seen that the international law doctrines of territorial sovereignty have rarely been subject to economic analysis, the same cannot be said of municipal property law. Although law and economics has lavished less attention on property than other common law subjects (Merrill and Smith 2001), the economic literature on legal property rights remains far richer than the corresponding literature on the doctrines of territorial sovereignty. Economic analysis of property law thus presents a potentially useful source of future studies of territorial sovereignty law.

Prescription and Adverse Possession

Perhaps the clearest potential parallel between territorial sovereignty and property can be found in the doctrines of prescription and adverse possession. International law awards territorial sovereignty to states that enjoy long and peaceful possession of territory of another state, even where the possession is wrongful. Municipal property law has two equivalent doctrines: adverse possession, which awards title to a long-time wrongful possessor of the land of another, and prescription, which awards use rights in the form of easements to long-time wrongful users of the land of another.

To be sure there are some important differences between the property and international law doctrines. In essence, the property doctrine of adverse possession transforms open trespassers into owners of land, so long as the trespassers' possession lasts long enough and abides by the additional conditions of being continuous, exclusive, and 'actual', as well as other technical requirements. In other words, adverse possession only grants title where the possession is 'adverse' or 'hostile', that is, without the permission of the true owner. International law's doctrine of prescription, at least formally, ignores questions of adversity. According to Jennings (1963), prescription 'comprehends both a possession of which the origin is unclear or disputed, and an adverse possession which is in origin demonstrably unlawful'.

Several different economic theories have been offered to justify the property doctrine of adverse possession, though none commands universal assent. Traditionally, adverse possession has been justified either on the grounds that it is necessary to clear away uncertain old titles for which there is insufficient evidence or that it encourages efficient transfers of property from slothful owners who neglect their property rights to trespassers who invest labor and other assets in developing the land (Bouckaert and Depoorter 1999; Netter, Hersch and Manson 1986).

These days, the former rationale is generally dismissed as outdated. Modern Western property systems are accompanied by extensive record keeping, which coupled with modern information technology make it possible to prove even very old title claims (Bell and Parchomovsky 2016). However, the latter rationale is also problematic, since there is no reason to believe that a non-consensual high-impact use is necessarily more efficient than an absentee non-use (Bouckaert and Depoorter 1999).

Newer rationales for the adverse possession doctrine thus focus on different, though related, explanations related to reducing the costs of errors. Netter, Hersch and Manson (1986) argue that adverse possession rules attempt to reduce the costs of title clearance by lowering the costs of investigating title (to a limited period of time) as well as by lowering the costs of keeping old records. These cost reductions come at the expense of inefficient owner monitoring of property to ward off potential trespassers. The optimal adverse possession rule aims for a statutory period that balances these costs.

Miceli (1997) focuses on a different type of error: surveying errors along the boundaries of properties with neighbors. Miceli argues that adverse possession incentivizes true owners to survey their boundaries correctly, and to police errors quickly, lest title be lost. Miceli and Sirmans (1995) use a similar analysis to justify the particular doctrinal components of adverse possession. In either event, cheaper record keeping and cheaper monitoring indicate a shorter term of limitations, while more expensive record keeping and monitoring suggest lengthening the limitations period.

These rationales seem partially to fit the doctrine of prescription in international law. There is no centralized registry for recording title claims of territorial sovereignty. Borders are often long and surveying can be costly. Oftentimes, boundaries are the result of events that occurred centuries ago. At the same time, monitoring encroachments can be quite costly, not only because of the length of the borders, but also because lack of centralized enforcement means title-holders must often use self-help to repel encroachers.

All this suggests that adverse possession can be quite useful in clarifying title and reducing the costs of searching for evidence of title. Because both record keeping and boundary monitoring are expensive, long periods of limitation are indicated. This, indeed, matches the law of prescription, which employs longer periods than are customary in municipal adverse possession law, although there is no agreed upon limitations period.

However, this justification for prescription rules breaks down when one considers the fact that voluntary cessions of title are relatively rare in the international arena. Because transactions are so rare, the gains for potential conveyors produced by clarifying title and wiping away the need for old title searches are minimal. While this suggests that prescription ought not to be seen in the same light as adverse possession, it reinforces the idea that prescription periods ought to be lengthier than the corresponding adverse possession periods in municipal property law.

First Possession

Another parallel discussion between property and territorial sovereignty law concerns doctrines of acquiring title by first possession. Territorial sovereignty awards title to first possessors (or occupiers) of territory without a sovereign. Similar rules apply in the municipal property context. The doctrine of 'discovery' awards title to the first occupier of unowned land. Certain assets – in particular wild animals and 'fugacious' minerals –are subject to a rule of capture or occupancy that grants title to the first person to reduce the items to possession.

The major justifications for first possession or capture rules are straightforward: the rule of capture reduces the evidentiary and administrative costs associated with establishing title (Epstein 1979). Capture rules, however, suffer from a characteristic flaw: they transfer items from the commons to private property item by item, as each is captured, exacerbating the 'tragedy of the commons'. The 'tragedy of the commons' is a phenomenon labeled by Hardin (1968), in which property that is owned by no one (open access, or, less precisely, property in the commons) is likely to be over-used since each item removed from the commons rebounds to the full benefit of the taker, while the losses associated with the removal are spread across all users of the commons. The tragic result is premature exhaustion of the resource. The classic solution for this problem is allocation of property rights to the entire commons, removing the incentive for piecemeal exploitation (Demsetz 1967). Ostrom (1990) observed that in many cases, collective governance may prevent excessive exploitation. Such governance can generally take hold only where a preexisting community can rely on existing rules of the community to reduce the enormous transaction costs associated with the collective governance mechanism.

As it turns out, there is little reason to worry about the tragedy of the commons as it relates to territorial sovereignty in land. Historically, one can identify elements of a tragedy of the commons during the 'Age of Discovery' when European states discovered lands previously unknown to them while denying territorial sovereignty to non-European states. However, the era has passed, and while it has left behind a variety of territorial disputes, it has also accounted for nearly all the lands of the world. Today, while the discovery doctrine continues to award title over land to first possessors, there are precious few undiscovered lands that are not already subject to the territorial sovereignty of a state. The one large land mass that is not under state sovereignty today – Antarctica – is subject to the Antarctica Treaty (1959) under which signatories agree that no new claims of territorial sovereignty can be asserted while the treaty is in force. Together with attendant treaties and guidelines, the Antarctica Treaty permits a variety of uses of the land (primarily scientific) while undermining the utility of acts of possession aimed merely at establishing sovereignty rights.

Benvenisti (2002) has identified an interesting area of international law where the tragedy of the commons may persist: transboundary resources. Technically speaking, the doctrines that apply to transboundary resources are not doctrines of territorial sovereignty. In issues of transboundary resources, the legal question is more akin to property than to sovereignty. The question is not what state may exercise its sovereign power over the resource, but rather, what state has the right to exploit the resource.

One of the basic assumptions of territorial sovereignty is that the state that has sovereignty over any given land, has full rights to exploit the resources in that land, underneath it, and above it. Transboundary resource issues in land arise where a single resource is present under multiple jurisdictions (such as a large pool of underground oil), or where the resource is not stationary (such as running water or wildlife). In such cases, absent an agreement between the states, each state may fully exploit the resource within its land. A related set of problems occurs where the resources are at sea. While the right to exploit resources in land is generally plenary and in the hands of the title-holder, rights to exploit resources at sea are more complicated. Resources found in the open seas are generally open to a first possession rule, while resources in coastal seas are subject to a more complicated regime, granting only some rights to the nearest coastal state. Thus, where no treaty changes the baseline rule, all states may fish as much as they want in the open seas. Within territorial waters, coastal states have greater exclusive rights. Once again, these are not, strictly speaking, questions of territorial sovereignty, but, rather, something more akin to international property law.

Because transboundary resources may be fully exploited by states within their territorial boundaries, or on the open seas, resources may be subject to over-use due to the tragedy of the commons. For instance, oil in an underground pool extending under multiple states is essentially subject to a first possession rule among the states over the pool. Each state enjoys full rights over the oil it extracts, but cannot prevent extraction and exploitation by other states within the other states' territory. Likewise, fish in the open seas may be fully exploited once captured, but no state may block the exploitation by another state. Thus, occasionally, the result is exactly the wasteful exploitation of resources anticipated by the tragedy of the commons. Some fisheries in the open seas, for example, have been exhausted by over-fishing, and some common water resources have been overdrawn. International law has no systematic rule for covering such cases, but several agreements cover specific cases or types of resources. Benvenisti (2002) argues for more systematic cooperation to avoid tragedies of the commons.

While systematic cooperation does emerge in some situations (Ostrom 1990; Axelrod 1984), Benvenisti's argument is best seen as aspirational rather than descriptive. There is little reason to suspect that more systematic cooperation is in the process of emerging. Given this state of affairs, the best explanation of the persistence of rules of first possession may best be a concession to an uncomfortable reality: in a world with limited ability to enforce the law, it may be best for the law to accommodate a reality of exploitation through possession in order to maintain its salience (Bell 2015). In other words, given that states can enjoy the benefits of resources on the basis of possession, even if unrecognized by law, if the law is to remain salient, it has to give some legal recognition to a possession it cannot combat.

Fragmentation and Anti-Commons

Yet another potential source of enrichment of the discussion of property can be found in the literature on the fragmentation of property rights. Anti-commons, first explored at length by Heller (1998), and again by

Heller (2008) are phenomena that potentially afflict property rights that are excessively fragmented or divided. Heller (1998) first observed the phenomenon in post-Communist Russia, where he found large supermarkets struggling to maintain their businesses, while street peddlers right next to the supermarkets succeeded. Heller hypothesized that because the supermarkets had too many owners with too many veto rights, they could not be managed efficiently, while the street peddlers' businesses were subject to only one owner's decisions. More generally, Heller argued that where ownership rights are excessively divided in a single asset, or where an asset is physically divided into too many small units, the assets will be under-consumed, due to the high transaction costs among the many owners. Heller described this as the opposite of commons: where commons suffer from a lack of an owner with exclusion rights, and therefore fall prey to over-consumption, anti-commons suffer from an excess of owners with exclusion rights, and therefore fall prey to under-consumption.

Buchanan and Yoon (2000) formalized Heller's results, showing that commons and anti-commons are symmetrical phenomena that result from mismatches between usage and exclusion rights. Where the same owner has both full usage and exclusion rights, there is little worry of inefficient dissipation of value. Where owners have full usage rights but insufficient exclusion rights, the commons problem arises, leading to excessive use. Where owners have full exclusion rights but insufficient usage rights, the anti-commons problem arises, leading to sub-optimal use.

Heller (2008) worried about the tendency of assets to find themselves under-utilized as a result of trends toward anti-commons and 'gridlock'. Parisi (2002) and Parisi, Depoorter and Schulz (2006) offered the formal version of this observation, arguing that asymmetric transaction costs mean that anti-commons will be more common than commons, and that property suffers from 'entropy' – in this context, a 'one-directional bias that leads towards increasing property fragmentation'.

Anti-commons are less easily identified in the context of territorial sovereignty than in property. Earlier eras saw a great deal of geographic fragmentation of territorial sovereignty among numerous tiny states, and one might argue that European feudal principalities prior to unification of states such as Germany and Italy were marked by anti-commons problems. However, in the modern era, such geographic fragmentations are difficult to find.

It is possible to argue, however, that functional anti-commons have been created by the division of sovereign powers over many entities. The European Union and its associated institutions, for instance, have created situations where some kinds of decisions regarding territory are subject to multiple veto-holders. One might argue that this creates the potential for sub-optimal use of territory.

Numerus Clausus

A different aspect of the fragmentation of property rights is highlighted by the *numerus clausus* doctrine. The *numerus clausus* doctrine is central to property law, though theorists have struggled to justify it. In international law, the doctrine does not exist as such, though similarities can be found, and it is possible to try to justify the parallels. The *numerus clausus* doctrine specifies that only certain kinds of property forms can be recognized by the law, and that if parties try to specify a set of rights outside the recognized list, that set of rights will only be enforceable as contractual arrangements between the parties but not as property arrangements binding the world. Merrill and Smith (2000) attempted to explain the doctrine in economic terms as a measure for reducing information costs. In general, when parties tailor rights to their tastes, we may assume that they do so in a manner that maximizes their utility. However, property rights, unlike contractual rights, are *in rem* and prevail against the world. As a consequence, when parties create idiosyncratic property rights, they impose costs on third parties who are indirectly affected by the rights. This is because once the possibility of idiosyncrasies exists, parties to transactions in other assets will have to expend efforts to ascertain the nature of the rights they are acquiring. The result is that there is an optimal amount of standardization in property rights, which balances parties' need for flexibility in defining rights and third parties' need for certainty about the rights of others.

Merrill and Smith argue that the *numerus clausus* doctrine is not intended to block fragmentation of property rights. In their accounting, clever use of the standardized types of property rights can divide rights in nearly every way; however, the building blocks must always be the standard units of property.

In a way, the law of territorial sovereignty has an even more restrictive rule of *numerus clausus* than property. While the rules of territorial sovereignty have become somewhat blurry over the years, there remains a core of Westphalian thought which views territorial sovereignty as absolute. In the classic Westphalian view of sovereignty, there is only one type of sovereignty – the absolute authority of a state over its territory. The classic view does allow for a variety of cases in which another state may have temporary powers to act as a sovereign over territory under the territorial sovereignty of another state, such as leases, belligerent and pacific occupation, or other rights of administration. The classical view has also partially given way as confederations such as the European Union have blurred the sovereignty lines between states and the international organizations empowered by those states, as well as by treaty regimes that have bypassed states and directly addressed individuals. Nonetheless, in many ways the traditional rule remains. The creation of new kinds of territorial sovereignty remains rare. Arguably, the past century has only seen two new types of arrangements: mandates and trusteeships.

Does Merrill and Smith's theory explain the limited number of types of territorial sovereignty? Frankly, it seems doubtful. Admittedly, in contrast to the many domestic land title registries, there is no central registry of territorial sovereignty claims. This would seem to favor Merrill and Smith's argument that reducing the types of sovereign territory is important for reducing the costs of information gathering to third parties. On the other hand, every other factor mitigates against Merrill and Smith's approach. There are very few voluntary transactions of territorial sovereignty, meaning that there are not likely to be many third parties affected by idiosyncratic sovereignty rights. Additionally, while there is no central registry for territorial sovereignty land claims, there are central registries for legal instruments. Treaties are filed with the United Nations. Judgments of the International Court of Justice and other courts and arbitral panels are centrally recorded and easily accessed.

If one finds Merrill and Smith's theory persuasive, it is possible to argue that with greater information now available about idiosyncratic types of territorial sovereignty, international law should now be willing to offer greater flexibility regarding different types of sovereign status of land.

Succession and Servitudes

A more attenuated kind of parallel between property analysis and territorial sovereignty can be found in issues of succession to state obligations.

The law of servitudes in property law recognizes a set of obligations that 'run with the property'. A properly constructed servitude binds not only the parties that created the original obligation, but also those that succeed to the parties' interest in the burdened and benefited property rights. One way of looking at servitudes is as a tool for dividing property rights by use. For instance, the creation of a right of way easement over Blackacre divides the asset into two units: the easement, and the rest of the rights in Blackacre less the easement (Stake 1999). However, not all agreements to allow passage over Blackacre are intended to create a new property right; some are intended only to allow passage while maintaining the unity of ownership in Blackacre. In addition, the law may seek to block certain divisions of use rights as they inefficiently fragment property.

The law of servitudes is complex. Servitudes can only be enforced against successors in interest if a variety of conditions are met, including privity among the original parties and their successors in interest, intent of the party, and a sufficient 'touch and concern' relationship with the burdened land. Dnes and Lueck (2009), like Parisi, Depoorter and Schulz (2006) describe the law as having a reputation as a 'Byzantine tangle of doctrine', while arguing that a coherent logic for the law can be found in information economics. Together with Depoorter and Parisi (2003), all describe servitude laws as aimed at rescuing property from the excessive fragmentation that can result from asymmetric transaction costs and asymmetric information. Rules of 'touch and concern', for instance, ensure that the servitudes will be of a type that can be anticipated by future acquirers of property rights. Dnes and Lueck stress that the development of more sophisticated registration systems for property rights allows the relaxation of the restrictions of servitude rules.

Servitudes exist in the law of territorial sovereignty as well. Servitudes denote territory under the sovereignty of one state that are 'made to serve the interests of territory belonging to another state' (Malanczuk 1997). Unfortunately, while there is a body of law in property that defines the nature of servitudes and how they arise, servitude law is much vaguer in international law. Indeed, while the term servitude is borrowed from property law, the law of territorial sovereignty adopts neither the requirements of property law (such as 'touch and concern' and privity), nor its key feature: that the obligations of servitudes 'run with the land' to successors in interest to the property rights.

The uncertain nature of servitudes in international law these days makes it difficult to know whether agreements that limit the exercise of territorial sovereignty (such as rights of passage) are terminable. Indeed, under current thought, servitudes in the sense they are found in property law – as permanent fragmentations of property rights – cannot exist at all. At least in one view, any current agreement creating an obligation in the nature of a servitude over territorial sovereignty is evaluated under the equivalent of municipal contract law, i.e., as an ordinary treaty obligation to be interpreted according to the rules found in the Vienna Convention on the Law of Treaties (1969). To interpret the servitudes otherwise would violate the principle of sovereign equality of states (Marchisio 2011).

However, even as treaty obligations, servitudes can persist. The rules of state succession often carry over treaty obligations to successor states. The law of state succession is in some disarray, making absolute statements on the matter difficult, but there is a significant body of law establishing that states can succeed to rights and obligations of prior states, even where the successor state does not inherit the legal personality of the predecessor. The clearest example can be found in the treatment of international borders. Successor states, even those that do not inherit their predecessor's legal personality or any of its treaty rights and obligations, remain bound by their predecessor's boundary agreements (Zimmerman 2006).

The importance of binding servitudes in international law is similar to that of property law. Servitudes allow the division of territorial sovereignty into smaller units – a particular use right extracted from a larger generalized sovereign right. In some cases, such divisions of sovereignty can be more efficient than standard larger units of sovereignty.

However, it is more difficult to draw an analogy between property and territorial sovereignty on one of the central concerns of servitudes: the many rules that limit the creation and enforceability of servitudes. Limitations in property law stem from concerns about asymmetric information and fragmentation. The concerns about information in particular would seem to have little relevance to issues of territorial sovereignty. There are few voluntary transfers of territorial sovereignty, leaving few cases where potential acquirers will be deterred by the cost of detecting and verifying unknown servitudes. Treaties about servitudes, like all other treaties, are centrally filed and generally available, making the cost of detection low even in those cases where voluntary transfers occur. Likewise, excessive fragmentation of territorial sovereignty seems unlikely to arise in many cases. Nonetheless, excessive fragmentation can arise in territorial sovereignty, and this may be seen as animating a general hostility to servitudes 'running with the land'.

THE FUTURE OF ECONOMIC ANALYSIS OF TERRITORIAL SOVEREIGNTY

Why Sovereignty is Not Like Property

While economic analyses of property law provide several interesting points of comparison with territorial sovereignty, economic analysis of property law cannot be imported wholesale to the field of territorial sovereignty. This is not only because there are important and striking doctrinal differences between sovereignty and property, but more importantly because the functions served by the two doctrines are fundamentally different.

Ordinary observers often overlook the differences between territorial sovereignty and property to such an extent that they confuse the content of the two doctrines. Newspaper reports refer to state 'ownership' of territory when they intend to describe state sovereignty. At times, courts examine issues of sovereignty and property as if they were interchangeable. At least lexically, property and sovereignty share many of their most basic concepts. However, similarity in terminology of the two fields of law can sometimes obscure more than it reveals.

Property rights, according to Barzel (1997) consist of the ability to derive utility or consume value from an asset. Among the many basic justifications for legally recognizing property rights, two are of particular importance, and they are intimately connected. The first reason is to assist in keeping assets in the hands of the owner who most highly values them. The legal recognition of property assets, and the protection of those assets against involuntary transfer, permit owners to invest in the creation and development of assets. Stability in ownership thus encourages, within many settings, optimal investment in the assets (Bell and Parchomovsky 2005). Secondly, and relatedly, protection of title in property rights encourages the transfer of such assets, from time to time, to optimal users. With the ability to protect title and transfer it to others only in voluntary transactions, owners can transfer assets when a potential buyer offers a price exceeding the value of the asset to the seller. If transaction costs are sufficiently low, this encourages the holding of assets by owners who most highly value them (Shavell 2004).

By contrast, territorial sovereignty concerns the ultimate power over people and objects within territorial bounds. The allocation of territorial sovereignty is not intended to maximize the utility that can be extracted from domestic populations and lands by rulers. Rather, it is intended to clarify the lines of authority, and prevent conflicting commands of sovereigns. To be sure, some aspects of territorial sovereignty are similar to property. Sovereigns have a claim to property ownership over all otherwise unowned assets within the territorial bounds of their sovereignty. Thus, discussions about transboundary resources that are owned by states can share some parallels to property discussions. However, this is an exception rather than the rule. The primary concern of territorial sovereignty is governance over individuals.

For this reason, property rules that clarify title and thereby encourage optimal extraction of utility by an owner's use and transfer of assets do not translate well into the context of territorial sovereignty. Because territorial sovereignty has subjects – the persons subject to the power of the sovereign with the given territorial bounds – territorial sovereignty rules necessarily are concerned with regulation of the behavior of self-aware individuals rather than the management of inert assets.

Unsurprisingly, some doctrines in territorial sovereignty cannot be illuminated at all by reference to property law. Take, for instance, self-determination. Self-determination is among the most controversial and confusing areas of modern international law. In its most expansive sense, the principle of self-determination establishes the rights of peoples to rule themselves within sovereign territories. However, the translation of this right into legal doctrine is not entirely straightforward. A broad version of the doctrine would allow local populations a right of secession, i.e., the right to take territorial sovereignty away from the current title-holder and vest in themselves. This broad version is not the generally accepted view of self-determination. Arguably, self-determination only provides substantive legal rights where it is established by *lex specialis* (as in the case of trust territories or mandates) or where the concerned territories are colonial possessions (Cassese 1995). In other cases, as Klabbers (2006) writes, self-determination is best understood as a procedural right that gives 'entities [] a right to see their position taken into account whenever their future is being decided'.

This is a problem entirely unlike any faced by property law. In the modern world of property, where slavery is forbidden, assets do not develop the desire for changes in the structure of ownership over themselves.

More generally, property issues almost always presume a background of sovereignty as a separate subject. Legal property rights are developed not solely by the markets but by the background rules of the government as regulator. The rules of territorial sovereignty concern the behavior of the regulator. The rules of property concern the behavior of the regulated. Obviously, the mode of analysis cannot be the same. To take a very simple example, a rule of property that simplifies the transfer of land may help optimize utility from property by lowering the costs of transferring property. However, the same rule may be problematic in the context of territorial sovereignty where the transferred land is populated by subjects who have no voice in the altered sovereign structure. Property rules should encourage utility-maximizing exploitation of assets. Territorial sovereignty rules, by contrast, should at least in part encourage optimal governance.

For this reason, it is not possible to copy directly economic analyses of property rights to the field of territorial sovereignty.

FUTURE DIRECTIONS

A better direction for future analyses of territorial sovereignty must take into account the nature of sovereigns as rulers rather than owners. We can view the resulting analyses as a continuum, stretching from property to territorial sovereignty. At one end lies private property, which is concerned solely with assets. In the middle lie items like state-owned property, which concern extracting value from assets as well as issues of regulation and the promulgation of rules over others. Finally, at the other end lies territorial sovereignty, which primarily concerns the capacities of the state as regulator, rather than owner.

Taking account of the state as regulator is crucial for understanding the proper place of doctrines like self-determination, which, under certain circumstances, gives territories and their attendant populations the right to demand a reconsideration of existing arrangements of territorial sovereignty. Self-determination is incomprehensible in a property analysis; in a world without slavery, assets cannot rebel against their owners. However, in an analysis of sovereignty, questions of the optimal scope of the state's powers are crucial.

Similarly, taking account of the way the state's power is exercised is important for analyzing the doctrines of allocating territorial sovereignty. Since sovereignty entails control over people as well as for resources, the way states exercise their authority over individuals must necessarily affect the doctrines that apply to the acquisition and maintenance of territorial sovereignty. To return to an earlier example, there is ample reason to argue that the doctrines of territorial acquisition should not be identical for democratic and autocratic states.

Economic analysis of territorial sovereignty remains in its infancy. Selective incorporation of property analysis can help, but ultimately, analysis of territorial sovereignty must forge its own path.

REFERENCES

Articles and Books

Alesina, Alberto and Enrico Spolaore. 2006. 'Conflict, Defense Spending, and the Number of Nations' 50(1) *European Economic Review* 91–120.

Alesina, Alberto and Enrico Spolaore. 2003. *The Size of Nations*. Cambridge, MA: MIT Press.

Alesina, Alberto and Enrico Spolaore. 1997. 'On the Number and Size of Nations' 112 *Quarterly Journal of Economics* 1027–56.

Alesina, Alberto, Enrico Spolaore and Romain Wacziarg. 2001. 'Economic Integration and Political Disintegration' 90 *American Economic Review* 1276–96.

Alesina, Alberto and Romain Wacziarg. 1998. 'Openness, Country Size and the Government' 69 *Journal of Public Economics* 305–22.

Axelrod, Robert. 1984. *The Evolution of Cooperation.* Basic Books.

Barzel, Yoram. 1997. *Economic Analysis of Property Rights*, 2nd edn. Cambridge University Press.

Bell, Abraham and Gideon Parchomovsky. 2005. 'A Theory of Property' 90 *Cornell Law Review* 531–615.

Bell, Abraham and Gideon Parchomovsky. 2016. 'Of Property and Information' 116 *Columbia Law Review* 237–86.

Bell, Abraham. 2015. 'Title in the Shadow of Possession', in Yun-Chien Chang (ed.), *Law and Economics of Possession.* Cambridge University Press.

Benvenisti, Eyal. 2002. *Sharing Transboundary Resources: International Law and Optimal Resource Use.* Cambridge University Press.

Benvenisti, Eyal. 1996. 'Collective Action in the Utilization of Shared Freshwater: The Challenges of International Water Resources Law' 90 *American Journal of International Law* 384–415.

Benvenisti, Eyal and Amihai Cohen. 2012. 'Public International Law', in Uriel Procaccia (ed.), *The Economic Approach to Law.* Nevo Publishing (Hebrew).

Besson, Samantha. 2008. 'Sovereignty', in Rüdiger Wolfrum (ed.), *The Max Planck Encyclopedia of Public International Law.* Oxford University Press, online edition www.mpepil.com.

Bouckaert, Boudewijn and Ben W. F. Depoorter. 1999. 'Adverse Possession – Title Systems', in Boudewijn Bouckaert and Gerrit De Geest (eds.), *Encyclopedia of Law and Economics.* Cheltenham, UK and Northampton, MA, USA: Edward Elgar, online edition encyclo.findlaw.com/.

Buchanan, James and Yong J. Yoon. 2000. 'Symmetric Tragedies: Commons and Anticommons' 43 *Journal of Law and Economics* 1–14.

Cassese, Antonio. 1995. *Self-Determination of Peoples: A Legal Reappraisal.* Cambridge University Press.

Demsetz, Harold. 1967. 'Toward a Theory of Property Rights' 57 *American Economic Review* 347–59.

Depoorter, Ben W. F. and Francesco Parisi. 2003. 'Fragmentation of Property Rights: A Functional Interpretation of the Law of Servitudes' 3(1) *Global Jurist Frontiers* 1–41.

Dnes, Antony and Dean Lueck. 2009. 'Asymmetric Information and the Law of Servitudes Governing Land' 38 *Journal of Legal Studies* 89–120.

Epstein, Richard A. 1979. 'Possession as the Root of Title' 85 *Georgia Law Review* 1221–43.

Hardin, Garrett. 1968. 'The Tragedy of the Commons' 162 *Science* 1243–48.

Heller, Michael. 2008. *The Gridlock Economy: How Too Much Ownership Wrecks Markets, Stops Innovation, and Costs Lives.* New York, NY: Basic Books.

Heller, Michael, 1998. 'The Tragedy of the Anti-commons: Property in Transition from Marx to Markets' 111 *Harvard Law Review* 621–88.

Jennings, Robert Yewdall. 1963. *The Acquisition of Territory in International Law*. Manchester University Press.

Klabbers, Jan. 2006. 'The Right to be Taken Seriously: Self-Determination in International Law' 28 *Human Rights Quarterly* 186–206.

Kokott, Juliane. 2011. 'States, Sovereign Equality', in Rüdiger Wolfrum (ed.), *The Max Planck Encyclopedia of Public International Law*, Oxford University Press, online edition www.mpepil.com.

Krasner, Stephen. 1999. *Sovereignty: Organized Hypocrisy*, Princeton University Press.

Malanczuk, Peter. 1997. *Akehurst's Modern Introduction to International Law*, 7th revised edn. London: Routledge.

Marchisio, Sergio. 2011. 'Servitudes', in Rüdiger Wolfrum (ed.), *The Max Planck Encyclopedia of Public International Law*, Oxford University Press, online edition www.mpepil.com.

Merrill, Thomas W. and Henry E. Smith. 2001. 'What Happened to Property in Law and Economics?' 111 *Yale Law Journal* 357–98.

Merrill, Thomas W. and Henry E. Smith. 2000. 'Optimal Standardization in the Law of Property: The *Numerus Clausus* Principle' 110 *Yale Law Journal* 1–70.

Miceli, Thomas J. 1997. *Economics of the Law: Torts, Contracts, Property, Litigation*. New York: Oxford University Press.

Miceli, Thomas J. and C. F. Sirmans. 1995. 'An Economic Theory of Adverse Possession' 15 *International Review of Law and Economics* 162–73.

Nesi, Guiseppe. 2011. 'Uti Possidetis Doctrine', in Rüdiger Wolfrum (ed.), *The Max Planck Encyclopedia of Public International Law*, Oxford University Press, online edition www.mpepil.com.

Netter, Jeffry M., Philip L. Hersch and Willam D. Manson. 1986. 'An Economic Analysis of Adverse Possession Statutes' 6 *International Review of Law and Economics* 217–27.

Ostrom, Elinor. 1990. *Governing the Commons: The Evolution of Institutions for Collective Action*. New York, NY: Cambridge University Press.

Parisi, Francesco. 2002. 'Entropy in Property' 50 *American Journal of Comparative Law* 595–632.

Parisi, Francesco, Ben Depoorter and Norbert Schulz. 2006. 'Duality in Property: Commons and Anticommons' 25 *International Review of Law and Economics* 578–91.

Posner, Eric. 2006. 'International Law: A Welfarist Approach,' 73 *University of Chicago Law Review* 487–543.

Ratner, Steven R. 1996. 'Drawing a Better Line: Uti Possidetis and the Borders of New States' 90 *American Journal of International Law* 590–624.

Shavell, Steven. 2004. *Foundations of Economic Analysis of Law*. Harvard University Press.

Shaw, Malcolm. 1997. 'Peoples, Territorialism and Boundaries' 3 *European Journal of International Law* 478–507.

Simmons, Beth A. 2005. 'Rules over Real Estate: Trade, Territorial Conflict, and International Borders as Institution' 49 *Journal of Conflict Resolution* 823–48.

Stake, Jeffrey Evans. 1999. 'Decomposition of Property Rights', in Boudewijn Bouckaert and Gerrit De Geest (eds.), *Encyclopedia of Law and Economics*,

Cheltenham, UK and Northampton, MA, USA: Edward Elgar, online edition encyclo.findlaw.com/.
Zimmerman, Andreas. 2006. 'State Succession in Treaties', in Rüdiger Wolfrum (ed.), *The Max Planck Encyclopedia of Public International Law*, Oxford University Press, online edition www.mpepil.com.

Cases

Islands of Palmas Arbitration (*U.S.* v. *Netherlands.*), 2 R.I.A.A. 829 (1928).
Legal Status of Eastern Greenland (*Denmark* v. *Norway*), 1933 P.C.I.J. (ser. A/B) No. 43 (April 5).
Reference re Secession of Quebec, [1998] 2 S.C.R. 217.

Conventions and Treaties

Antarctic Treaty, December 1, 1959, 12 U.S.T. 794, 402 U.N.T.S. 71.
United Nations Convention on the Law of the Non-Navigational Uses of International Watercourses, May 21, 1997, 36 I.L.M. 700.
Vienna Convention on the Law of Treaties, May 23, 1969, 1155 U.N.T.S. 331; 8 I.L.M. 679 (1969).

PART II

Sources of Law

4. The economic analysis of international treaty law

Francesco Parisi and Daniel Pi

Until the beginning of the twenty-first century, economic analysis of international law was a lamentable rarity, despite the ever-growing influence of law and economics in most other subject-areas of legal scholarship (Dunoff and Trachtman 1999). At least two factors potentially contributed to this unfortunate circumstance. First, international law scholars may have been unfamiliar with the tools used by law and economics scholars, raising a methodological barrier.[1] Second, the normative, political, and doctrinal nature of traditional international law scholarship may have misled law and economics scholars into believing that international law was a too informal, impenetrable or otherwise unfruitful subject for economic analysis. Recent researches happily find that neither of these prejudices were justified.[2]

In this chapter, we review some approaches to international treaty law from an economic perspective, offering critical commentary and extensions to those approaches along the way. In Section I, we lay out some of the basic background material on treaty law. In Section II, we discuss the signaling function of treaties. In Section III, we discuss treaty formation and accession. In Section IV, we consider the evolution of treaty law over time, giving particular attention to the issues of ratification and fragmentation. Finally, in Section V, we summarize the results of the chapter and identify areas where further research is needed.

[1] One barrier may have been the mistaken belief that law and economics necessarily entails (or is entailed by) a conservative political perspective. See Dunoff and Trachtman 1999. Another barrier – bizarrely – may have been terminological confusion over the word 'positivist', which means different things to an international law scholar and a law and economics scholar.

[2] To be clear, the economic analysis of international law has found purchase not in addressing normative questions, but rather by sidestepping them to analyze the payoffs and strategic behavior of the parties. See, e.g., Parisi and Fon 2009; Goldsmith and Posner 2003.

I. INTRODUCTION: SETTING UP THE FRAMEWORK[3]

The principles of modern treaty law are enumerated in the 1969 Vienna Convention on the Law of Treaties (the 'Vienna Convention').[4] Prior to its entry into force in 1980, the rules governing treaty formation and legality were the subject of customary law. However, the state of the customary law of treaties in the period between World War II and the Vienna Convention was murky, and the introduction of a uniform, enumerated set of principles was sorely needed.[5]

Most of the articles of the Vienna Convention were derived from the customary law that preceded it, with the exception of those concerning reservations and accession.[6] Consequently, most non-parties now recognize the enumerated principles of the Vienna Convention as at least having the force of customary law (i.e., they treat the Vienna Convention as a restatement of the customary law of treaties).[7] It is worth noting here that (as is the case with contract law) the articles of the Vienna Convention are *default rules*. Any particular treaty may explicitly reject or modify the default rules to tailor the constraints of a particular legal agreement to its particular purpose and context. The Vienna Convention governs treaties only when disputes arise, the resolution of which was either not contemplated by the parties *ex ante*, or which the written agreement failed to articulate.

What is a Treaty?

The Vienna Convention defines a 'treaty' as being, 'an international agreement concluded between States in written form and governed by

---

[3] Much of the material in this section is derived from Dunoff and Trachtman 1999 and Dunoff 2000.

[4] Vienna Convention on the Law of Treaties, May 23, 1969, 1155 U.N.T.S. 331 (entered into force January 27, 1980). Most scholars classify the Vienna Convention as a declaratory treaty, inasmuch as it reduces to treaty form previously existing customary rules governing the formation of international treaties. As we will discuss later in this chapter, notwithstanding its mostly declarative nature, the Vienna Convention makes several innovations on a few specific issues.

[5] See G.A. Res. 478, U.N. GAOR, 5th Sess., November 16, 1950. See also Hylton 1994.

[6] Vienna Convention, arts. 19–23.

[7] Briggs 1979. But see Frankowska (1988), arguing that the view that the Vienna Convention largely formalizes customary law is overly reductive.

international law, whether embodied in a single instrument or in two or more related instruments and whatever its particular designation'.

We may therefore distinguish treaties from other forms of non-legal international agreements, such as, 'memoranda of understanding, non-binding resolutions, exchanges of notes, joint communiqués, joint declarations, *modi vivendi*, political agreements, administrative agreements, voluntary guidelines, handshakes, verbal promises, unperfected acts, principles, declarations of principles, "best practices," exchanges of letters, unspoken rules, gentlemen's agreements, and side letters' (Goldsmith and Posner 2003).

The characterization of treaties as being legally recognized agreements between parties often leads to a comparison with contractual agreements and amenable to the application of contract law principles (Posner and Sykes 2013).[8] We mentioned already one of the similarities: that many of the rules governing both realms are regarded as 'default rules', which can be modified by express agreement. However, the law and practice of treaty formation has evolved autonomously, undermining possible analogical applications of contract law principles to treaties. It is therefore easy to overstate the relationship between treaty law and contract law. For instance, principles central to contract, such as consideration, are entirely absent in treaty law. In areas where they do share similarities, the prevailing doctrine often diverges. Moreover, there does not exist an effective 'international government' to enforce treaty law in the same way that domestic courts enforce contract law.

More profoundly, one of the core contributions of law and economics to contract law – the concept of 'efficient breach' – is entirely antithetical to the international law doctrine of *pacta sunt servanda*. Indeed, theorizing about breach and liability, so fruitful a ground for the economic analysis of contracts, is quite absent in the realm of treaty law. There is good reason for this, apart from the lack of an 'international government' to enforce treaty obligations. The cost of breach in the case of contract law can usually be monetized with some degree of precision. Thus, expectation damages or reliance damages may be inferred from market value, and the promisee made whole. However, it is frequently unclear how to monetize the stakes in the interactions between nations. For

---

[8] See e.g., World Trade Organization, *Japan – Taxes on Alcoholic Beverages, Report of the Appellate Body,* WT/DS8/B/R, WT/DS/10/AB/R, WT/DS11/AB/R (October 4, 1996) ('The WTO Agreement is a treaty – the international equivalent of a contract').

example, if a nation 'breaches' a human rights treaty, then it is unclear how (or why) other parties to the treaty should be 'compensated' for the violation.[9]

Given the absence of compensatory or injunctive remedies for unfulfilled treaty obligations, Goldsmith and Posner (2003) further argue that treaties might be better analogized to letters of intent rather than contracts. This view of treaties is plausible, and suggests a different framework for the economic analysis of treaty law – that it should be viewed in terms of cooperation, coordination, and signaling.

Why Form Treaties?

In Section III of this chapter, we will discuss nations' incentives for forming or acceding to treaties. However, before proceeding to this somewhat more complex question, it is worth asking why nations choose to use the treaty instrument rather than customary law.[10] International customary law arises from regular conduct that becomes reified as law through *opinio juris* – the recognition by participating states that the prescribed conduct is 'binding'.

Treaties have several advantages and disadvantages as compared with custom. The first and most obvious is expediency. Whereas a custom often takes time to develop, requiring repeated rounds of cooperation to crystalize as a recognizable legal obligation, explicit bargaining and agreement may offer considerable advantages in terms of speed.[11]

Second, since customary law develops from actual interactions between parties, the boundaries of customary obligation may be vague. For example, a customary norm that nations should not molest or capture enemy fishing vessels during war does not necessary contemplate what counts as a 'fishing vessel', nor indeed what exceptions might apply

---

[9] But see Dunoff and Trachtman (1999), discussing the possibility of 'efficient breach' in the context of the GATT/WTO system, when damages can be monetized.

[10] For a more complete discussion on customary international law, see Parisi and Pi, Chapter 6 in this volume.

[11] Treaties are not, of course, the only mechanism for explicit bargaining and agreement. See Section II of this chapter for a discussion on the comparative merits of treaties versus informal agreements. See also Goldsmith and Posner 2003.

(Goldsmith and Posner 2000; Posner and Sykes 2013).[12] Express agreement to explicit terms cures these deficiencies, forcing parties to articulate precisely what they believe the bounds of the agreement are.

Third, by relying on the treaty as an instrument for cooperation, states automatically invoke the default rules of the Vienna Convention, further reducing uncertainties as to their obligations.

Fourth, once established, customs may be difficult to modify, and exiting from customary obligations may be legally difficult or impossible. Treaties generally allow parties to formally withdraw, as do the default rules provided by the Vienna Convention, in case withdrawal is not explicitly articulated in a treaty's terms.[13] Thus, treaties may be more flexible to changing circumstances than customary law.

However, treaties also have some disadvantages relative to customs. First, express bargaining and agreement imposes a cost. Decentralized cooperation arising from customary practice has the advantage of revealing parties' preferences and willingness to cooperate without negotiating costs. When those costs are very high, allowing cooperation to emerge organically may entail superior payoffs to treaty formation.

Second, customary law is often thought to evolve toward efficient outcomes. (Sykes 2004). Kontorovich (2006) points out, however, that many of the indices of efficiency fail to obtain in the context of customary international law; however in the subset of cases where such conditions are present, customary international law may plausibly lead to efficient outcomes. By contrast, bargaining power, biases, and conflicting political factors may pollute the treaty negotiation process, possibly leading to inferior outcomes.

Normativity

One of the main obstacles to analyzing treaties from an economic perspective seems to be the heavily normative groundwork underlying much of traditional treaty law. Let us therefore consider at the level of utmost generality how the traditional approach to treaty law differs from the economic approach.

A frequent theme among international law scholarship has been that states may be 'bound' by their commitments to other states (or to universal moral norms). This appeal to moral notions seems motivated principally by the absence of centralized law-making and enforcement

---

[12] *The Paquete Habana*, 175 U.S. 677 (1900).

[13] Vienna Convention, art. 56.

mechanisms in the international arena. The problem is that in the absence of a centralized international legal regime, it is difficult to describe and explain the role of 'law' in guiding or binding the conduct of nations. Traditional international law scholars have chosen to address the problem by introducing normative and moral factors as substitutes for those critical elements of what we ordinarily regard as 'law'.

The economic approach offers a different explanation for compliance with international 'law'. The economic analysis begins with the assumption that states act to advance their own interests, and that international agreements – including treaties – serve as useful mechanisms for effecting those goals. The reason why states are 'bound' by international law is analyzed in terms of self-interest rather than any sort of normative obligation.

To be sure, the two views are not wholly incompatible. Dunoff (2000) acknowledges that the expressive component may be acutely important in the international arena. For example, it is difficult to imagine that the International Criminal Court will have terribly much deterrent effect on dictators determined to carry out a program of mass killings. And indeed, it is not obvious how economic analysis can be made useful in understanding the expressive component of law in such types of cases. However, Dunoff argues that much of international law is *not* merely expressive, and those normative, expressive, and moral functions of international law should not be regarded as proof of the inappropriateness of economic analysis on matters of international law, but rather as limitations. Moreover, Dunoff points out, what economic analysis *can* explain, it seems to explain very well.

Goldsmith and Posner are also open to a pluralistic conception of the role of economic analysis in international law. However, while they acknowledge that normative factors may play a role in conjunction with the forces identified by economic analysis, they harbor deep skepticism as to its effect on behavior (Goldsmith and Posner 2003). Whatever their effect on behavior, Goldsmith and Posner argue, it seems likely that normative, quasi-moral factors will be overwhelmed by self-interest, to the extent that their influence will be *de minimis*. Historical observation, they wryly aver, lends little credibility to the claim of traditional international law scholars that nations are ever bound by anything else.

Finally, before proceeding it bears remarking on one final point about methodology. Recall that traditional international law scholarship answered the descriptive question – why states tend to comply with international law – with an appeal to normativity, whereas law and economics scholars answer the descriptive question with a descriptive analysis (of incentives).

One additional reason put forth in the literature for the late arrival of economic analysis in the realm of treaty law may arise from a trifling point of jargon. Law and economics scholars refer to the descriptive answer they give as 'positivist' (in contradistinction with 'normative').[14] However, 'positivism' for international law scholars means something entirely different: a dogmatic, state-centric view of international relations (Gross 1948). Thus, Dunoff and Trachtman (1999) propose that hostility toward law and economics in international law scholarship may be partly attributable to mere confusion over terminology. What law and economics scholars proudly call 'positivist' (descriptive analysis) means something entirely different from what many international law scholars call 'positivist' (a Westphalian conception of international relations, often associated with a reductive realism).

Elements of Treaties

Treaties are agreements between nations to undertake some cooperative activity (for example, mutual defense, reducing pollution, nuclear disarmament, open trade, or pooling resources). Nations may enter into such agreements in one of two ways: (1) they may be one of the original signatories to the treaty; or (2) they may accede to a preexisting treaty.

When nations become *signatories* to a treaty, they indicate their political support for the agreement; however, the agreement is not legally binding until the treaty is codified in written form and the signatory nation *ratifies* it. Ratification processes differ by state and involves some official assent to participation in the agreement.

In ratifying a treaty, a nation may articulate *reservations*, *understandings*, or *declarations*, which express unwillingness to abide by certain terms of the treaty (or a limitation on the extent to which the party is willing to participate). States that introduce reservations are still formally parties to the treaty, though they are not fully bound by the treaty's terms.

The original signatories to a treaty may control the conditions limiting when other nations may subsequently accede. We follow Parisi and Fon in distinguishing three treaty types, with respect to their openness to accession by non-signatory states: (1) open; (2) semi-open; and (3) closed (Parisi and Fon 2009). Open treaties allow any nation willing to accept the terms of a pre-existing treaty to join it. Semi-open treaties require a majority of parties to approve the admission of a new entrant

[14] See e.g., Parisi 2013.

into the treaty. And closed treaties require unanimous approval of member states to admit a new party into the treaty.

II. COOPERATION, COORDINATION AND SIGNALING

Let us begin by considering international agreements generally. International agreements may be 'binding' to varying degrees. Treaties, of course, represent an extremum on the spectrum. On the other end, we find informal instruments, such as 'unspoken rules' and 'gentlemen's agreements'. Recognizing this spectrum of degrees of commitment prompts two questions. First, why do nations engage in international agreements? Second, how do they select among the many forms of agreement.

Why Form International Agreements?

Goldsmith and Posner argue that parties are motivated to form international agreements for the same reasons they comply with customary laws – self-interest.[15] When parties express commitment to a course of action, it may be because: (1) there simply exists a *coincidence of interests*; (2) weaker nations may have been *coerced* by more powerful nations; (3) *cooperation* may yield a greater net benefit in the long term (as in an iterated prisoners' dilemma); or (4) complementary choices may resolve *coordination* problems (Goldsmith and Posner 2000; 2003). The first two cases are theoretically less interesting, and we will therefore devote our attention to how international agreements solve cooperation and coordination games.

Cooperation games are typified by the 'prisoners' dilemma'. In its most general form, both players have two choices available to them: cooperation or defection. A player's payoff is maximal when he defects, while the other player cooperates, and likewise a player's payoff is minimal when he cooperates, while the other player defects. Between the two extremes, the players' second-best payoffs are when both parties cooperate, and their third-best payoffs are when both parties defect. In equilibrium (i.e., when both players select choices that maximize their payoffs regardless of what the other player does), both parties will defect, because regardless of what the other player chooses, a player will receive a greater payoff from defecting (i.e., if one player cooperates, the other

---

[15] See Goldsmith and Posner (2000) and the discussion in Parisi and Pi, Chapter 6 in this volume.

player can get the maximal payoff by defecting; if the other player defects, the other player must cut his losses so that he is not made a 'sucker', and also defect).

However, when the prisoners' dilemma is repeated over many rounds of interaction between the same players, the analysis changes. Defection is no longer an equilibrium strategy, and parties may be better off 'trusting' each other not to defect, thereby maximizing both players' payoffs over many rounds (Aumann 1959; Axelrod 1984). Goldsmith and Posner (2003) argue that international relations may sometimes be modeled as iterated prisoners' dilemmas, and that cooperative behavior may represent a payoff-maximizing strategy in the long term.

Strictly speaking, such agreements should not be regarded as solutions to the iterated prisoners' dilemma; one of the premises of the prisoners' dilemma being that the players are not allowed to communicate. Nevertheless, the point of the comparison remains compelling – nations may employ international agreements to overcome the threat of 'defection', where mutual cooperation is a socially optimal (privately second-best) outcome.

Coordination games are more straightforward. A coordination problem arises when either player would prefer to make a choice complementary to the other player's choice. Such situations often arise in choosing standards – for example, railroad gauges. Nations may have slight preferences for one railroad gauge over another, but their principal concern will be that they are the same as neighboring nations, so trains traveling across the border will be able to operate on the other countries' rail system.

One solution to coordination games is the concept of 'focal points' (Schelling 1960). The classic example of a coordination game is the 'Battle of the Sexes', where a couple agrees to meet at a concert the next day. Unbeknownst to them, two concerts are playing the following day – one jazz and one classical. Of course, they may both enjoy either concert alone, but they would rather attend the same concert together, whichever it may be. Thus the dilemma. However, let us suppose that on the same night that they had agreed to meet at a concert, they had also been arguing about whether Evgeny Koroliov's recording of Bach's *Well-Tempered Klavier* was superior to Glenn Gould's. Recalling the discussion, they may both choose to go to the classical concert, hoping to find the other there. Memory of the unrelated discussion gives salience to 'classical music', leading both parties to 'guess' classical.

Goldsmith and Posner argue that international agreements may serve as focal points for future conduct in the same way. Of course, this also circumvents the assumption that the players cannot communicate –

nulling the very problem giving rise to coordination games. A more perspicuous analysis might be that international agreements give parties a way of avoiding the coordination problem in the first place. In any event, the point is again that self-interest is what ends up motivating compliance with the agreement.

Legalization

Goldsmith and Posner's (2003) reasoning seems to explain the majority of occasions where international agreements arise, as against the traditional explanations of international law scholars (who appeal to the 'normative pull' of treaty commitments and vague speculation about universal morality). However, this leaves open the question why nations choose one *kind* of international agreement over another. Why do nations agree to formal treaties rather than settling things with a handshake between leaders?

The traditional answer is that treaties have more 'normative pull' than handshakes. Goldsmith and Posner point out that in the absence of an international enforcer, such an explanation has little merit. Instead, they point to the signaling function of treaties to explain when and why legally binding agreements are preferred to informal ones.

This issue arose in real world events, when United States (US) President George W. Bush was negotiating the Strategic Offensive Reductions Treaty ('Treaty of Moscow') with Russian President Vladimir Putin (Goldsmith and Posner 2003).[16] Bush proposed 'sealing the deal' with a handshake, but Putin and the US Senate pressed for a formal written treaty with ratification by both the US Senate and Russian Duma.

As we averred earlier, international agreements may be regarded as a spectrum, with handshakes and unspoken agreements on the informal side, and treaties on the formal side. Generally, the more formal an agreement, the higher the transaction costs. This begs the question why nations would ever desire the most onerous of instruments for international agreement. Goldsmith and Posner offer two explanations. First, as a purely practical matter, the designation of an agreement as a 'treaty' triggers the machinery of the Vienna Convention, relieving parties of having to articulate the many possible contingencies and procedures that a satisfactory agreement might require. That is, it allows parties to import the default rules of the international law on treaties. Moreover, since

---

16 Strategic Offensive Reductions Treaty, May 24, 2002, US–Russ., art. I, S. Treaty Doc. No. 107–8 (2002).

treaty ratification incorporates the agreement into the laws of the member nations, disputes may be adjudicated in domestic courts.

Second, the higher transaction costs involved in forming a treaty serve an important signaling function. Treaty ratification meaningfully expresses greater commitment than an executive's hortatory statements, demonstrating the desirability of the agreement to other institutions within a nation's government. Moreover, when treaties are put to a vote, democratic nations deliver useful information to prospective partners about how committed the country as a whole is to pursuing the agreed conduct. Further information about contingencies and potential concerns may arise in committee debates and possibly in media coverage, providing further evidence of support (or the lack of support) for the treaty terms.[17]

Thus, contrary to the traditional account that treaties are more binding because they have greater 'normative pull', the economic analysis is that treaties signal a greater interest in cooperation. Rather than pre-committing themselves to some course of conduct, treaties simply signal how desirable the conduct would be. Parties to a treaty are thus not less likely to break the agreement because the treaty has 'normative pull', but rather because a nation would only ratify a treaty if it were very strongly committed to the agreement in the first place.

The significance of these factors is far-reaching. Assurance that a treaty is desirable to a large part of a partnering nation is especially desirable in democratic nations, where compliance may require acquiescence of legislative bodies, and where new leaders may be elected, who might not necessarily have the same preferences or priorities. Thus, Bush's commitment to nuclear disarmament, however sincere, would be insufficient to guarantee either that the US would follow through with its promise, or that subsequent presidents would share Bush's enthusiasm for it. Ratification of the Treaty of Moscow signaled to the Russians that there was broad support in the legislature for such an agreement, and that future leaders would likely share that objective.

Moreover, because treaty terms are often vague, with no bright line separating compliance and noncompliance, the effect of signaling greater voluntary commitment to the principles of the agreement may be far

---

[17] Of course, these factors may be outweighed by expediency. For example, the resolution of the Cuban Missile Crisis in 1962, which required swift action to avert escalation of the conflict, involved informal agreements between the US and the Soviet Union.

more meaningful than whatever 'legal obligation' is conferred by ratification. In an environment without enforcement mechanisms, communicating enthusiasm for an agreement may be more significant than any degenerate sense of being 'bound'.

Finally, it is also worth mentioning reputational effects. A nation that routinely breaks its treaty obligations will find it difficult to enter into new treaties, and a desire for 'good standing' in the international community may motivate a greater degree of compliance for treaties than, say, joint communiqués or letters of intent. Again, however, the problem arises that the absence of a bright line separating compliance from noncompliance may allow nations to assert compliance, without adhering to the other party's expectations.

III. FORMATION AND ACCESSION

As we discussed in Section I, there are two ways that nations may participate in a treaty: (1) they may be one of the original signatory states; or (2) they may accede to a preexisting treaty. In this section, we will discuss the economic analysis of treaty formation and treaty accession.[18]

Formation

We begin our analysis of treaty formation where Goldsmith and Posner left off, with the premise that parties enter into and comply with treaties principally out of self-interest. This insight begs the question what conditions must exist for parties to enter into a treaty.

With the exception of the small number of treaties having only an expressive purpose, treaties are formed to convey benefits to parties. However, there may be dispute about the level of effort that a treaty requires. For example, signatories to the Kyoto Protocol agreed to reduce their greenhouse gas emissions to meet predetermined benchmarks, contingent on their wealth and technological development.[19] However, those benchmarks are likely privately suboptimal for most or all of the parties. Some nations would have preferred higher benchmarks, while

---

[18] Much of the material in this and the subsequent section are drawn from Parisi and Fon 2009.

[19] United Nations Framework Convention on Climate Change, Third Conference of the Parties, December 11, 1997, 37 I.L.M. 22.

others may have preferred lower benchmarks. Likewise, the aforementioned Treaty of Moscow called for the US and Russia to reduce their nuclear stockpiles to between 1,700 to 2,200 operationally deployable warheads.[20] The benchmarks may be regarded as the requisite 'effort' demanded by the treaty, and both parties may have preferred different effort levels.

Let us therefore consider what the threshold for acceptability might be for a nation contemplating joining a treaty. The nation may undertake the activity unilaterally, exercising a privately optimal level of effort. In the case of greenhouse gas emission, for example, governments may see benefits in the health of the local environment, the air quality in that nation's cities, and political support from domestic environmental groups. However, the nation may also have an interest in reducing global greenhouse gas emissions. Here, the nation's unilateral conduct will have only a fractional effect on the overall output of greenhouse gasses. Thus, there will also be a benefit when other nations follow the same course of conduct.

Thus, the opportunity cost of joining a treaty is the benefit that a nation would see by investing an optimal level of effort unilaterally. For a nation to agree to a treaty, the added benefit of having other nations behaving cooperatively must offset the suboptimal payoff from increasing or reducing its effort to meet the treaty terms and the transaction cost of negotiating the treaty (Parisi and Fon 2009).

Let us call the prescribed level of effort called for by a treaty its 'content'. Ordinarily, we may expect that a treaty's content will be the Nash bargaining solution to the N-state treaty negotiation, taking into account the parties' bargaining power and threat points (i.e., the threshold where opportunity costs exceed the benefit of joining the treaty).

Naturally, when parties are heterogeneous (i.e., when the privately optimal treaty content for one party diverges from the privately optimal treaty content for the other(s)), states with greater bargaining power will therefore realize greater gains from the treaty, while states with less bargaining power will be left near or at their threat points.

When parties are heterogeneous, but are roughly equal with respect to bargaining power, then the margin for agreement may be precariously

---

[20] Or to update the example given in Goldsmith and Posner (2003), we might more topically mention the New Strategic Arms Reduction Treaty (New START), between the United States of America and the Russian Federation on Measures for the Further Reduction and Limitation of Strategic Offensive Arms, US–Russ., April 8, 2010, S. Treaty Doc. No. 111-5, which calls for a further reduction to 1,500 to 1,750 warheads.

narrow. Both parties exerting equal bargaining power will increase the cost of negotiation, and the opportunity costs will therefore increase. Thus, the initial range of effort levels that would be beneficial to prospective parties must be sufficiently large, to ensure sufficient bargaining space for parties to achieve agreement. Nevertheless, most treaties tend to be of this variety, presumably because there tends to be greater need for cooperation or coordination in such cases (discussed in Section II).

Finally, when the parties are homogeneous (i.e., when the optimal treaty content is similar as between the two parties), then obviously bargaining power will be irrelevant, and parties will simply set the treaty content to their private optima. That is, the treaty will be privately optimal for both parties and aggregate welfare will be maximal. An added benefit of such treaties is that transaction costs will be minimal, increasing the expected benefit of the treaty.

Accession

Recall from Section I our tentative classification of treaties with respect to their degree of openness to the accession of non-signatory states: (1) open; (2) semi-open; and (3) closed. We will consider each possibility in turn (Parisi and Fon 2009).

An open treaty leaves prospective acceding states with a 'take it or leave it' choice. This may be desirable where broad multinational cooperation is desirable. The cost–benefit analysis for a state contemplating accession is essentially the same as it was for the original signatories: if the benefit of cooperation outweighs the cost of undertaking sub-optimal effort (note that transaction costs will tend to be low for acceding states, since the treaty terms will already have been established by the original signatories), then the nation will accede.

Original signatories may opt to make their treaty open to accession, if the benefit of being joined by future participants would be substantial. In this case, parties may set the treaty content in anticipation of future nations joining the treaty. For example, suppose two nations, A and B are contemplating a treaty to reduce greenhouse gas emissions. And suppose that A would prefer a benchmark x, whereas B would prefer a benchmark y. Now, let us also suppose that A and B anticipate that C will accede some time after the treaty has been formed. Say that C prefers a benchmark reduction z.

If A and B want C to join, then they may set a benchmark that is the Nash bargaining solution to negotiations between A, B and C. That is, they may factor in C's preferences *in absentia*, to entice C to join the treaty at some later time. Again, this circumstance will only arise in cases where the value of having more participants outweighs the opportunity cost of forming a closed bilateral treaty.

Let us now consider semi-open treaties, which allow accession only upon majority approval by nations already participating in the treaty. Here, public choice principles are determinative. When a state requests accession to a preexisting treaty, the parties will assess whether the benefit of the treaty with N+1 members outweighs the opportunity cost – the value of the treaty with N members – plus transaction costs. If this is the case for the median voter, then the prospective signatory will be allowed to accede.

If the acceding nation requests changes in the treaty content, then once again the median voter's preferences are determinative. If the changes proposed by the acceding state represent an improvement in the payoffs for the median voter, then the acceding state will be permitted to join with the requested changes in treaty content. In some cases, it may arise that a treaty with N+1 member states would represent a net benefit to the median voter state, but that the requested changes would not. In this case, the acceding state is left with a 'take it or leave it' choice, similar to that in an open treaty.

Finally, let us consider closed treaties. Under closed treaties, all of the signatory states hold veto power over admitting new states to the treaty. Thus, the opportunity costs for all of the current parties must be outweighed by the benefit of admitting an additional member. If the acceding state requests modifications to the treaty terms, then the treaty content will again be the Nash bargaining solution, with the acceding state.

Of course, it may often be the case that acceding nations will have less bargaining power than the nations currently parties to the treaty have collectively. Thus, nations contemplating accession may form blocs with other prospective participants, which have similar preferences. This may explain why, for example, expansion of European Union membership often involves multiple nations joining at once rather than individually.

We conclude with an observation about the relationship between the number of participants and treaty content. When the number of participants and the treaty content are complementary, then there will be greater returns to effort the more nations participate in the treaty. In such cases, the privately optimal treaty content will increase for all parties, and even when the acceding state does not demand modifications, states should emend the treaty content when a new state accedes.

Contrariwise, when the relationship between the number of participants and the treaty content are substitutes, then there will be parties that will need to exert less effort individually to effect the desired result. In such cases, the privately optimal treaty content will decrease for all parties, and again states should amend the treaty content when a new state accedes.

IV. RESERVATIONS AND FRAGMENTATION

We mentioned earlier that the main substantive innovation of the Vienna Convention, not present in the customary law of treaties, was the mechanism of matching reservations, allowing states to join multilateral treaties, while selectively reserving certain treaty terms, to which they refuse to be bound (or reducing the extent to which they agree to cooperate). That is, nations may still be parties to a treaty, while declaring a lower level of compliance for themselves for certain elements of the treaty.

However, this creates two problems. First, if reservations are not allowed, then there may be a foregone benefit when prospective participants are faced with a 'take it or leave it' choice, where the benefits of full ratification are less than their opportunity costs. In this circumstance, the prospective participant will decline to ratify the treaty, and both the prospective party to a treaty and the existing parties may miss out on mutual benefits that would have arisen from partial ratification. Second, if reservations are allowed, then nations may behave strategically, introducing reservations to reduce their burden, while obtaining the full benefit of the treaty. This creates a prisoners' dilemma scenario. Since no party will want to be made a 'sucker', they will all try to undercut each other, introducing reservations that place a greater balance of benefits on themselves, while leaving other nations to shoulder the burdens. This will lead to a ratcheting down effect, which may obliterate the treaty entirely, but will at minimum shift the treaty content further from the social optimum (in a downward trajectory).

Article 21 of the Vienna Convention resolves these problems by allowing states to introduce reservations, but with the caveat that other nations will be no more obligated to the reserving nation than the reserving nation is to the others. That is, 'matching reservations' preserve reciprocity, preventing one nation from unilaterally exerting less effort than set by the terms of the treaty. If party *A* introduces a reservation, committing itself to $s - n$ effort (where s is the level of effort called for by the treaty), then parties *B*, *C*, and *D* are still bound to commit s effort with respect to each other, but only $s - n$ with respect to *A* (and only *A*). This ensures that nations will only introduce reservations to the extent that it improves their private welfare, preventing free-riding and the strategic problem of the prisoners' dilemma.

Thus, the matching reservations under article 21 improve social welfare. However, matching reservations will often fail to yield socially *optimal* behavior. To see that this is the case, consider a two-party example (this is analytically convenient, and the results will be generalizable to multilateral treaties, though in practice the matching reservations notion has little meaning in a bilateral treaty – a reservation in that context simply reduces to a change in treaty content). Suppose that the privately optimal treaty content for *A* is *s*, and the privately optimal treaty content for *B* is *t*. Let us say that with respect to the contemplated treaty, *A* is a high-cost, low-benefit participant, and therefore $s < t$. Assuming the parties' payoffs are continuous functions, the socially optimal treaty content will be some intermediate value, $s < r < t$. However, the mechanism of matching reservations allows the reserving state to reduce the treaty obligation (suboptimally) to *s*. This may often be an improvement over a 'take it or leave it' approach, in which case the effort required by the treaty may be zero (i.e., without the ability to introduce reservations, the party simply declines to participate in the treaty). Nevertheless, it is still less than the socially optimal level.

This does not foreclose the possibility that matching reservations may *sometimes* produce socially optimal outcomes. For example, if *A* and *B* have the same preferences (i.e., their private optima align), then reducing the treaty obligation to their private optima will maximize social welfare. The two-party model is less helpful here, for this begs the question why either party needed to employ the mechanism of matching reservations, rather than simply setting the treaty content at the mutually optimal level in the first place. More meaningfully, if there are other parties, *C* and *D*, who prefer higher effort levels, then the matching reservations will at least make the treaty *with respect to A and B* optimal, though the relationships between *A* and *C*, *A* and *D*, *B* and *C*, and *B* and *D* will be suboptimal. The same holds true when *A* and *B* have privately optimal treaty content that is above the effort level set by the treaty terms.

Objections

States may also object to reservations introduced by other states. Posner and Sykes (2013) point out, for example, that the Netherlands objected to the US reservation to article IX of the Convention on the Prevention and

Punishment of the Crime of Genocide.[21] The US required consent before any dispute involving the US as a party was tried before the International Court of Justice, which the Netherlands argued undermined the purpose of the treaty (Posner and Sykes 2013).

However, the legal status of objections is unclear. It seems that objections to a reservation do not entail that the reserving state is not accepted as a member of the treaty. Likewise, the objecting member does not cease to be a member. Nevertheless, the threat of objections may create uncertainty about the integrity of the agreement, creating disincentives for nations to reserve unless their interests are substantially affected.

Fragmentation

The introduction of matching reservations may threaten the integrity of treaties. Consider the perspective of the highest-cost state, which derives the least benefit from cooperation in the treaty. When that party introduces reservations, the only response available to the other parties will simply be to reciprocate. But the effect will be that the highest-cost party will have achieved a first-best result from the treaty.

The next highest-cost state will likewise have incentives to introduce reservations, which reduce the effort level required by the treaty, reducing the extent of the treaty obligation with respect to every other treaty member, except the highest-cost state, who preferred an even lower effort level.

If every state follows this course, the treaty will effectively fragment into a network of bilateral treaties, each favoring the higher-cost party. This result is particularly undesirable for nations that derive much benefit from cooperation. Thus, nations may take steps to mitigate fragmentation of a treaty at its formation. The most obvious and straightforward method would simply be to disallow reservations. Recall that the Vienna Convention enumerated *default* rules for treaties – parties remain free to articulate alternative rules explicitly. One such articulation would simply be to deny prospective members the option to reserve in the first place.

Another possible countermeasure available to low-cost/high-benefit nations would simply be to offer side deals to high-cost/low-benefit nations. That is, if nation *A* receives a greater benefit from cooperation than nation *B*, then *A* may pay *B* not to introduce a reservation,

---

[21] Convention on the Punishment and Prevention of the Crime of Genocide, December 9, 1948, Status, http://treaties.un.org/pages/ViewDetails.aspx?src=TREATYandmtdsg_no=IV-17chapter=4andlang=en (accessed June 7, 2011). Eleven other nations have also objected to the US reservation.

compensating *B* for the reduced payoff of abiding by the higher effort level required by the treaty. Coasean bargaining may simply reduce the effective heterogeneity of parties, such that if the marginal cost to *B* of increasing *B*'s effort to meet the treaty obligation is less than the marginal benefit to *A* of increasing *B*'s effort, then *A* can compensate *B* up to the socially optimal point. This may be accomplished either informally or in the treaty language itself. For example, the Montreal Protocol on Ozone-Depleting Substances calls for wealthier nations – whose populations are more sensitive to environmental concerns – to subsidize the compliance costs of poorer nations.[22]

Third, nations may avoid fragmentation by forming agreements limited to participation by homogeneous nations, i.e., where the costs and benefits for all the parties are similar. By making the treaty closed to new participants, low-cost/high-benefit nations may avoid the problem of treaty fragmentation that may arise from multilateral agreements with heterogeneous parties. We may observe such limited membership in regional economic development and trade treaties between nations of comparable wealth and technological development.

Lastly, where broad cooperation is important to the objective of a treaty (e.g., human rights treaties, environmental treaties and disarmament treaties), states may opt to tailor treaty content to the economic and technological development of states, avoiding fragmentation by setting variable requirements in the terms of the treaty itself. Examples of this include the aforementioned Kyoto Protocol, which sets variable greenhouse gas reduction goals, contingent upon a nation's economic and technological development, and the World Trade Organization, which tailors 'special and differential' treatment to favor poor and developing nations (Fukasaku 2000; Hoekman, et al. 2003).

To conclude this section, it may be useful to characterize what a high-cost/low-benefit nation is. Very often, such nations are economically and technically less developed. This may explain why wealthier nations at the time of the Vienna Convention lobbied against allowing unilateral reservations, while less developed nations lobbied for them. Since the matching reservations mechanism allows higher-cost nations to obtain optimal (or near-optimal) payoffs from a treaty, poorer nations, who are often unable to participate in international cooperation, or who derive little benefit from it, are benefited. However, it is not necessarily the case that a nation's marginal costs and benefits from international cooperation

[22] Montreal Protocol on Substances that Deplete the Ozone Layer, September 16, 1987, 26 I.L.M. 1541.

correspond to wealth. For example, the US in its relationship with its partners in the North American Free Trade Agreement, is a highest-cost/lowest-benefit nation with respect to intellectual property.[23]

Termination

Participation in treaties may be terminated at will. Sometimes treaties state explicitly the formal requirements for withdrawal. Otherwise, the Vienna Convention provides default rules for withdrawal, which may be implied from the language of the treaty of its 'nature' (for example, a treaty concerning a joint enterprise may be considered terminated when the underlying purpose of the agreement – the joint effort – is completed).[24]

Posner and Sykes observe that the ease of termination may provide yet another explanation for why breach remedies are virtually nonexistent in the law of treaties – a nation may simply declare that it is withdrawing from an agreement before doing whatever it wishes to avoid 'breaching' (Posner and Sykes 2013). A treaty, they write, 'is best understood as the terms of cooperation as long as states are willing to cooperate' (Posner and Sykes 2013). States may avoid the reputational consequences of 'breaching' or strategically withdrawing from an agreement by offering side payments to other parties to the treaty to 'renegotiate' the terms, or simply to permit withdrawal from the treaty obligations without protest. Posner and Sykes liken this to employee termination, where an employee wishes to avoid the reputational effects (and possible legal ramifications) of firing an employee, and employees wish to avoid the stigma of being fired; the two parties may simply work out a deal, so that it appears the employee left voluntarily. This benefits both the former employee and employer, though it imposes an externality on future employers (i.e., it internalizes the positive externality of the information).

V. CONCLUSION

In this chapter, we have summarized several developments in the economic analysis of treaty law. The late arrival of law and economics in addressing international law generally still leaves innumerable opportunities for scholars in search of fertile areas of research. In their pioneering

[23] North American Free Trade Agreement, December 17, 1992, US–Can.–Mex., 32 I.L.M. 289.

[24] Vienna Convention, art. 56.

work, Goldsmith and Posner (2003) contend that international agreements generally could be explained without appealing to vague, quasi-moral, universal norms, but rather to rational self-interest. We then distinguished treaties from less formal international agreements, discussing why parties to an agreement might prefer more or less formal mechanisms for communicating the intention to behave cooperatively. In Sections III and IV, we described Parisi and Fon's work, developing Goldsmith and Posner's game-theoretic framework as it applies specifically to treaty formation, ratification and reservations (Parisi and Fon 2009).

The economic analysis of treaty law is still in its early stages, and there remain many opportunities for innovation for researchers interested in using economic methods to understand treaties. Several questions in international treaty law are in need of illumination by the categories and analytical instruments of economic analysis, ranging from the optimal scope of treaty law vis-à-vis other formal and informal sources. Another virtually overlooked dimension in the current literature is that of the optimal size of international treaties. Bilateral treaties and treaties with fewer participants can more easily be tailored to the needs of the participants. For other treaties, however, the benefits of tailored treaty content are more than counterbalanced by the benefit obtainable through widespread treaty participation. Other areas of interest for economic analysis concern the interaction between customary and treaty rules, and the rules governing the adaptation of international law to changed circumstances.

REFERENCES

Aumann, Robert J. 1959. 'Acceptable Points in General Cooperative *n*-Person Games', in A.W. Tucker and R.D. Luce (eds.), *Contributions to the Theory of Games* (AM-40) vol. IV, Annals of Mathematics Study, Princeton University Press, 287–324.

Axelrod, Robert. 1984. *The Evolution of Cooperation*, New York, NY: Basic Books.

Briggs, Herbert W. 1979. 'United States Ratification of the Vienna Treaty Convention' 73 *American Journal of International Law* 470.

Dunoff, Jeffrey L. 2000. 'Some Costs and Benefits of Economic Analysis of International Law' 94 *American Society of International Law Proceedings* 185.

Dunoff, Jeffrey L. and Joel P. Trachtman, 1999. 'Economic Analysis of International Law' 24 *Yale Journal of International Law* 1.

Frankowska, Maria. 1988. 'The Vienna Convention on the Law of Treaties Before United States Courts' 28 *Virginia Journal of International Law* 281.

Fukasaku, Kiichiro. 2000. 'Special and Differential Treatment for Developing Countries: Helping Those who Help Themselves', in S.M. Murshed (ed.), *Globalization, Marginalization and Development*, Abingdon, UK: Routledge, 156–70.

Goldsmith, Jack L. and Eric A. Posner. 2003. 'International Agreements: A Rational Approach' 44 *Virginia Journal of International Law* 113.

Goldsmith, Jack L. and Eric A. Posner. 2000. 'Understanding the Resemblance Between Modern and Traditional Customary International Law' 40 *Virginia Journal of International Law* 639.

Gross, Leo. 1948. 'The Peace of Westphalia, 1648–1948' 42 *American Journal of International Law* 20.

Hoekman, Bernard, Constantine Michalopolous and Alan Winters. 2003. *Special and Differential Treatment for Developing Countries: Towards a New Approach in the WTO*, World Bank: mimeograph.

Hylton, Daniel N. 1994. 'Default Breakdown: The Vienna Convention on the Law of Treaties' Inadequate Framework on Reservations' 27 *Vanderbilt Journal of Transnational Law* 419, 421.

Kontorovich, Eugene. 2006. 'Inefficient Customs in International Law' 48 *William and Mary Law Review* 859.

Parisi, Francesco. 2013 'Positive vs. normative law and economics', in F. Parisi. *The Language of Law and Economics: A Dictionary*, Cambridge, UK: Cambridge University Press.

Parisi, Francesco and Vincy Fon. 2009. *The Economics of Lawmaking*, New York, NY: Oxford University Press.

Posner, Eric A. and Alan O. Sykes. 2013. *Economic Foundations of International Law*, Cambridge, MA: Harvard University Press.

Sykes, Alan O. 2004. 'International Law', in Mitchell Polinsky and Steven Shavell (eds.), *Handbook of Law and Economics*, Philadelphia, PA: North Holland.

Schelling, Thomas. 1960. *The Strategy of Conflict*, Cambridge, MA: Harvard University Press.

5. Soft law

Andrew T. Guzman and Timothy Meyer

INTRODUCTION

The topic of international soft law has long confounded both legal scholars and political scientists. Although the term soft law has been in the legal lexicon since at least the 1970s, there is still no consensus on its meaning or its role in the international legal system. In an attempt to summarize existing views on the subject, we identify three different approaches to situating soft law within the international legal landscape.

One group of scholars, the traditional legal positivists, tends to dismiss soft law. They do so not because they think the norms at issue are irrelevant, but because they consider these norms to be beyond the scope of what should concern legal scholars.[1] Prosper Weil, for example, once argued that the kinds of obligations that flow from soft law are indeterminate because they 'are neither soft law nor hard law: they are simply not law at all'.[2] In a similar manner Jans Klabbers argued that soft law is fundamentally incoherent as a theoretical construct and is, at best, a superfluous addendum to the binary conception of law and legality.[3] Jean d'Aspremont has gone so far as to contend that maintaining the binary distinction between law and non-law is necessary for the international legal system to maintain its ability to regulate state behavior.[4]

---

[1] *See* Anthony D'Amato, *International Soft Law, Hard Law, and Coherence*, Northwestern Public Research Paper No. 08-01 (2008).

[2] *See* Prosper Weil, 'Towards Relative Normativity in International Law?', 77 *Am. J. Int'l L.* 414–15 n. 7 (1983).

[3] *See* Jans Klabbers, 'The Redundancy of Soft Law', 65 *Nordic J. Int'l L.* (1996).

[4] Jean d'Aspremont, *Formalism and the Sources of International Law: A Theory of Ascertainment of Legal Rules* 30 (Oxford: Oxford University Press 2011) (arguing that in the absence of formal criteria to distinguish law from non-law, legal rules 'cannot be clearly ascertained' and therefore 'will fall short of generating any change in the behavior' of states).

Oscar Schacter is somewhat more tolerant of soft law, but views it as a clear second best relative to hard law.[5]

The positivists' position, however justified as a doctrinal matter, does not make soft law disappear. It offers no answer to the important questions of what agreements such as the Universal Declaration of Human Rights, the Helsinki Final Act, and the Basle Accords actually do and why they are used by states. Whether or not the use of the word 'law' in the term 'soft law' is objectionable, one cannot deny that it is pervasive in international affairs. Not even the most committed legal positivists could deny that these agreements, and many others, are meaningful and worthy of study. Their objection to the term 'soft law' is based on a fear that it erodes the clear distinction between that which is legally binding and that which is not. They seek, in other words, to protect the special status of international law as distinct from political or other commitments.

A second group of legal scholars uses traditional tools of legal analysis to examine non-binding legal obligations.[6] The result has been a wide range of observations and claims about soft law, but no central theoretical core or broad consensus about its place in the international legal system. For some scholars, soft law is considered a quasi-legal way to organize inter-state relations, which offers advantages of flexibility and cost savings.[7] Dinah Shelton describes soft law as a 'social rather than legal norm'.[8] Similarly Cynthia Lichtenstein notes that soft law is more akin to a set of expressive, non-binding normative preferences announced by the international community.[9]

Others in this group are more interested in how various sub-state or inter-state actors interact with soft law. For example, Cynthia Williams describes how industry groups voluntarily create reporting schemes and governance principles to better adapt to an environment where authority

---

[5] Oscar Schacter, 'Comment, The Twilight Existence of Nonbinding Agreements', 71 *Am. J. Int'l L.* 296, 304 (1977).

[6] *See generally* Anna di Robilant, 'Genealogies of Soft Law', (2006) 54 *Am. J. Comp. L.* 499 (exploring the different historical roots of modern soft law).

[7] *See* Hartmut Hillgenberg, 'A Fresh Look at Soft Law', 10 *Eur. J. Int'l L. 499* (1999); John J. Kirton and Michael J. Trebilcock, *Hard Choices, Soft Law: Voluntary Standards in Global Trade, Environment, and Social Governance* (Brookfield, VT: Ashgate 2004) (exploring which fields have adopted soft law as de rigueur and why).

[8] Dinah Shelton, 'Soft Law', in *Routledge Handbook of International Law* (David Armstrong, ed. New York, NY: Routledge 2009).

[9] Cynthia Crawford Lichtenstein, 'Hard law vs. Soft Law: Unnecessary Dichotomy?' (2001) 35 *Int'l L.* 1433, 1434.

is diffuse.[10] Richard Bilder argues that foreign policy officials often equate soft law with international norms. In doing so, they approach soft law with a pragmatic mindset – that is to say, foreign policy officials are more interested in the integrity of their own policy positions rather than necessarily complying with the underlying norms embodied by a specific piece of soft law.[11] And Armin Schäfer suggests that international organizations themselves may promulgate soft law as a way to facilitate cooperative compromises in situations where states would not normally agree to a hard law rule.[12] In other words, although states may be unable initially to agree to a set of hard law rules, they may be amenable to a soft law surveillance and standard-setting regime. With enough time, this soft law regime may provide default rules in a given area or become codified into hard law. Indeed, even the European Union, perhaps the international institution that most resembles a national government in terms of the scope of its powers, uses soft law and various forms of non-legal discourse to induce states to comply with goals.[13]

More recently, a third group – in which we place ourselves – has taken to examining soft law through the lens of social science.[14] These scholars include both institutionalists and constructivists, who, despite methodological disagreements, share an interest in soft law and a belief that it can both have tangible effects on state behavior and improve the ability of states to cooperate. They have argued that the traditional legal positivist view of a binary conception of law and legality focuses too much on form, at the expense of function. Though they do not deny the binary distinction between that which is binding under international law and that which is not, they point out that sovereign state behavior is influenced by a wide range of international legal instruments and institutions and a

---

10 *See* Cynthia A. Williams, 'Civil Society Initiatives and "Soft Law" in the Oil and Gas Industry', (2003–2004) 36 *N.Y.U. J. Int'l. L. and Pol.* 457.

11 Richard B. Bilder, 'Beyond Compliance: Helping Nations Cooperate' in *Commitment and Compliance: The Role of Non-binding Norms in the International Legal System* (Dinah Shelton ed., New York, NY: Oxford University Press 2000) at 65, 67 (noting that officials may see soft law as an expression of preferences as well as an instrumental tool).

12 Armin Schäfer, 'Resolving Deadlock: Why International Organisations Introduce Soft Law', (2006) 12 *Eur. L.J.*, 194.

13 David M. Trubek and Louise G. Trubek, 'Hard and Soft Law in the Construction of Social Europe: The Role of the Open Method of Co-ordination', (2005) 11 *Eur. L.J.*, 343, 356.

14 To be fair, there is no stark distinction between those we place in our third group and those in our second. The difference is more one of degree than one of kind.

proper understanding of the international system requires consideration of all of them.[15]

In a seminal institutionalist article on soft law, Kenneth Abbott and Duncan Snidal propose thinking of international agreements as relatively hard or soft along three dimensions: obligation, precision and delegation.[16] They argue that states make deliberate choices about the form of their legal obligations, including by altering the bindingness of the obligation, by adjusting the degree of vagueness, and by choosing whether to delegate enforcement and interpretation. Reducing the strength or depth of an obligation can be useful because it may offer benefits in the form of reduced transaction costs, increased flexibility, and enhanced cooperation.[17] Importantly, though Abbott and Snidal discuss degrees of 'hardness' in law, they do not dispute the binary nature of legal obligation that is of concern to positivists. They agree that international commitments are either binding or non-binding. They refer to this binary feature, however, as the bindingness of the obligation. In a significant (and sometimes confusing) distinction with other scholars, they use the terms 'hard law' and 'soft law' to refer to the combined effect of obligation, precision and delegation.[18]

Building off Abbott and Snidal's work, rational institutionalist scholars have suggested that states deliberately choose to employ soft law for a host of different reasons. These reasons include, among others, wanting to avoid the higher sanctions associated with violations of hard law, wanting to delegate authority to a third party in order to ensure some flexibility to change rules in the future, and using soft law as a way to counterbalance existing hard law rules that states may find disagreeable.[19] Soft law, in short, is easier and cheaper to negotiate and violate than hard law.

---

[15] *See* Charles Lipson, 'Why are Some International Agreements Informal?', 45 *Int'l Org.* (1991); Kenneth W. Abbott and Duncan Snidal, 'Hard and Soft Law in International Governance', (2000) 54 *Int'l Org.* 421; Kenneth W. Abbott, Robert O. Keohane, Andrew Moravcsik, Anne-Marie Slaughter and Duncan Snidal, 'The Concept of Legalization', (2000) 54 *Int'l Org.* 401 (hereinafter Abbott, Keohane, et al.); Andrew T. Guzman and Timothy L. Meyer, 'International Soft Law', (2010) 2 *J. Legal Analysis*; Andrew T. Guzman, *How International Law Works* (New York, NY: Oxford University Press 2008).

[16] Abbott and Snidal, *supra* note 15, at 422.

[17] Abbott and Snidal, *supra* note 15, at 423.

[18] *See* Abbott, Keohane, et al., *supra* note 15.

[19] Andrew T. Guzman, 'The Cost of Credibility: Explaining Resistance to Interstate Dispute Resolution Mechanisms', (2002) 31 *J. Legal Studies* 303; Timothy L. Meyer, 'Soft Law as Delegation', (2008) 32 *Fordham Int'l L.J.*

Constructivists, on the other hand, tend to look at soft law as a manifestation of, and mechanism for, various forms of socialization between states. These manifestations and mechanisms can include persuasion, norm diffusion, and acculturation, internally as well as externally, between states. As such, constructivist scholars take the position that soft law can have a much greater impact upon states and societies than its mere application in courts or at high-level political decision-making processes.[20]

WHAT IS SOFT LAW?

As noted above, any discussions of soft law must start with an acknowledgement that there is no consensus definition of the term. In fact, there is no meaningful sense in which one can say that there is a single 'true' definition of soft law. Predictably, this has led to a modest amount of analytical confusion despite the fact that the issue is ultimately semantic. Clarity, however, requires that we not confuse different definitions with different substantive arguments. It is therefore important to be explicit about how we will use the term 'soft law.'

Abbott and Snidal's definition, discussed above, has been particularly influential. They define hard and soft law with respect to what they term 'legalization' and what we might call the compliance-pull of an obligation. The key insight to be extrapolated from their definition is that

---

888–942; Gregory C. Shaffer and Mark A. Pollack, 'Hard vs. Soft Law: Alternatives, Complements, and Antagonists in International Governance', (2010) 94 *Minnesota L. Rev.* 706–99; *See also* Christine Chinkin, 'Normative Development in the International Legal System', in *Commitment and Compliance: The Role of Non-Binding Norms in the International Legal System* (Dinah Shelton ed., New York, NY: Oxford University Press 2000) at 31 (regarding hardening of soft law); Lipson, *supra* note 15.

[20] Martha Finnemore and Stephen J. Toope, 'Alternatives to "Legalization": Richer Views of Law and Politics', (2001) 55 *Int'l Org.* 743; Ryan Goodman and Derek Jinks, 'How to Influence States: Socialization and International Human Rights', (2004) 54 *Duke L.J.* 621; Ryan Goodman and Derek Jinks, 'Toward an Institutional Theory of Sovereignty', (2003) 55 *Stanford L. Rev.* 1749; John Gerard Ruggie, 'What Makes the World Hang Together? Neo-utilitarianism and the Social Constructivist Challenge', 52 *Int'l Org.* (1998); Beth Simmons, 'International Efforts Against Money Laundering', in *Commitment and Compliance: the Role of Non-binding Norms in the International Legal System* (Dinah Shelton ed., New York, NY: Oxford University Press 2000) at 245 (noting that the Financial Action Task Force recommendations on combating money laundering depend mainly on peer pressure to bring countries into line).

different aspects of an international agreement, which can vary along a continuum between what they consider fully legalized obligations and fully hortatory norms, can influence the ability of a rule to alter behavior. States, behaving in a functionalist way, choose to locate a given international agreement along the continuum in order to better achieve cooperative goals.[21] As discussed above, Abbott and Snidal consider three variables that states can adjust in order to change the degree of legalization: obligation, precision and delegation. As any or all of the three dimensions are weakened, the resulting rule becomes increasingly 'soft', by which they mean a less powerful legal commitment. Ultimately, if one goes far enough the commitment becomes merely political.

They define obligation as the degree to which international actors are legally bound by rules or commitments. Precision deals with the degree of ambiguity in any given set of rules, and delegation refers to the grant of authority to third parties to judge the relevant rules and state behavior.[22] In their view, obligation, precision and delegation are the defining characteristics of legalization. As the level of legalization increases, the law 'hardens'; as legalization decreases, the law 'softens'. Because Abbott and Snidal use the terms hard and soft law to refer to the extent of this 'hardness', it follows that 'the choice between hard law and soft law is not a binary one'. As we show below, Abbott and Snidal's position is consistent with the views of other writers focusing on the compliance pull of a commitment that use different terms.[23]

Kal Raustiala offers an analysis of soft law that is superficially quite different from Abbott and Snidal's but, once the terminological confusion is cleared up, leads to very similar conclusions. In an attempt to avoid confusion over terms, Raustiala makes a distinction between what he calls 'pledges' and 'contracts'. Contracts, which we call hard law, are legally binding commitments under international law and correspond roughly to what Abbott and Snidal call obligation. Pledges are everything else. By adopting this binary categorization, Raustiala rules out any intermediate categories of 'bindingness', which is consistent with a conventional international law perspective. Having committed to the distinction between binding and non-binding, he observes that 'there is no such thing as "soft law"'. Although stated provocatively, what he

---

21 *See also* Lipson, *supra* note 15.

22 *See* Abbott, Keohane, et al., *supra* note 15.

23 Abbott and Snidal, *supra* note 15, at 422.

means here is simply that an agreement is law only if it is binding. If it is not binding it is not law at all, and so cannot be 'soft' law.[24]

Here again we run into a semantic distinction. Raustiala rejects the notion that one can categorize international law as hard or soft because all international law is, by definition, binding. In this sense, he is resisting the particular vocabulary used by Abbott and Snidal. He is not, however, dismissing the entire class of quasi-legal norms commonly known as soft law. He merely seeks to make clear that they are not 'international law' in the formal sense.

Beyond this disagreement over terms, however, Raustiala's conclusions sound a lot like Abbott and Snidal's. He proposes a framework within which states vary their commitments along three dimensions: legality, substance and structure. Legality, as we have already noted, is binary. The substance dimension is a sliding scale, dealing with how much change from status quo behavior an agreement requires from states. Structure mostly deals with the underlying mechanisms for monitoring compliance and violation of the agreement.[25] As we can see, although Raustiala's categories are not identical to Abbott and Snidal's, substantively they can be largely reconciled with obligation, precision and delegation.

Our own definition of soft law, and the one used in the rest of this chapter, aligns with Abbott and Snidal's and Raustiala's concepts of obligation and legality – a commitment is either formally binding or it is not. We embrace the binary, doctrinal distinction between binding and non-binding agreements, but focus our inquiry on why states choose the soft law form of agreements, and how that choice affects the impact of a rule.[26] Stated clearly, our definition of soft law is 'those nonbinding rules or instruments that interpret or inform our understanding of binding legal rules or represent promises that in turn create expectations about future conduct'.[27] One of the advantages of adopting a binary approach to legality that is in line with the above scholars is that it gives us the opportunity to consider how legal form – meaning the choice of hard or

---

[24] Kal Raustiala, 'Form and Substance in International Agreements', (2005) 99 *Am. J. Int'l L.*, 581, 586–7.

[25] *Ibid.*, at 581.

[26] *See generally* Guzman and Meyer, *supra* note 15; Andrew T. Guzman and Timothy L. Meyer, 'International Common Law: The Soft Law of International Tribunals', (2009) 9 *Chicago J. Int'l L.* 515.

[27] Guzman and Meyer, *supra* note 15, at 174.

soft law – along with monitoring, dispute resolution, and substance, 'affect the compliance-pull of an agreement'.[28]

Our focus on the relationship between what we term soft law – meaning non-binding commitments – and the effectiveness or compliance-pull of an agreement places the spotlight squarely on the question of how and why non-binding 'soft law' can 'shape states' expectations as to what constitutes compliant behavior'.[29] The operating assumption is that, all else being equal, states take binding (hard law) agreements more seriously than non-binding (soft law) agreements. That said, the mere fact that an agreement is non-binding is insufficient to predict how it will affect state behavior. Bindingness is just one of several variables that matters. In fact, this is in keeping with the consensus view, which notes that the legal status of an agreement (i.e., hard or soft law) interacts with others elements, including the substance, precision, structure, delegation, monitoring, and more, to determine the impact of the agreement on states.

WHAT DOES SOFT LAW DO?

No doubt because the definitional disagreements are more semantic than substantive, scholars have forged ahead and explored various aspects of the function and forms of international soft law rather than argue about the definition of terms. For purposes of the present survey, discussions of what soft law does and why states use it can be divided into three broad categories: contractual explanations of the use of soft law; discussions of the relationship between domestic legal structures and the choice of soft law; and the role of soft law in managing complexity within the international legal system.[30]

---

[28] Andrew T. Guzman, 'Design of International Agreement', (2005) 16 *Eur. J. Int'l L.* 579, 584.

[29] Guzman and Meyer, *supra* note 15, at 175.

[30] The literature discussing the relative merits of hard and soft law is large. *See generally* John J. Kirton and Michael J. Trebilcock, 'Introduction', in *Hard Choices, Soft Law: Voluntary Standards in Global Trade, Environment, and Social Governance* (John J. Kirton and Michael J. Trebilcock eds., Brookfield, VT: Ashgate 2004) 3, 9; Abbott and Snidal, *supra* note 15, at 434–54; Lipson, *supra* note 15, at 500–1, 514–27; David M. Trubek, Patrick Cottrell and Mark Nance, 'Soft Law, Hard Law and EU Integration', in *Law and New Governance in the EU and the US* (Grainne de Burca and Joanne Scott eds., Oxford, Portland OR: Hart 2006) 65, 73–4; Hartmut Hillgenberg, *supra* note 7, at 501, 504; Guzman, *supra* note 28; Guzman, *supra* note 15, at 142–7; Guzman and Meyer,

The first category focuses on compliance-related concerns and includes explanations of soft law that stem from the notion that states seek to lower the costs of both compliance with and potential violations of an agreement. The underlying notion is that states prefer to capture the largest gains (increased cooperation) at the lowest risk possible (cost in the event of a violation). The second category includes explanations that focus on the effects of domestic politics and legal institutions on international cooperation. These explanations are contingent on the domestic political and judicial institutions having sufficient purchase on the executive's power to enter international obligations. The third category looks to systemic effects of states' use of soft law. The international legal system is notoriously fragmented, consisting of myriad overlapping and non-hierarchical obligations.[31] The system is also beset by competing interests among states as to the degree of commitment their obligations should reflect. This last set of explanations often stress how states can use the soft law form to manage complexity across legal instruments and achieve system-wide changes to international rules and obligations.

Contractual Explanations of Soft Law

Contractual approaches generally start with the observation that states are risk averse, or at least risk neutral, and seek to maximize potential gains while minimizing potential losses. This leads to several theories about why states use soft law. First, soft law may have lower contracting costs than hard law.[32] Potential hard law agreements are subject to intense scrutiny because states understand that the reputational costs for a potential breach are higher than if the state breaches a piece of soft law. Since reputational costs for potential breach are high, states are more constrained in their behavior after signing the agreement. This dynamic influences the amount of effort states put into negotiating the initial

---

supra note 15; Shaffer and Pollack, *supra* note 19; Mary Ellen O'Connell, 'The Role of Soft law in a Global Order', in *Commitment and Compliance: the Role of Non-binding Norms in the International Legal System* (Dinah Shelton ed., New York, NY: Oxford University Press 2000); Chinkin, *supra* note 19, at 26; Dinah Shelton, *supra* note 11; Raustiala, *supra* note 24, at 582; Martin Koppel, 'The Effectiveness of Soft Law: First Insights from Comparing Legally Binding Agreements with Flexible Action Programs', (2009) 21 *Geo. Int'l. Envtl. L. Rev.* 821, 823–6.

[31] Kal Raustiala & David G. Victor, 'The Regime Complex for Plant Genetic Resources', (2004) 58 *Int'l Org.* 277.

[32] Abbott and Snidal, *supra* note 15, at 434.

agreement. Relatedly, when enforcement and *ex post* scrutiny of state behavior is predicted to be high, as is true of hard law agreements relative to soft law agreements, states tend to bargain harder.[33] By contrast, since states may perceive lower reputational costs for breaching soft law in the future, they may put fewer resources into the negotiation and incur lower contracting costs than they otherwise would.

Second, soft law allows states to temper the expected losses from potential violations. This 'loss avoidance theory' points out that while higher violation costs in the international arena serve to discourage violations, they represent a net loss for the parties to the agreement – they are not zero-sum transfers. As such, when a violator is hit with reputational losses, the counterparty receives no offsetting gain. Sanctions in international law are, in other words, negative sum. States will therefore sometimes prefer soft law over hard law because the joint costs in the event of a violation are lower. Specifically, states are more likely to choose soft law if the marginal costs of violations exceeds the marginal benefits of increased compliance with the underlying agreement.[34] The same basic argument provides an explanation for why states do not use dispute resolution or monitoring more often.

We can see this dynamic playing out in certain specialized areas of international law. Chris Brummer, for example, describes how the law of international finance often takes the form of best practice standards or other soft law agreements.[35] Each state must weigh the benefits of compliance against the costs of non-compliance, including reputational, market, and institutional costs. In the context of capital markets, Brummer argues, the costs of violation can be high for both the breaching and non-breaching party.[36] By choosing a soft law form, states reduce the costs associated with violation.

Third, states may choose soft law over hard law as a strategy to deal with uncertainty. When states face an uncertain landscape and expect to be affected in a similar fashion by future changes, states may want to design an institution that can adapt to changes faster and more easily than

---

[33] James Fearon, 'Bargaining, Enforcement, and International Cooperation', (1998) 52 *Int'l. Org.* 269, 270.

[34] Guzman, *supra* note 19.

[35] Chris Brummer, *Soft Law and the Global Financial System*, 5 (New York, NY: Cambridge University Press 2012).

[36] *Ibid.*, at 153.

unanimity allows.[37] The 'delegation theory' of soft law explains how states can employ soft law to give one or more states the ability to make de facto amendments to the agreement.[38] Influential members of an agreement can refuse to comply and demand that other parties accept some alternative arrangement. In some circumstances, this leads to a welfare-enhancing change and, by side-stepping the need for formal amendment or unanimous consent, it greatly reduces the risks that a beneficial amendment will be held up or prevented by one or more states that prefer the status quo. This form of quasi-coercive amendment requires that existing arrangements be breached by one or more parties. Choosing a soft law obligation reduces the cost of this breach, making it easier for a state to trigger the amendment. States, then, may opt for soft law if they want to make it easier for leading states to engage in this form of amendment. In effect, they delegate the power to amend to some subset of states.

Fourth, some scholars offer uncertainty coupled with risk aversion as a reason states may choose soft law over hard law.[39] When faced with uncertainty about the future, any commitment can have unpredictable distributional consequences. If states are risk averse with respect to such commitments, they may prefer a soft law agreement that they can exit at lower cost rather than a hard law agreement.

We do not find this explanation entirely persuasive, however, and neither the loss-avoidance theory nor the delegation theory requires that states be risk averse, rather than risk neutral. As one of us has argued elsewhere, it is more sensible to model states as risk neutral, rather than risk averse, with respect to international legal obligations. States have many such obligations and are well diversified with respect to their international commitments. Furthermore, the cost of a violation is almost always limited. States, then, have a diverse portfolio of obligations and the costs of violation are almost never terribly large. Under these circumstances they will be better off to behave in a risk neutral fashion and simply try to maximize the expected gains from the commitments.[40]

Fifth, states may use soft law as a way to solve coordination games. In short, states may look to soft law to create a focal point around which all

---

[37] *See* Timothy Meyer, 'Shifting Sands: Power, Uncertainty, and the Form of International Legal Cooperation,' (2016) 27 *Euro. J. Int'l L.* 161; O'Connell, *supra* note 30, at 109–10 (regarding experimentation through soft law).

[38] *See* Meyer, *supra* note 19.

[39] *See* Raustiala, *supra* note 24, at 582.

[40] For a more detailed discussion of why states should be modeled as risk neutral, see Guzman, *supra* note 15, at 122–6.

involved can coordinate their activities.[41] For example, it would be of no benefit to anyone if all states handled air travel procedures differently. Thus the International Civil Aviation Organization promulgates standards that increase efficiency and safety for air travel worldwide. Because states have no incentives to defect, they can coordinate around the same standard with the knowledge that other states have also received the same information regarding the standards.[42] In simple coordination games, of course, it is possible to coordinate without any form of agreement or even any direct communication at all. This raises the question of why soft law is used for coordination rather than some other strategy such as unilateral statements by leading states or simply repeated practice. The answer is that coordination is often achieved through these other methods. When coordination is more complicated, however, it becomes convenient to produce a written document or in some other way memorialize the specific of the cooperation. To cite just one of many possible examples, the International Criminal Police Organization (Interpol) was formed in 1923 and today operates based on a 'Constitution' adopted in 1956. This Constitution is actually a soft law document.[43] Interpol's work includes facilitation of informational exchange, maintenance of a secure communications network, management of DNA, fingerprint, and other databases, a twenty-four hour command and coordination center, and so on. These activities are fundamentally about coordination, but would be difficult to carry out without a negotiated and agreed upon common text to address governance, management, budget, and more. Soft law, then, comes to be used because it is the most convenient coordination tool.

Domestic Politics and Soft Law

The second camp of explanations deals with the impact of domestic law and politics on the choice of international legal form. The most obvious of the predictions is that the choice of hard or soft law is the result of domestic interest group politics.[44] Raustiala and others have argued that those in favor of an international commitment will generally prefer hard

---

[41] Guzman and Meyer, *supra* note 15, at 188.

[42] *See* Richard H. McAdams, 'The Expressive Power of Adjudication', (2005) *U. Ill. L. Rev.* 1045.

[43] There is, in fact, some debate about its legal status, but we put that aside for present purposes. Mario Savino, 'Global Administrative Law Meet 'Soft' Powers: The Uncomfortable Case of Interpol Red Notices', (2011) 43 *N.Y.U. J. Int'l L. and Pol.* 263, 271–2.

[44] Raustiala, *supra* note 24, at 595–97.

law over soft law, even when soft law might better achieve their substantive objectives.[45] When domestic politics is strongly supportive of an international agreement, then, the state will prefer that it be a treaty. When the domestic politics are more complicated, however, soft law may be more attractive. If there are competing interest groups – one wanting hard law, the other preferring no commitment at all – domestic leaders may find that the best outcome in political terms is a compromise involving soft law. Proponents of an international agreement may be satisfied (or at least not too dissatisfied) and opponents may be willing to live with a soft law agreement.

Perhaps the most classic perspective on soft law takes the position that states enter into soft law agreements because they 'are faster to adopt, easier to change, and more useful for technical matters that may need rapid or repeated revisions'.[46] The broad statement benefits from some unpacking. It seems clear that soft law can be easier and faster to accomplish as a practical matter because hard law often involves some formal domestic procedures, such as ratification. This reality is imposed either by the practice of states who prefer that hard law include ratification or some other form of delay, or by domestic requirements that insist on some domestic process after an agreement is reached. In the United States (US), for example, the treaty clause of the Constitution requires a two-thirds vote of the Senate. In countries like the US, where the ratification process is often not fully within the control of the executive branch, soft law may be used by the executive to avoid entanglements with the legislature or because the ratification process is onerous in some other way.[47] For example, the US insisted that key greenhouse gas emissions reductions obligations in the 2015 Paris

---

[45] *Id.* at 596; Douglass Cassel, 'Inter-American Human Rights Law, Soft and Hard' in *Non-Binding Norms*, *supra* note 11.

[46] *See* Shelton, *supra* note 8.

[47] *See* Chinkin, *supra* note 19, at 26. Of course, in many countries the executive branch can create hard law and still bypass the legislature. In the US this can be accomplished in some issue areas through the use of sole executive agreements. Moreover, legislatures retain oversight functions that allow them to supervise the executive's decision to enter into soft law agreements. For example, Basle II – a soft law agreement revising capital adequacy standards for big banks – was never fully implemented in the US because of congressional hostility to the accord, see Pierre-Hugues Verdier, 'U.S. Implementation of Basel II: Lessons for Informal International Law-Making', in *Informal International Lawmaking* (Joost Pauwelyn, Ramses Wessel and Jan Wouters eds., Oxford: Oxford University Press 2012).

Agreement be non-binding so that the agreement would not require the approval of the US Senate.[48]

However, international law does not itself require any domestic process and requires only some expression by the relevant states of a consent to be bound.[49] Furthermore, not all domestic systems require ratification of treaties as a domestic legal matter, and some, like the US, do not require it in all cases. The US can, under certain circumstances, enter into binding international agreements as sole-executive agreements, meaning the President can make the commitment without any involvement by Congress.[50] The most sensible view, then, is that there are often meaningful constraints on the ability of states to enter into hard law commitments without some formal domestic process, but they are certainly not always insurmountable.

A related argument is that, as a practical matter, treaties tend to be negotiated and signed by relatively high-ranking officials, whereas soft law agreements are often entered into by lower-ranking personnel.[51] We are not aware of any empirical study suggesting that treaties – a broad category that includes both agreements made by heads of state and cabinet level officials, as well as agreements made through an exchange of diplomatic notes authorized at lower levels of government – are in fact more likely to be entered into by high ranking officials than are soft law agreements. Moreover, there is no particular constraint on the ability of lower-ranking government officers to bind the state. To the extent that soft law is in fact more likely to be made by lower level officials, states either choose to send lower-ranking officials when the agreement will be soft law, or they tend to prefer soft law when lower-ranking officials negotiate the agreements. This is a plausible explanation of the choice of soft law over hard law only if one state fears the lower-ranking officials will exercise poor judgement and it is too expensive to send more senior

---

[48] Daniel Bodansky, 'The Paris Climate Change Agreement: A New Hope?' (2016) 110 *Amer. J. Int'l L.* (forthcoming).

[49] Vienna Convention on the Law of Treaties, art. 11, May 23, 1969, 1155 U.N.T.S. 331.

[50] The boundaries of what the President can do through sole-executive agreements remains controversial. *See* John Yoo, 'Rational Treaties: Article II, Congressional Executive Agreements and International Bargaining', (2011) 97 *Cornell L. Rev.* 1, 41; Bradford R. Clark, 'Domesticating Sole Executive Agreements', (2007) 93 *Va. L. Rev.* 1573, 1654–60; Michael D. Ramsey, 'Executive Agreements and the (Non) Treaty Power', (1998) 77 *N.C. L. Rev.* 133, 218–35.

[51] Lipson, *supra* note 15, at 508–09.

personnel. This is possible, but seems a thin explanation in a world of instantaneous and virtually costless communication.

With respect to the more general claim that soft law is easier to change, our view is that this is captured by the above discussion of what we call the delegation theory.[52] Soft law, or at least soft law agreements (as opposed to decisions of tribunals or statements by international organizations), can generally be amended only with unanimous consent – something that is also true of hard law. The delegation theory points out that generating consent for a change may be easier in the case of soft law because the cost of violating or exiting the rule and, in effect, depriving participants of the status quo ante is lower. Removing the status quo can make states more likely to consent to change. The key difference, though, is between the costs of exit and violation, not the domestic costs associated with amendment procedures. With the exception of this form of amendment, soft law seems no easier to change than hard law.

Significantly, when the executive uses soft law to avoid the legislature, other states may infer that the associated promise is less credible because it lacks support from the legislature. In other words, the choice of hard and soft law, or at least the decision to seek ratification through the legislature, may provide a signal about the political support a particular promise has and, therefore, the likelihood of a future breach. This approach views the choice of hard law as a costly signal of commitment. For instance, passing a treaty in the US Congress generally requires far more political capital from the President than if he simply signed an executive agreement.[53] The result is that the President can strategically choose to put an international agreement up for the advice and consent to ratification of the US Senate as a way to signal strength of commitment. Of course, the implication of the domestic politics explanations is that it requires an examination of the specific circumstances surrounding each and every international agreement to see if the executive in a particular member state negotiates for a specific form of agreement in order to circumvent its legislature.[54]

Examinations on this level of specificity have yielded insights into when states may be more amenable to using or implementing soft law. For example, empirical work has shown that democracies are more likely

---

52 *See* Meyer, *supra* note 19.

53 Lisa Martin, 'The President and International Commitments: Treaties as Signaling Devices', (2005) 35 *Presidential Stud. Q.* 440, 447–8.

54 Raustiala, *supra* note 24, at 595–9.

to implement the soft law Basel Accords than are non-democracies.[55] While this study does not look at the initial choice between hard and soft law, it provides further support for the notion that domestic institutions and preferences matter in explaining how states interact with soft law.

Soft Law and Managing Complexity

The third camp focuses on soft law's effect on the international legal system as a whole, and in particular on the relationship between legal instruments. This category holds a fairly diverse set of ideas about soft law, and may not represent the views of any single commentator. They include approaches that can be termed functionalist and constructivist, as well as some that represent traditional thinking among international law scholars. The real defining feature of the category is that the explanations are based on states using soft law to govern the web of often complementary and sometimes conflicting obligations they face from multiple legal instruments.

Scholars first started generating this third camp of explanations as a response to legal positivists' critique that soft law is incoherent and has negative consequences for the integrity of the international legal system.[56] A common argument is that soft law can be used to buttress, support, and fill out related, pre-existing hard law obligations.[57] As Dinah Shelton writes 'it is rare to find soft law standing in isolation; instead it is used most frequently either as a precursor to hard law or as a supplement to a hard law instrument.'[58] Memoranda of understanding between states, for example, can clarify how states will implement a treaty. In a series of papers, Pollack and Shaffer argue that hard and soft law should not only be viewed as either substitutes (states choose between them) or complements (soft law supports hard law), but also as antagonists. Specifically, states will sometimes use soft law to undermine existing hard law regimes, and vice-versa.[59] For example, a state that wants to change an

---

[55] *See* Daniel E. Ho, 'Compliance and International Soft Law: Why Do Countries Implement the Basle Accord', (2002) 5 *J. Int'l Econ. L.* 647–88.

[56] *See* Weil, *supra* note 2; Klabbers, *supra* note 3.

[57] *See, e.g.*, Jeffrey L. Dunoff, et al, *International Law: Norms, Actors, Process* 95 (2d ed. 2006).

[58] Dinah Shelton, 'Law, Non-Law, and the Problem of Soft Law,' in *Commitment and Compliance: the Role of Non-binding Norms in the International Legal System* 1, 10 (Dinah Shelton ed., New York, NY: Oxford University Press 2000).

[59] *See* Shaffer and Pollack, *supra* note 19, at 708–9.

underlying hard law regime in a specific field may promote antagonistic soft law norms. If the state is successful in introducing these antagonistic soft law norms, then the hard law regime is weakened. Similarly, states can introduce hard law agreements that, given the circumstances, cause related soft law regimes to harden into something resembling legal obligations. On both situations, hard and soft law are used antagonistically in the sense that one is used to undermine the benefits of the alternative legal form. Soft law is used to reduce the reliability and compliance-pull of hard law and hard law is used to stiffen soft law norms.

One of the interesting implications of conceiving of hard and soft law as antagonists is that it highlights the mechanism by which non-state actors can exert significant influence to shape international legal regimes on particular issues. Non-state actors, such as non-governmental organizations or intergovernmental organizations, can strategically use soft law to harden or weaken an existing hard law regime. One of the best examples of this is the movement from the 1960s onward to define the usage of nuclear weapons as against international law. A group of non-nuclear-weaponized states cooperated with non-governmental organizations to introduce United Nations (UN) General Assembly (UNGA) resolutions declaring the threat to use and usage of nuclear weapons as illegal under international law. The effort culminated with the group successfully passing a UNGA resolution in 1994 requesting an advisory opinion from the International Court of Justice regarding the legality of nuclear arms usage.[60] While the court's decision was intricately equivocal on the legality of nuclear weapons usage, no one would doubt that all interested states were extremely concerned that this attack on the legality under existing hard law rules of using or threatening to use nuclear weapons was effective. In short, actors can sometimes strategically use hard and soft law in an antagonistic fashion to further their own vision of what the international legal regime should be.

An additional advantage of soft law, though not one we dwell on here, is that soft law agreements can include parties that are unable to sign treaties, including international secretariats, business groups, non-governmental organizations, and so on.[61]

Finally, discussions of soft law most commonly refer to international agreements that fail to rise to the level of formal treaties. One should not,

---

[60] *See* Gregory C. Shaffer and Mark A. Pollack, 'Hard Versus Soft Law in International Security', (2011) 52 *B. C. L. Rev.* 1147, 1181.

[61] *See* Shaffer and Pollack, *supra* note 19, at 719.

however, ignore soft law created by international institutions, including that created by international tribunals and other international organizations. In past work, we have considered the role of tribunal decisions.[62] We define 'international common law' as the set of non-binding rulings or standards issued by international tribunals created by hard law obligations. At a minimum, these rulings and standards influence state expectations as to the nature of compliant behavior with the underlying hard law. When tribunal decisions depart from the relevant legal text, they can also create what are, in practice, new (soft law) rules.

One of the great advantages of international common law is the relative ease with which an international institution can promulgate new legal rules or fill in gaps of understanding without the need for the unanimous consent of states. Furthermore, it may be possible to give the tribunal sufficient freedom to do its job while retaining enough control for states to accept the associated sovereignty costs.[63] As such, international common law should be particularly prevalent in areas where the laws on an issue are vague and some states would prefer to move toward deeper cooperation as time goes on.[64] In the next section, we extend this analysis to soft law created by international organizations, which we term 'international legislative soft law'.[65]

INTERNATIONAL LEGISLATIVE SOFT LAW

In the remainder of this chapter, we develop a theory of why states create soft law through international legislative institutions, by which we mean intergovernmental institutions that create international instruments through deliberation, negotiation, and ultimately voting.[66] These institutions include the UN Security Council (UNSC) and the UNGA, which

---

62 *See* Guzman and Meyer, *supra* note 15, at 201.

63 *See* Andrew T. Guzman, 'International Organizations and the Frankenstein Problem,' (2013) 24 *Euro. J. Int'l L.* 999; *but see* Andrew T. Guzman and Jennifer Landsidle, 'The Myth of International Delegation', (2008) 96 *Cal. L. Rev.* (noting that non-trivial instances of delegation are actually quite rare).

64 *See* Guzman and Meyer, *supra* note 15, at 204.

65 This is related to the large and important literature on Global Administrative Law. *See* Benedict Kingsbury, Nico Krisch and Richard B. Stewart, 'The Emergence of Global Administrative Law', (2005) 68 *L. and Contemp. Probs.* 15.

66 *See* Timothy Meyer, 'From Contract to Legislation: The Logic of Modern International Lawmaking', (2014) 14 *Chicago J. Int'l Law* 559.

scholars have treated like legislative bodies.[67] We also include institutions such as the Conference of the Parties (COPs) (or Assembly of the Parties, etc.) to multilateral agreements, such as the COPs to the UN Framework Convention on Climate Change (UNFCCC), the Convention on the International Trade in Endangered Species (CITES), and the so-called Chemicals Conventions.[68] These institutions, while not commonly thought of as legislative bodies, exhibit the same basic features as domestic legislative institutions. They often divide their work into committees, they grant agenda-setting powers to key positions such as committee chairs as a way to break cycling over different alternatives, and they have voting rules they follow in the adoption of particular instruments.[69]

These international legislative institutions do the bulk of their work in the form of soft law. Moreover, the move toward legislative soft law in international affairs reflects an effort to enhance international law's effectiveness by weakening the status quo bias inherent in hard law rules to which each state bound must consent.[70] Accounts of why states frequently employ soft law do not distinguish between the different institutional environments in which international lawmaking occurs. Scholars often treat soft law instruments produced through treaty-like bargaining in the same fashion that they treat soft law produced by international institutions. We argue, however, that international institutions offer advantages in the production of soft law that are distinct from soft law produced through other means. In particular, states can use institutionally produced soft law to send each other costly signals about how they interpret the content of binding legal obligations. Using institutionally-produced soft law in this way enhances international law's effectiveness because it allows states to communicate their expectations as to what constitutes unlawful behavior, and therefore what kinds of actions are likely to produce sanctions. International legislative institutions – institutions in which states vote on the creation of legal instruments in accordance with standing procedural rules – offer particular advantages to states considering using soft law. In particular, they

---

67 *See e.g.*, Erik Voeten, 'Clashes in the Assembly', (2000) 54 *Int'l Org.* 185.

68 *See* Meyer, *supra* note 79 (arguing that many modern multilateral treaties exchange arms-length contractual bargaining for legislative bargaining within continuing bodies such as a COP).

69 *Ibid.*

70 *Cf.* Andrew T. Guzman, 'Against Consent', (2012) 52 *Va. J. Int'l L.*; Guzman, *supra* note 70; Timothy Meyer, 'Power, Exit Costs, and Renegotiation in International Law', (2010) 51 *Harv. Int'l L.J.* 379.

allow states to create soft law over the objections of dissenters – something not possible with contractual soft law – while still retaining the bargaining advantages that come with a multilateral forum in which many states participate and in which issue linkages are possible, a feature lost when other kinds of institutions such as tribunals are used to make soft law. In what follows, we develop our theory of international legislative soft law. We begin by explaining how our theory builds on our earlier work on the soft law that emerges from international tribunals. We then show that international legislative institutions commonly work through soft law and explain why this is so.

Our theory of international legislative soft law builds on our earlier work on international common law, discussed briefly above.[71] Our work on international common law was motivated by a puzzle. The existence of an international tribunal with jurisdiction over disputes is often considered to be a hallmark of legality in an international regime.[72] Yet international tribunals rarely have the ability to make decisions that have prospectively binding effect and most international tribunals do not have formal rules of binding precedent that would give retrospective decisions prospective effect. The International Court of Justice, for example, hears advisory cases, but even when acting within its contentious jurisdiction the International Court of Justice's decisions have no binding force beyond the parties and facts of the particular dispute. More generally, the decisions of tribunals and less adversarial adjudicative bodies, such as the UN Human Rights Committee, often do not have binding legal effect even with respect to the parties and the facts before the tribunal.[73]

We argued that the use of soft law by international tribunals can be explained as a move by cooperation-minded states to circumvent the consent requirement in international law that generally prevents treaties with expansive membership from requiring significant changes in status quo behavior by states. States often wish to develop the law by establishing more detailed expectations as to what counts as compliance with existing binding rules. But efforts to set such expectations through formal lawmaking are stymied by the need to obtain the consent of all affected parties. Moreover, unilaterally announced interpretations of legal rules may be self-serving and thus are liable to be discounted as cheap talk. States thus need a mechanism to develop expectations as to what counts as compliance with binding legal rules that cannot be defeated by

[71] *See* Guzman and Meyer, *supra* note 15.
[72] Abbott and Snidal, *supra* note 15.
[73] *See* Guzman and Meyer, *supra* note 15.

the consent required that goes along with the creation of binding rules. Submission to the jurisdiction of a tribunal through a jurisdictional protocol or through a UNGA resolution referring an issue to the International Court of Justice's advisory docket is such a mechanism. By submitting to a tribunal's jurisdiction, states send a costly signal that their expectations as to what counts as compliance with the underlying legal rules for all states will be shaped by the decision of the tribunal. These expectations about compliant behavior apply to all states that are bound by the underlying binding rules, regardless of whether they have accepted the tribunal's jurisdiction. For example, the fact that the US rejected the jurisdiction of the International Court of Justice in the *Nicaragua* case did not mean that the International Court of Justice's decision did not affect the US' obligations under international law. Other states understood the decision in that case to illuminate what international law requires regarding the use of force, even for those states that reject the International Court of Justice's jurisdiction. Since states themselves provide the sanctions that generate compliance in international law, it is these expectations that drive compliance with legal rules. Cooperation-minded states can delegate authority to tribunals to issue non-binding decisions that create a gloss on the underlying binding legal rules, a gloss that affects the obligations of even those states that have not consented to the jurisdiction of the tribunal.[74]

Our theory of international legislative soft law begins by noting an important similarity between international tribunals and international legislatures. Like international tribunals, international legislatures produce an enormous amount of soft law relative to the amount of hard law they produce. A small number of international legislative bodies have the power, in certain circumstances, to make hard law through legislative-like voting. The most obvious example is the UNSC, which is empowered to 'make recommendations, or decide what measures shall be taken … to maintain or restore international peace and security'.[75] The distinction between 'recommendations', which are non-binding, and 'decisions', which are binding, reflects the fact that the Security Council is empowered to make both hard and soft law. Similarly, treaties like the Montreal Protocol allow the COP to make binding changes to technical aspects of the treaty through super-majority voting.[76] Scholars have noted, however,

---

74 *Ibid.*

75 Charter of the United Nations art. 39, (1945) 1 U.N.T.S. XVI.

76 *See* Laurence R. Helfer, 'Nonconsensual International Lawmaking', (2008) *Ill. L. Rev.* 71, 84–5.

that the number of institutions that can make rules that formally bind non-voting or dissenting states is relatively small.[77]

Less rare, and significantly less noted, is the power to make non-binding rules, often through supermajority voting. Perhaps the most prominent example of a legislative institution with soft lawmaking power is the UNGA, which is empowered to 'make recommendations to the Members of the United Nations or to the Security Council'.[78] These recommendations are made through either a majority or two-thirds vote, depending on the subject matter.[79] Other representative examples include the COPs to the Cartagena Protocol on Biosafety and the Nagoya Protocol on Access to Genetic Resources, which are charged with 'mak[ing] recommendations on any matters necessary for the implementation of this Protocol'.[80] Indeed, as far back as 1959 the Antarctic Treaty charged its member states, which convene in conferences known as the Antarctic Treaty Consultative Meetings, with 'formulating and considering, and recommending to their Governments, measures in furtherance of the principles and objectives of the Treaty'.[81]

Legislative soft law can be used to radically change or expand the obligations created by an international treaty. The CITES COP is an instructive example. CITES authorizes the COP to, among other things, make decisions as to whether a species should be listed in Appendix I or II of the Convention. Listing in either appendix determines the level of controls imposed on trade in the listed species. The Convention also empowers the COP to 'make recommendations' for improving the effectiveness of the Convention.[82] Since 'recommendations' are not

---

[77] *See* Guzman, 'Against Consent', *supra* note 83; Helfer, *supra* note 89.

[78] UN Charter art. 10.

[79] UN Charter art. 18.

[80] Cartagena Protocol on Biosafety art. 29.4(a), (2000) 39 I.L.M. 1027; Nagoya Protocol on Access to Genetic Resources and the Fair and Equitable Sharing of Benefits Arising from their Utilization art. 20.4(a) (2010), UNEP/CBD/COP/DEC/X/1, available at www.cbd.int/abs/text/; *see also* Convention on Wetlands of International Importance Especially as Waterfowl Habitat art. 6, (1971) 11 I.L.M 963 ('The Conference of the Contracting Parties shall be competent … to make general or specific recommendations to the Contracting Parties regarding the conservation, management and wise use of wetlands and their flora and fauna').

[81] Antarctic Treaty art. IX (1959), 402 U.N.T.S. 71.

[82] Convention to Regulate International Trade in Endangered Species of Flora and Fauna art. XI, (1973) 993 U.N.T.S. 243. The COP's other powers are primarily administrative in nature, such as making provisions for the Secretariat's operation.

legally binding, the COP's authority to bind member states would seem limited to subjecting species to the strict trade controls spelled out in the Convention for species listed in Appendix I,[83] or the slightly less strict controls that apply to Appendix II species.[84] Yet despite this paucity of a legal mandate, the CITES parties have used the COP as a legislature to erect a complicated series of compliance institutions and modifications to the formal requirements for listed species.[85] Most notably, the COP created a compliance system in which roles are assigned to the COP itself and a body created by the COP, which is referred to as the Standing Committee.[86] The compliance mechanism can result in non-binding recommendations from the Standing Committee to the Parties to suspend trade with a particular party if the party is, in the view of the Standing Committee, violating CITES either in the way it administers CITES trade controls or by failing to file reports mandated by the Convention.

Although only soft law recommendations, the decisions of the COP and the Standing Committee have proven relatively effective at generating compliance. For example, when faced with a possible suspension from trading for failing to file the necessary reports over a period of three years, Dominica, Rwanda and Vanuatu quickly brought themselves into compliance.[87] Similarly, the COP has greatly expanded its ability to impose controls on endangered species by effectively amending the Convention to ignore the categorical choice between listing a species in Appendix I or II or not listing it at all. Instead, the COP will sometimes transfer a species from Appendix I to Appendix II (a move that eases trade controls) subject to restrictions known as 'annotations'. These annotations, nowhere authorized by the Convention itself, allow the COP to create trade controls that are tailored to species-specific concerns. Because they are not authorized by the Convention, these annotations can be considered a form of soft law – a non-binding gloss on the underlying categories established by CITES.

What explains states' decision to grant this kind of expansive soft-lawmaking authority to legislative bodies? The answer to this question turns on states' need to communicate credible information to each other about their expectations as to what constitutes compliance with binding

---

[83] CITES art. III.

[84] CITES art. IV.

[85] Daniel Bodansky, *The Art and Craft of International Environmental Law*, 158–59 (Cambridge, MS: Harvard University Press 2010).

[86] CITES COP Decision 12/84 and 14/3.

[87] Chris Wold, 'Trade in Endangered Species', (2004) 14 *Yearbook Int'l Env. L.* 375, 381.

legal rules. Absent such information, states are unable accurately to assess what they need to do in order to avoid sanctions for violating legal rules, and law therefore loses much of its ability to affect state behavior. For reasons we explain below, in many cases legislative soft law is the most effective means of establishing and conveying critical information about state expectations.

To begin, recall that enforcement in international law is decentralized. Sanctions for legal violations, to the extent they are imposed at all, are imposed only by states themselves against their peers.[88] This fact places each state in a position akin to that of a judge in the domestic system. It assesses whether other states are complying with the law, and if not, what action to take. States might, for example, impose retaliatory or reciprocal sanctions, or they might update their assessment of another state's reputation for complying with its legal obligations.[89] On a rationalist account of international law, it is the possibility of these sanctions that provides the incentive to comply with international legal rules.[90] This creates an informational conundrum for states in deciding whether to comply with international legal rules because the odds that a state will be sanctioned for violating a legal obligation turns on, among other things, whether other states will perceive a specific act to violate the legal obligation in question. Put differently, a state's incentives to comply with legal obligations are determined by what *other* states believe the law requires, rather than what the state itself believes it has consented to.

Viewed in this light, it becomes apparent that the efficacy of international law requires that states have a means to communicate their expectations as to what legal obligations require.[91] Absent such a means of communication, the threat of sanctions for legal violations will not incentivize changed behavior because states will not be able to predict what actions their peers will view as unlawful and thus likely to provoke sanctions.[92] A significant part of what international legal process does is provide the opportunity for states to send costly signals to each other about what they believe the law requires. The ability to send costly signals allows states to distinguish between self-serving statements about what the law requires and sincere statements about what the law requires.

---

88 *See* Guzman, *supra* note 15.

89 *Ibid.*

90 *Ibid.*

91 Timothy Meyer, 'A Communicative Theory of International Law', (2012) 13 *Melb. J. Int'l L.* 921.

92 *Ibid.*

Based on the latter, states are able more accurately to determine what actions are likely to be viewed as unlawful, and therefore to provoke sanctions.

For example, the President of the US might claim that China is violating World Trade Organization (WTO) rules by dumping solar panels on the US market even if US government trade lawyers do not believe the law is so clear on this point. Such a public statement is not necessarily very informative as to the sincere view of the US government, however, because the statement itself is not costly to the US. When the US initiates a WTO dispute with China over the same issue, the informational signal becomes much stronger because sending the signal is costly. The initiation of the dispute is costly for the US, both in terms of the actual costs of the dispute, but also because the dispute seeks to elevate the US position to a principle to which the US itself will be held in future disputes. Because the US was willing to incur these costs to send the signal, the presumption arises that the US must feel particularly strongly about the content of the message.

Like litigation, the process of bargaining over and creating obligations involves sending signals about expectations. When bargaining over legal obligations, the most potent tool states have to signal expectations to each other is their own consent to a legal obligation. It carries with it a reputational pledge to abide by the text of the convention, which in turn carries with it an incentive to be truthful, as well as the possibility of retaliatory or reciprocal sanctions.[93] Many international agreements also carry with them domestic costs, either political costs owing to domestic ratification procedures or economic or legal costs flowing from changes to the domestic regulatory environment.[94]

Consent to a legal obligation alone is, however, inadequate to support the kind of costly communication that is necessary for international law to function. First, even the most precise legal obligations are indeterminate, and international legal obligations are usually far from precise. To require that consent to a legal obligation be the primary means of communication would be to require that treaties be amended every time states wanted to send each other costly signals about their expectations as to what constitutes compliance with pre-existing obligations. Second, formal consent to legal obligations can be too costly to effectively serve its role as a signaling device, particularly where divisive issues are

---

[93] *See* Guzman, *supra* note 15, at 58–9.

[94] *See* Martin, *supra* note 54; Melissa Durkee, 'Persuasion Treaties', (2013) 99 *Va. L. Rev.* 63.

concerned. Domestic political or legal conditions may prevent amendment on hot-button issues, denying states the opportunity to credibly signal important private information about what they expect other states to do to comply with their legal obligations. Moreover, the reputational consequences of committing to a firm set of expectations may chill communications by constraining a state's own future actions. The result is that effective communication about legal expectations requires a method of communication that is neither so cheap that self-serving and sincere statements cannot be distinguished, nor so expensive that it can only rarely be used.

Delegations to international institutions to create soft law help solve this problem by creating a structure in which states can send signals to each other about their legal expectations that are costly, and thus credible, but not so costly that they can only rarely be sent. To return to the example of dispute resolution and international common law, delegating to international tribunals the ability to expound the law in a non-binding fashion is a costly signal because states lose some control over the content of the law's evolution. Precisely because of this, states' arguments made before tribunals and the decision to abide by tribunal decisions, especially adverse ones, send credible signals that a tribunal's jurisprudence informs the underlying legal obligation.[95]

Joining international legislative institutions with the power to create soft law is another kind of costly signal. Submitting to the jurisdiction of legislative institutions is costly in two ways. First, having agreed that a particular body is tasked with adopting rules and monitoring the implementation of an agreement, a state has pledged some reputational capital to abide by the decisions of that body. That is, a state has signaled to other states that the decisions of the legislative body should form part of the basis for expectations about how that state will behave. Failing to live up to the expectations established by the legislative body thus results in a reputational sanction in the same way that failing to abide by the expectations established by a tribunal does. This means states can use legislative soft law to both develop and amend hard law by signaling shifts in expectations as to what counts as compliant behavior. For example, the 1951 Refugee Convention codifies the rule of *non-refoulement*, which states that a state may not return a person to a place where she might be tortured or face persecution.[96] *Non-refoulement* is

---

[95] Guzman and Meyer, *supra* note 15.

[96] Convention Relating to the Status of Refugees, July 28, 1951, 189 U.N.T.S. 137 (entered into force April 22, 1954).

subject to a number of exceptions, but after the Cold War states began to worry that the exceptions were not broad enough to permit states to deny refugee status to terrorists acting on behalf of non-state organizations.[97] Rather than amend the treaty, however, the UNGA passed a resolution defining acts of terrorism as 'contrary to the purposes and principles of the United Nations', one of the exceptions to the principle of *non-refoulement* found in the Refugee Convention.[98]

Second, legislative soft law decisions lack some of the procedural safeguards that go with hard law obligations. As a consequence, legislative soft law decisions can – like the soft law decisions of international tribunals – affect states that would be able to avoid a comparable hard law obligation.[99] Hard law obligations made by legislative bodies often come with procedural checks that allow states to opt out of the obligations. For example, even where legislative institutions make binding decisions through supermajority voting, often the institution will either require state ratification of the decision before the state is bound or will at least allow the state to reserve its way out of the obligation.[100] These kinds of procedural checks do not apply to soft law obligations. To illustrate, CITES allows parties to enter reservations to listing decisions.[101] But reservations are themselves legally binding instruments and cannot be entered against soft law decisions. There is no mechanism in CITES legally to opt out of a recommendation from the CITES Standing Committee that all CITES parties refuse to accept CITES permits and certificates required under CITES for trade in protected species. When the Standing Committee takes such action, as it did in 2003 when it notified CITES parties of 'significant problems' in the issuance of CITES-mandated export permits by the Democratic Republic of the Congo, the target state has no recourse as it would with a binding obligation.

---

97 James C. Hathaway and Colin J. Harvey, 'Framing Refugee Protection in the New World Disorder', (2001) 34 *Cornell Int'l L. J.* 257, 263.

98 Measures to Eliminate International Terrorism, G.A. Res. 51/210, Annex 2, GAOR 52nd Sess., UN Doc. A/RES/52/165 (January 16, 1997).

99 *See* Guzman and Meyer, *supra* note 15 (arguing that soft law created by international tribunals affects the obligations of states that have not consented to the jurisdiction of international tribunals).

100 *See* Helfer, *supra* note 89; International Convention on the Regulation of Whaling art. V(3) (providing a 90-day period for states to object to decisions of the International Whaling Commission before becoming bound).

101 CITES art. XV(3).

Of course, if soft lawmaking in international legislative institutions worked in exactly the same way as in international tribunals, there would be little reason to prefer one over the other. But soft law created through international legislative institutions differs in several important respects from that created by international tribunals. First, states are able to engage in bargaining over the creation of soft law in international legislative institutions much more directly than they are in tribunals. While states can obviously negotiate a resolution to a dispute, they cannot directly negotiate the terms of the tribunal's decision. Legislative institutions offer the possibility of introducing new issues as the negotiations are ongoing and offer the possibility of linking different legal rules under the institution's jurisdiction more easily than a tribunal can. While a tribunal may consider issues that arise late in litigation, many tribunals are reluctant to do so and are generally reluctant to consider issues outside the scope of those raised by the parties. Legislative institutions are comprised of the parties themselves, however, and so are more suitable for ongoing negotiations and are more malleable in terms of crafting compromises. Second, legislative institutions are better suited for participatory soft lawmaking than are tribunals. Although many states can participate in litigation before international tribunals, legislative institutions allow for broader participation among members states because member states need not assert an interest in the particular issue under debate. Legislative institutions thus offer a different kind of bargaining forum from litigation, one in which the parties collectively have more control over the outcome and the negotiations are more flexible because they are not subject to the stricter procedural rules, particularly regarding the agenda, that prevail in tribunals. At the same time, any individual party may actually have less control in a legislative institution, precisely because of the greater number of parties involved and the fact that the agenda is not fixed in the way it is within a dispute resolution proceeding.

Third, many legislative institutions offer the possibility of varying the legal effect of an instrument during the course of negotiations. This feature is critically different from tribunals. Where a tribunal is concerned, the bindingness of the tribunal's decisions is determined at the time the institution is created, or at the latest at the time the dispute is submitted to the tribunal (for example, a decision in a contentious case at the International Court of Justice is binding on the parties to the dispute, while an advisory opinion is not). This essentially removes legality as a feature subject to modification when tribunals make decisions about substantive obligations. Tradeoffs between form and substance in tribunals must be made sequentially, rather than simultaneously. Legislative institutions allow the possibility of simultaneous trading off of substantive obligations and legal form. A COP might, for example, choose to adopt a series of soft law instruments that elaborate a compliance mechanism for the agreement, or they might choose to adopt an amendment to be given binding legal effect. Which legal form they choose might affect the content of the substantive obligations adopted, with states willing to adopt more stringent soft law obligations. The ability to decide these two issues simultaneously has both costs and benefits. On the one hand, it expands the bargaining space by making more agreements possible at different points in time. On the other hand, it also removes the disciplining role of sequential decision-making, introducing the possibility of cycling over alternatives.

Consider by way of example the decision to create the compliance mechanism for the Kyoto Protocol. The UNFCCC COP serves as the meeting of the parties to the Kyoto Protocol, and thus as its legislative body.[102] The Kyoto Protocol, like many other treaties, empowers its COP to 'make, within its mandate, the decisions necessary to promote its effective implementation' and '[m]ake recommendations on any matter necessary for the implementation of this Protocol'.[103] The COP thus has soft lawmaking authority expressly granted to it. At the same time, the Kyoto Protocol also provides that:

> The [COP] shall, at its first session, approve appropriate and effective procedures and mechanisms to determine and to address cases of non-compliance with the provisions of this Protocol ... Any procedures and mechanisms under this Article entailing binding consequences shall be adopted by means of an amendment to this Protocol.[104]

This provision creates dual authority for the COP. It supplements the general grant of soft law authority above with authority specifically to make soft law decisions regarding compliance (because only procedures and mechanisms involving binding consequences must be made through amendment, leaving non-binding procedures to the COP). It also authorizes the COP to activate the amendment process if it wishes to create binding legal obligations regarding compliance, and by extension would seem to require it to do so if it wished to create a compliance mechanism that resulted in binding sanctions.

---

[102] Kyoto Protocol to the United Nations Framework Convention on Climate Change art. 13, (1997) 37 I.L.M. 22.
[103] *Ibid.*
[104] Kyoto Protocol art. 18.

The Kyoto Protocol thus established a legislative forum for bargaining over how compliance issues under the Protocol would be contested. Indeed, the Kyoto Protocol is a famously incomplete agreement, deferring not only issues of compliance but also critical issues as to what would count in terms of states satisfying their emissions reduction obligations. For instance, in the Kyoto Protocol developed states agreed to binding emissions reductions and also agreed that net removals of greenhouse gases from forestry activities could be counted in emissions reduction and that states could use a variety of 'flexibility mechanisms' to trade emissions credits across countries or jointly satisfy their collective obligations.[105] Yet these obligations were open-textured, requiring subsequent interpretation and communication between the parties as to what behavior they actually expected of each other. Moreover, these gap-filling negotiations were occurring at the same time states with obligations were deciding whether to ratify the Kyoto Protocol, further complicating matters. The entry-into-force provisions of the Protocol – requiring 55 parties accounting for 55 percent of the carbon dioxide emissions for 1990 – were set in 1998 when the Protocol was initially opened for signature, but the actual expectations as to what would count as compliance with the Protocol's emissions targets continued to be negotiated in the COP. In 2001, the COP reached the Bonn Agreement and the Marrakech Accords, which filled in these gaps by adopting rules governing forestry accounting, emissions trading and joint implementation, and established one of the most elaborate compliance mechanisms in multilateral environmental agreements.[106]

Despite their names, these instruments are merely decisions of the parties and as such are not legally binding.[107] In particular, the enforcement branch of the Kyoto Compliance Mechanism has the ability to suspend a country's participation in emissions trading and, if it determines that a state has not met its emissions reductions obligations, applies a penalty to that state by reducing the state's allotted emissions in any subsequent emissions agreement and suspending the state from emissions trading.[108] These penalties certainly have the ring of binding rules, involving as they do the removal of legal rights contained in legal documents (such as the right to engage in emissions trading under the Kyoto Protocol or the right to emit a certain amount of greenhouse gases under future agreements), but they are nevertheless soft law because they

---

105 Kyoto Protocol arts. 3–4, 12, 17.
106 *See* Bodansky, *supra* note 98, at 248.
107 *Ibid.*, at 14, 87.
108 *See* the Bonn Agreement and Marrakech Accords of 2001.

were adopted by the COP pursuant to its soft lawmaking authority, rather than as formal amendments to the Protocol.[109]

The ability to negotiate simultaneously across this range of issues, and to be able to trade off the bindingness of the legal obligation against the substantive obligations, was key in successfully allowing the parties to bring the Kyoto Protocol into force. The parties had drafted a treaty that did not establish firm expectations as to what would count as compliance. They thus needed some mechanism to credibly signal to each other what they would consider to be compliant. Moreover, after the US announced it would not ratify the Protocol in 2001, it became necessary to get all the remaining major developed countries to ratify the Protocol in order to meet the requirement that states representing 55 percent of 1990 emissions ratify the agreement. Thus, the signaling function of subsequent instruments was necessitated both by the ambiguity in the Kyoto Protocol itself and the practical need to ensure entry into force.

And yet the typical means of sending costly signals – consent to binding amendments – was not politically feasible. States were seeking rules to reduce their commitments and, in light of the ratification problem, had the leverage to insist on it. Had binding amendments been the only option for elaborating the Kyoto Protocol, it seems likely that the Protocol would have never entered into force. Instead, the soft lawmaking authority of the Kyoto COP entered to provide states with a mechanism whereby they could elaborate their expectations as to what would count as compliance with a wide range of Kyoto's rules. In this way, the soft lawmaking authority of the Kyoto COP operated as a safety valve that may have saved the Kyoto Protocol. It provided the legislative tools that allowed expectations to be set at a reasonable cost.

CONCLUSION

The legalization of international affairs in recent decades has been accompanied by a proliferation of legal forms. Soft law instruments have become a favored tool of states in expanding their ability to regulate state behavior. Given the diversity of situations in which soft law is deployed and the different kinds of soft instruments that exist, no single theory can explain all instances in which soft law is used. Scholars have offered a number of valuable explanations that shed light on why states use

109 *See* Bodansky, *supra* note 98, at 14, 87.

instruments that have legal consequences but are not themselves binding legal instruments.

In this chapter, we have argued that the rise of international organizations is driven in part by the value of institutionally created soft law, and in particular international legislative soft law. Formal international law suffers from a status quo bias due to the general rule that a state must consent before it can be bound by a rule of international law. Institutionally created soft law can solve this problem by giving states a vehicle to convey cost-effective yet credible signals to each other about their expectations as to what counts as compliant behavior. Delegating authority to an institution is costly because one is bound by the institution's subsequent decisions. The costliness of this decision serves to enhance the credibility of the institution's subsequent elaboration of legal rules. International legislative soft law is particularly valuable because it allows states to use voting procedures, often along majoritarian lines, to effect changes in legal obligations. Scholars have noted that international legislative institutions are rarely empowered to make binding rules through majoritarian voting, but this misses the expansive role that international legislative soft law plays in many modern treaty regimes. Moreover, international legislative soft law offers particular advantages over other kinds of institutionally created soft law. Most notably, legislative soft law is created through explicit inter-state bargaining in a way that other kinds of institutional soft law are not, and legislative soft law allows states simultaneously to trade off legal form and substantive obligations in a way that cannot be done by, for example, international tribunals. The existence of international legislative soft law thus highlights a key way in which international law is creeping toward a system of majoritarian governance – a trend that would be missed by focusing only on hard law.

6. The emergence and evolution of customary international law

Francesco Parisi and Daniel Pi

The Statute of the International Court of Justice identifies three primary sources of public international law: (1) international conventions; (2) international custom; and (3) general principles of law.[1] In this chapter, we discuss the emergence and evolution of the second source, customary law, from the perspective of law and economics.

Let us begin by looking at what the term customary international law (CIL) means. The term 'custom' in a legal context describes normative practices that develop independently of the law in a decentralized manner, but which gradually take on an obligatory (legal) character. Customs become recognized as 'customary *law*' when they acquire binding force. In its most general form then, customary law is characterized by (a) decentralized formation, and (b) centralized enforcement.[2]

Customary law can be found both within domestic legal systems,[3] where it is becoming increasingly rare,[4] and in international law, where it

---

[1] Statute of the International Court of Justice, Art. 38(1).

[2] Francesco Parisi, *The Language of Law and Economics* (Cambridge, MA: Cambridge University Press, 2013).

[3] *See, e.g.*, Francis G. Snyder, 'Colonialism and Legal Form: The Creation of "Customary Law" in Senegal' 19 *J. Legal Pluralism* 49 (1981); T.W. Bennett, *Customary Law in South Africa* (Claremon, South Africa: Juta & Co. 2004); Lester B. Orfield, *The Growth of Scandinavian Law* (Clark, NJ: Lawbook Exchange, Ltd. 2002), xii–xiii, 171–4. *See also Trimarco v Klein*, 436 N.E.2d 502 (N.Y. 1982) (US tort case, where a building manager was sued for failing to install shatterproof glass in a shower door, and the court held, 'when proof of a customary practice is coupled with a showing that it was ignored and that this departure was a proximate cause of the accident, it may serve to establish liability.'); Victor E. Schwartz, et al., *Prosser, Wade, and Schwartz's Torts: Cases and Materials 186* (12th edn, Westbury, NY: Foundation Press, 2010) ('For the professions in general, evidence as to customary practice is admissible and may prove very influential. For the medical profession, it is usually found to be controlling and the jury are usually told that the plaintiff cannot recover unless

plays a major role.[5] The reasons why customary law should be especially important in an international context are complex and manifold, relating principally to the historical absence of a centralized law-making body and problems in effective adjudication and enforcement prior to the middle of the twentieth century.

Without digressing too deeply into the philosophical and historical reasons why international law failed to develop centralized law-making mechanisms,[6] it suffices to observe that the absence of 'global legislation' left a law-making vacuum in the international arena – a void which customary law filled. In contradistinction to conventions and treaty law, which are the product of express negotiation, the spontaneous emergence of regular, predictable behavior that characterizes custom arises naturally without cooperative deliberation, thus making it a particularly sturdy groundwork for legal development.

This ruggedness allows customs to flourish in 'lawless' environments. However, as we will discuss, this same trait can also prove to be a defect, insofar as it invites momentary opportunism, subverting the development of efficient rules.

Law and economics scholars have analyzed CIL from a number of different angles. In this chapter, we introduce some exemplars, which elucidate the elements of CIL and provide groundwork for future research. Before discussing the law and economics perspective on customary law, we begin with a very brief summary of its 'traditional' account. In Section II, we introduce a sketch of Goldsmith and Posner's seminal contributions on the topic. In Section III, we exposit a formal model of incentives in CIL. We conclude with a summary and suggestions for future research.

---

the plaintiff proves that the defendant's conduct was not in accord with recognized medical practice.'). *See generally*, James Holden, *The History of Negotiable Instruments in English Law* (London: Althone Press, 1955). But cf. John Baker, 'The Law Merchant and the Common Law before 1700' 38 *Cambridge Law J.* 295 (1979).

4 *See* Robert D. Cooter, 'Structural Adjudication and the New Law Merchant: A Model of Decentralized Law' 14 *Int'l R. of Law and Econ.* 215, 216 (1994).

5 *See supra* note 1.

6 Resolutions passed by the United Nations seem increasingly to resemble something like international legislation.

I. THE TRADITIONAL ACCOUNT

According to conventional international law theories, customary law is composed of two components: (1) uniform behavioral regularities ('usage'); and (2) the belief that the practice is legally binding ('*opinio juris*').[7] We will discuss each in turn.

Usage is the extensional component of custom – the activity of parties participating in it. It is the 'material element' of custom. It must be predictable, universal, and uniform.

However, it is important to recognize that not all usage is custom. Predictable, universal, uniform behavior may be the product of mere habit or coincidence.

Traditionally, what differentiates habitual practice from customary practice is *opinio juris sive necessitates* ('*opinio juris*'), the intentional component of custom.[8] The precise characterization of *opinio juris* has posed a number of theoretical problems in the international law literature, generating a considerable quantity of scholarly debate. Ignoring the nuances that have hitherto preoccupied international law scholars, it suffices to observe that the function of *opinio juris*, whatever its more precise meaning may be, is to separate those behaviors that are merely coincidental or habitual conduct from behaviors that are undertaken to satisfy a recognized legal obligation.

The intersection of uniform behavior and *opinio juris* is what we call 'custom'. When recognized by law, it is provides the content of 'customary law', and the obligations become binding. However, international law has typically recognized two exemptions. First, the 'persistent objector doctrine', which excuses a state from the obligation of a customary practice if that state publicly and consistently declined to comply with the custom during the formative phase of the law (i.e. before the uniform behavioral regularity 'ripened' into a legal obligation). Second, the 'subsequent objector doctrine', which excuses a state from the obligation of a customary practice with respect to another state if and only if the other state acquiesces to a reduced obligation.

---

[7] *See* Anthony A. D'Amato, *The Concept of Custom in International Law* (Ithaca, NY: Cornell University Press 1971), 47–56.

[8] *See ibid.* at 66–73.

II. THE GAME THEORETIC ACCOUNT

Goldsmith and Posner[9] dismiss the theoretical problems concerning *opinio juris*, which had historically preoccupied international law scholars, as being 'the subject of an enormous literature that endlessly (and in our opinion unproductively) debates definitional issues …'.[10] Contrary to the conventional view, they argue that a game theoretic model furnishes a better explanation of customary practices.

Goldsmith and Posner's alternative view is principally an attack on the function and importance of *opinio juris*. They develop their argument by selecting universally recognized exemplars of 'custom' and explaining them in terms of incentives and disincentives.[11] While a number of antecedents exist in the literature,[12] Goldsmith and Posner's analysis is the starting point for most recent law and economics analyses of CIL.[13] Their analysis articulates four categories of behaviors:

1. *Coincidence of interest.* There may be common usage where parties have positive incentives to behave in the same way, regardless of how other parties behave.
2. *Coercion.* One party may simply threaten or otherwise forcibly coerce parties to behave in a particular way, thereby *forcing* compliance.
3. *True cooperation.* Parties may exhibit regular behavior, when they are faced with a cooperation problem, as in an iterated prisoner's dilemma, where the long-term interests of the parties are to cooperate rather than defect.
4. *Coordination.* Parties may exhibit similar behavior in response to coordination problems, where behaving similarly yields greater benefits than behaving differently.

---

[9] 'A Theory of Customary International Law' 66 *U. Chicago L. Rev.* 1113–77 (1999).

[10] *Ibid.* at 1118.

[11] *Ibid.* at 1139–67 (reducing the widely recognized customs of neutral shipping, diplomatic immunity, and territorial boundaries at sea to self-interested maximizing behavior).

[12] *See e.g.*, Alan O. Sykes, '"Mandatory" Retaliation for Breach of Trade Agreements: Some Thoughts on the Strategic Design of Section 301' 8 *B.U. Int'l L.J.* 301 (1990).

[13] *See also*, Jack L. Goldsmith and Eric A. Posner, 'Understanding the Resemblance between Modern and Traditional Customary International Law' 40 *Va. J. Int'l L.* 639 (2000); Jack L. Goldsmith and Eric A. Posner, 'Further Thoughts on Customary International Law' 23 *Mich. J. Int'l L.* 191 (2001).

The consequence of this analysis is that much of what traditional international law recognizes as custom may not in fact be the result of accession to the force of international law, but rather simply self-interested behavior.[14]

Goldsmith and Posner do not offer a rigorous account of how CIL changes over time. Rather, they use the malleability of CIL as evidence that parties' apparent recognition of the binding force of customary law is illusory. That is, the fluidity of changes in customary law is taken to demonstrate how little binding force custom has, strengthening their claim that apparent compliance with legal obligations may be better explained by parties' private cost–benefit maximizations.[15]

III. PARTICIPATION, SCOPE, AND TIMING OF EMERGING COOPERATIVE CUSTOMS

The main lines of research on CIL in law and economics take the Goldsmith and Posner papers as a launching point. In this section, we will discuss recent developments in the economic analysis of CIL, which elaborate on the hypothesis that state parties adopt usage out of rational

---

[14] Goldsmith and Posner, *supra* note 9, at 1138 ('Our theory contemplates that behavioral regularities will arise at an international level, but it suggests that these regularities will lack the robustness posited by the traditional account. We identify four main strategic situations in which behavioral regularities are likely to emerge: … [W]e claim that they – rather than the notion of universal state practices followed from a sense of legal obligation – account for the CIL identified by courts and scholars.')(citations omitted).

[15] The Goldsmith and Posner articles have provoked much discussion with traditional international law scholars. *See e.g.*, Mark A. Chinen, 'Game Theory and Customary International Law: A Response to Professors Goldsmith and Posner' 23 *Mich. J. Int'l L.* 143 (2001), who argues that while Goldsmith and Posner's model may be a true description of how CIL emerges, the traditional view may be viewed extensionally (Goldsmith and Posner call it a 'positivist' view). Goldsmith and Posner (2001), *supra* note 13, respond to Chinen, pointing out that the point of the traditionalist view is that *opinio juris* is essential to custom, and that this view cannot be reconciled with a purely game theoretic account. The nuances of that discussion, however, would require a far longer and digressive discussion than we can accommodate in the space of this chapter. *See also*, Andrew T. Guzman, 'Saving Customary International Law' 27 *Mich. J. Int'l L.* 115 (2001).

self-interest rather than a sense of legal obligation.[16] Operating on that premise, the question arises: what are the precise determinants of whether (and to what extent) parties participate in the customary usage? Accordingly, this section will proceed in two parts: (1) the emergence of CIL; and (2) the evolution of CIL.

A. The Emergence of CIL

The analysis of CIL in terms of incentives cashes out in two ways: (1) participation; and (2) effort level. We start from the premise that a nation will only adopt an emerging custom if that custom promises to yield a net benefit over time. Likewise, when fulfilling its obligations under the emerging custom, we assume that nations will be willing to expend resources up to the point where further commitment would not increase its expected future benefits.[17]

Terminology

Let us begin by defining terms. Call each occasion triggering performance of an emerging customary act an 'incident', and denote incidents 't_1, t_2, t_3, …', ordered chronologically such that any t_n is immediately succeeded by t_{n+1}. Let t_0 denote the time period preceding the first incident.

Let us refer to the party bearing the burden of performance during an incident as the 'obligor', the party that reaps the benefit as the 'beneficiary'; uninvolved parties are 'spectators'. Presumably, nations' roles will change from incident to incident over time, such that the beneficiary during one incident may become the obligor in some subsequent incident. Call this condition 'role reversibility'.

Exemplar

Let us now describe an exemplar of CIL to ground our intuitions and test the validity of the model. Suppose that a set of maritime nations routinely loses shipping to storms, pirates, collisions with wayward icebergs, and other such mishaps. And suppose it would be possible to avoid (or at least mitigate) these losses if foreign nations adopted a policy of rescuing

---

16 Much of the material in this section is drawn from Francesco Parisi and Vincy Fon, *The Economics of Lawmaking* (Oxford: Oxford University Press, 2009), 129–205.

17 To be clear, the expected future benefits are the product of reciprocal efforts spent by other parties in effecting rescue when the obligor is in the position of being a beneficiary.

distressed ships in their environs. Such a condition is a paradigmatic case where CIL may emerge.

Net social benefit

Assuming that the cost (to the obligor) of aiding foreign vessels is less than the benefit (to the beneficiary) of preserved shipping, the emerging custom will yield a surplus. That is, where $C(e_n)$ is the cost of rescue, $B(e_n)$ is the value of the rescued shipping, and e_n is the effort expended by the obligor at t_n, the social welfare function at t_n will be:

$$S_{t_n} = B(e_n) - C(e_n) \tag{6.1}$$

Assume that r^s is the social discount rate. Now the social welfare function looking forward to future incidents will be:

$$S = \sum_{i=1}^{\infty} \frac{1}{(1+r^S)^i} S_{t_i}$$

$$= \frac{B(e_i) - C(e_i)}{r^S} \tag{6.2}$$

Finally, let us define B and C by:

$$\begin{aligned} B(e) &= be \\ C(e) &= ae^2 \end{aligned} \tag{6.3}$$

That is, the cost of rescue increases with additional effort at a growing rate, while the benefit increases at a fixed rate.[18]

Now consider the parties' private welfare functions. For any incident t_n, the private cost-benefit function of the obligor will be:

$$P_{t_n} = \frac{1}{r}(\underbrace{\beta_n pB(e_m)}_{\text{Future Benefits}} - \underbrace{qC(e_m)}_{\text{Future Costs}}) - \underbrace{C(e_n)}_{\text{Present Cost}} \tag{6.4}$$

---

[18] Observe that when these conditions fail to hold, then no optimal effort level will exist, since if $C(e) = ae$ then $S = (b - a)e$. If $b > a$ then socially optimal effort for any incident will be infinite, whereas if $b < a$ then socially optimal effort will be 0. Clearly, the latter case is irrelevant and the former case is implausible, since there will normally be diminishing returns to effort.

Where p is the probability the party will be a beneficiary, q is the probability that the party will be an obligor, r is the party's discount rate, and β_n is the probability that other nations will perform when they are obligors. Thus, the payoff will be the *expected future benefit* minus the *expected future cost* minus the *actual present cost*. Obviously, the welfare function of spectators and beneficiaries at t_n will not include present costs; and beneficiaries will have the additional term $B(e_n)$ added. Since the obligor is the only party who can effect adoption of the custom, however, we will ignore the incentives of spectators and beneficiaries for now. Finally, since the emerging custom is defined by practice,[19] generally speaking, e_m will equal e_n.[20]

Let us now generate some simple results, assuming away the effects of the probabilities and future discounting by setting $\beta = 1$, $p = q$, and $r = r^s$. After generating some baseline results, we will then consider what happens when we reintroduce these elements.

Participation

The first thing to notice is that at t_0, all the parties are in effect 'spectators'. Serendipitously, private incentives are aligned with social incentives at t_0: parties will favor the emerging custom if it represents a net social benefit (i.e., if the net private value is greater than the payoffs under a policy of 'self-help'), and they will decline to participate if the emerging custom represents a net social loss. So far so good.

However, upon the occurrence of an incident $t_{n>0}$, the obligor encounters an additional cost – the immediate cost of a present rescue – thus changing the obligor's incentives. More precisely, because $P_{t_n} = P_{t_0} - C$, the obligor will be less likely to adopt the emerging custom. That is, if $C > P_{t_0}$, then a party who was formerly in favor of the emerging custom will now be opposed to it.

Of course, common sense tells us that it will be a rare circumstance that the obligation to perform on *one* occasion will prove so onerous that the cost–benefit balance of a party will flip from 'for' to 'against' on account of it. Nevertheless, we can see from the model what conditions would contribute to such a transformation: (1) a high discount rate; and (2) a low benefit-to-cost ratio $\frac{pB}{qC}$. That is, cooperative spectators at t_0 decline to participate when they are cast in the role of obligors at $t_{n>0}$, and the cost incurred during a single rescue is so great that it overwhelms

[19] Since any particular CIL is defined by the *historical practice* of nations, the decision to exert effort level x at the protean stage of emergence has the effect of simultaneously defining and satisfying the nascent obligation.

[20] We will see in the next section, when we discuss the evolution of CIL, that things need not be so rigid.

the anticipated benefits of future participation in the custom. This occurs when either the value of the net future benefits is heavily discounted, or when the difference between expected future benefits and expected future losses is very small.

Effort level

However, a change in participation will be an extreme case. The more likely consequence of the change in incentives between t_0 and $t_{n>0}$ is that parties will continue to *participate* in the emerging custom, but reduce the *effort* they invest in it.

It follows from formula (6.2) that the optimum effort level of parties will be:

$$e^* = \frac{b}{2a} \tag{6.5}$$

And it follows from formula (6.4) that the privately optimal effort level of obligors will be socially optimal at t_0, and when $t_{n>0}$:

$$e^{**} = \frac{pb}{2a(p+r)} \tag{6.6}$$

Clearly therefore, since $e^* > e^{**}$ when $r > 0$,[21] any nation in the position of being a rescuer will invest socially suboptimal effort in effecting the rescue.[22]

Let us next consider what happens when we manipulate the probability variables p and q, the probability variable β, and discount rate r.

Probability and group size

The probability of being a beneficiary p, and the probability of being an obligor q may either be independent or interrelated. We will consider each alternative in turn.

First, suppose that p and q are independent. In the context of maritime rescue, an illustration can be seen when p is a function of the volume of a nation's shipping, while q is a function of the size of its coastline. The probabilities are independent in the sense that the size of a nation's coastline is not necessarily related to its relative share of foreign shipping.

---

21 Note $e^{**} = \frac{p}{p+r} e^*$.

22 Note, however, that when $r = 0$, the present cost of being an obligator at t_n washes out over time. $\lim_{m\to\infty} \frac{mpb}{mp2a - 2a} = e^*$.

It is easy to see from formula (6.4) that $\frac{\partial}{\partial p}P_{t_n} > 0$, and therefore that higher p has the effect of lowering the threshold for participation. And when we allow $p \neq q$, formula (6.6) becomes:

$$e^{**} = \frac{pb}{2a(q+r)} \tag{6.7}$$

and it is easy to see that $\frac{\partial}{\partial p}e^{**} > 0$. Indeed, if $p > q + r$ for a party, then it is possible that its privately optimal effort level will even *exceed* the social optimum (formula (6.5)).

The same holds true for q with respect to costs. Since $\frac{\partial}{\partial q}P_{t_n} < 0$, higher q has the effect of raising the threshold for participation. And obviously $\frac{\partial}{\partial q}e^{**} < 0$.

These results should not be surprising. A CIL obligating nations to rescue endangered boats near their waters will obviously impose a higher cost on nations with large coastlines, causing them to be less likely to participate in the custom during its formative stage and less eager to expend effort even if they do participate. Likewise, nations with high volumes of shipping have more at stake, and will thus benefit more from a CIL mandating rescue.

Now suppose there are two nations *A* and *B*, such that *A* has a large coastline and engages in a high volume of shipping, whereas *B* has a small coastline and engages in a low volume of shipping. Here we get the slightly surprising result that if p_A and q_A represent the probabilities of *A* being a beneficiary and obligor, respectively, and likewise p_B and q_B for *B*, such that $\frac{p_A}{q_A} \approx \frac{p_B}{q_B}$, then ironically *A* and *B* will share similar incentives, *ceteris paribus*, despite having divergent probabilities.

Now suppose instead that p and q are interrelated. How might this arise? One possibility is that all non-beneficiary nations at t_n collectively contribute to the cost of rescue. This may be accomplished directly, or it may be the result of the particulars of the fact-situation. For example, if the primary cost of rescue were not the actual act of saving an endangered ship, but instead the cost of maintaining patrols, then in effect, even nations who do not directly contribute to the rescue of the troubled vessel are 'contributing' to rescue generally at t_n by patrolling their waters in the relevant time frame. In such a case, there are no spectators, and $q = (1-p)$. The private welfare function (formula (6.4)) becomes:

$$P^{\dagger} = \frac{1}{r}\left(p\beta B - \frac{1}{N-1}(1-p)C\right) - \frac{1}{N-1}C \qquad (6.8)$$

where N is the number of involved nations. And optimal effort level (formula (6.6)) becomes:

$$e^{\dagger **} = \frac{bp(N-1)}{2a(1-p+r)} \qquad (6.9)$$

Now, we need only deal with the single probability, such that $\frac{\partial}{\partial p}e^{\dagger **} > 0$. The privately optimum effort, $e^{\dagger **} = \frac{p(\mathrm{N}-1)}{(1-p+r)}e^{*}$, and the social optimum will coincide when $p = \frac{1+r}{N}$. Since the average probability of being the beneficiary for any nation will be $p = \frac{1}{N}$, the privately optimal effort for the average party will be less than the social optimum.

It is interesting to observe that when nations collectively share the burden of the obligor, such that each party bears $\frac{1}{N}$ th the cost of rescue, then the larger the group, the lower the threshold for participation, and the greater the effort the obligors will be willing to exert. However, things are not so simple, for every increase in N entails a decrease in p. That is, whenever a party becomes involved in the emerging custom, it does not only take on a share of the costs. It also takes a share of the probability of being a beneficiary.

If we assume that probabilities are homogeneous, then the probability that any nation in a group of N will be a beneficiary for an incident t_n is $p = \frac{1}{N}$. Thus, substituting p in formula (6.8), and setting $\beta = 1$ gives us:

$$\mathrm{P}^{\ddagger} = \frac{B-C}{Nr} - \frac{C}{N-1} \qquad (6.10)$$

And formula (9) now becomes:

$$e^{\ddagger **} = \frac{b(N-1)}{2a(Nr+N-1)} \qquad (6.11)$$

And it is clear that increasing N results in a decrease in effort incentives, except in the unrealistic circumstance that $r = 0$.

Little reflection is required to see that this makes sense intuitively. If the cooperative activity is beneficial, then it creates some social surplus, which is divided amongst the parties. If another party joins the group, then it takes on some of the costs of the group, but also takes a portion of the benefits. In general, from the perspective of the other parties, having an additional bearer of costs will not offset the increased probability that parties will have to be obligors. Thus, incentives decrease, and parties will exert less than socially optimal effort.

Situations where $q \neq 1 - p$ may include defense in case of a hostile aggressor.[23] Here, it makes sense that the cost of rescue be multiplied by the coefficient $\frac{1}{N-1}$, since the beneficiary of the mutual defense is often not in a position to contribute to the rescue effort. However, in cases such as the duty to rescue at sea, it may be the case that the emerging custom operates as a sort of insurance, and all nations including the beneficiary may contribute an equal share to the rescue cost. Thus, when costs are divided evenly N ways, formula (6.11) becomes:

$$e^{o**} = \frac{bN}{2a(Nr + N - 1)} \tag{6.12}$$

and now the social optimum can be achieved when $Nr = 1$.

Even when the cost of obligors is not shared, such that $q \neq 1 - p$, it will generally be the case that q decreases as p increases (and vice versa). And generally, the effect of increasing N will be to decrease private incentives. Incidentally, this neatly comports with empirical anthropological evidence that small communities are more fertile environments for the emergence of efficient customs.[24]

Probability of reciprocation

Nations that initiate an emerging customary practice, or participate in it during its formative stages suffer an additional obstacle. For instance, a nation may expend effort in a costly rescue, expecting that by kicking off the customary practice, foreign nations will follow its lead and later rescue its vessels. Let us suppose therefore that, all other things being

---

23 The 1991 Gulf War is a good example of such a circumstance.

24 *See* Edna Ullmann-Margalit, *The Emergence of Norms* (Oxford: Oxford University Press, 1977); Robert C. Ellickson, 'The Market for Social Norms' 3 *American Law and Economics Review* 1–49 (2001); and Francesco Parisi, 'Customary Law' in *The New Palgrave Dictionary of Economics and the Law* (London: Palgrave McMillan, 1998), 131–48.

equal, the initiator is willing to accept an up-front loss for the anticipated benefits, if the practice were to become recognized as CIL.

However, there is always the possibility that other nations will decline to follow the lead of the initiator. We account for such probability with the multiplicand $0 \leq \beta_n \leq 1$. The effect of β is straighforward. It reduces the expected benefits by the probability that other nations will reciprocate when the initiator is in the position of beneficiary.

However, as we will discuss shortly, the effect of β decreases over time, such that $\beta_n < \beta_{n+1}$.

Discount rates and time

Likewise, the effect of discount rates will be fairly uncomplicated. The more heavily future values are discounted, the more onerous up front present costs will be, raising the participating constraint and decreasing the effort level incentives.

Now, clearly when a party's discount rate exceeds the social discount rate, $r > r^S$, that party will exercise less than the socially optimum effort level. But if $r < r^S$, then that party will expend more than the socially optimal level of effort, *ceteris paribus*.

Interestingly, this creates the possibility that discount rate differences can compensate for the initial cost of present rescue, as well as the effect of probabilities, for some subset of involved nations if $r \leq \dfrac{r^S(p\beta B - qC)}{B - C + Cr^S}$. Such drastic differences in discount rate are not unrealistic, since the economic circumstances that nations face may result in highly divergent opportunity costs.

Parties for whom the discount rate is sufficiently low will therefore expend socially optimal effort when they are obligors. However, this will be a rare coincidence, and in general the private discount rates for parties will have varying effects in relation to probabilities. In some cases, it will improve incentives, and in some cases it will exacerbate disincentives.

Another element in parties' incentives is *time*. Generally, an emerging custom must be practiced for some substantial period of time, before being recognized as binding law. In France, forty years of practice has been traditionally required before a rule may become legally binding. In Germany, thirty years.[25]

---

[25] *See* Gregory I. Tunkin, 'Remarks on the Juridical Nature of Customary Norms in International Law' 49 *Cal L. Rev.* 419–30 (1961); Nicolas M. Mateesco, *La Coutume dans les Cycles Juridiques Internationaux* (Paris: Pedone, 1947).

Suppose the threshold when an emerging custom becomes binding CIL is γ years. And suppose the frequency of incidents is f per year. The custom will therefore remain in a developmental stage until $t_{f\gamma-1}$. This has some interesting consequences. First, it follows directly that for the obligor at $t_{f\gamma-1}$, there is no risk that subsequent obligors will fail to follow its lead.[26] Thus $\beta_{n\geq f\gamma-1} = 1$. Moreover, in the precedent incident $t_{f\gamma-2}$, the obligor will recognize that $\beta_{f\gamma-1} = 1$, thereby improving the probability that the obligor at $t_{f\gamma-1}$ will perform. $\beta_{f\gamma-2}$ will thus be fairly high, though less than 1. If we assume that conditions are homogeneous for parties involved in the emerging custom, then we can generalize that $\beta_{n-1} < \beta_n$. Clearly, therefore, higher values of f and higher values of γ decrease the likelihood of custom formation.

Likewise, it will be the case that the discount rate r will be be a function of f, such that $\frac{\partial}{\partial f} r < 0$. This is because the discount rate applies to incidents rather than a fixed unit of time. To see that this is the case, consider if the emergent custom concerned the rescue of foreign astronauts in space.[27] Since emergencies in space are relatively rare occurrences, occurring fewer than once per decade, the frequency f will be very low $f \leq .1$, which means the discount rate would have to be very high.

Articulation

Traditional accounts of international law accord a significant role to 'promulgative articulation', as evidence of *opinio juris*.[28] This requires simply an express declaration of a nation's understanding of *what* customary behavior it believes it is satisfying and why.

From an economic perspective, the declared 'why' of a nation's actions are unimportant. The *real* reason, at least in a large number of cases, will simply be that such a custom will represent a long-term benefit to the party. However, articulation plays an important, though different, role in this context.

---

[26] This is true enough for present purposes, but *caveat lector*, the persistent objector doctrine and subsequent objector doctrine allow parties to opt-out under certain circumstances. This will be discussed further in the next section.

[27] This custom was articulated in United Nations General Assembly Resolution 1962 (XVIII).

[28] *See e.g.*, Anthony A. D'Amato, *The Concept of Custom in International Law* (Ithaca, NY: Cornell University Press, 1971). ('The simplest objective view of *opinio juris* is a requirement that an objective claim of international legality be *articulated* in advance of, or concurrently with, the act which will constitute the quantitative elements of custom.')

Observe that for any extensional act, there are an infinitude of intensional rules, with which the act will be consistent. For example, if a nation rescues a foreign ship that is sailing 10 miles from its shores, then it is simultaneously satisfying an obligation to rescue ships that are within 11 miles of its shores, an obligation to rescue ships that are within 12 miles of its shores, etc. Indeed, it may be satisfying a general obligation to save foreign *vehicles* generally. Or it may be more narrowly satisfying an obligation to rescue foreign *cargo* vessels.

By engaging in the rescue, a nation both defines and satisfies the obligation, which eventually crystalizes into a CIL. However, the ambiguity of mere action means that definition requires something more. It requires some indication of what the party believes the emerging custom to be.

Recall now that in the vast majority of circumstances discussed in the foregoing analysis in this section, $P_{tn} < S$ and $e^{**} < e^{*}$. And it is obvious from but a brief glance at formula (6.4) (reproduced below) why this should be the case.

$$P_{t_n} = \frac{1}{r}(\underbrace{\beta_n pB(e_m)}_{\text{Future Benefits}} - \underbrace{qC(e_m)}_{\text{Future Costs}}) - \underbrace{C(e_n)}_{\text{Present Cost}}$$

The principal reason why obligors at $t_{n>0}$ face a higher participation threshold and prefer lower effort levels is because they are faced with a present, undiscounted cost $C(e_n)$ when they act.

Now consider the payoff function at t_0. Prior to the first incident, everyone is the position of 'spectator', and no nation faces a present cost. In this case, the only difference between the payoffs for the parties and the social welfare function S (formula (6.2)) will be the presence of probabilities p, q and β; and the difference between r and r^S. Since r^S is merely a function of the r values of all the parties, and also because it cancels out in determining optimal effort levels, the more interesting source of divergence will be the probabilities.

First let us observe what the privately optimal effort level will be at t_0:

$$e_0^{**} = \frac{p\beta B}{2qa} \tag{6.13}$$

Now it is easy to see that privately optimal effort will approach socially optimal effort as $p\beta - q$ approaches zero. In other words, the more homogeneous the nations in the group are with respect to the emerging custom, the more likely it will be that an efficient custom will emerge.

Likewise, when parties are heterogeneous with respect to the probabilities, then it is less likely that the emergent custom will be efficient.

Articulation is thus a potential route to avoiding the first-mover problem encountered after incidents $t_{n>0}$. By declaring their preferred effort levels and defining their *ex ante* understanding of the emerging custom's obligations, CIL may in some cases be able to track efficiency.

It is important to note that this explanation does not make reference to parties' recognition of their practice as being *legally binding*. This is in contradistinction to traditional international law theories, which suggest that for articulation to be effective evidence of *opinio juris*, some expression of legal obligation is essential.

In practice, promulgatory articulation often lacks this element. For example, in the landmark customary law case *Paquete Habana v United States*,[29] the Court recognized the exemption of fishing vessels as prize captures during war, despite the fact that such restraint was often 'articulated' as being motivated by comity rather than legal obligation.

Coordination problems

The phenomena we have modeled thus far are coordination problems – iterated prisoner's dilemmas. However, as Goldsmith and Posner point out, there are at least three other conditions, describable in game theoretic terms, where customary practices may emerge. *Coordination problems* are the most salient of these alternatives.

A paradigmatic example of a coordination problem is the selection of a track gauge as a national standard.[30] Track gauges are the distance between the two rails of railroad tracks. For various reasons relating to cost and the stability of trains at certain speeds, nations may have different preferences with respect to gauge distances. However, these preferences pale in comparison to the advantage of having a uniform standard between neighboring nations.

That is, while nations may have weak preferences for one or another size of track gauge, these preferences will be overwhelmed by a strong preference that neighboring nations use the *same* track gauge – whatever it may be.

Coordination problems are often resolved when parties select their choices in response to *focal points*,[31] which arise in the absence of communication, and which make certain choices more salient.

---

[29] 175 U.S. 677, 694 (1900).

[30] See Goldsmith and Posner (1999), *supra* note 9.

[31] *See* Thomas C. Schelling, *The Strategy of Conflict* (Cambridge, MA: Harvard University Press, 1980), 57.

In a CIL context, the first mover provides a focal point, which subsequent adopters will tend to mimic. Thus, during the development of national railroads, the first among neighbors to adopt a track gauge will likely provide a focal point for the countries around it as they develop their own railroad networks.

In problems such as these,[32] promulgatory articulation may be a source of confusion if the articulated preferences of parties are inconsistent. Indeed, the problem may be exacerbated when parties formally engage in bargaining (as in treaty law), creating a significant transaction cost.

In problems such as these, unarticulated customary law may provide a more expeditious and elegant solution.

B. The Evolution of CIL

We turn now to the mechanisms available to states to 'opt out' of an emerging and established custom. These are, respectively, the 'persistent objector doctrine', and 'subsequent objector doctrine'. We will consider each in turn, before concluding with some more general remarks on stability and change.

Persistent objectors

During the formative stage of a CIL, before it ripens into a binding rule, nations may choose to opt out of the practice. Allowing such exemptions obviously opens the door to strategic behavior. A nation may passively observe the development of a custom, reaping the benefits of it when it finds itself in the role of beneficiary, only to refuse performance when it comes time to fulfill its obligations.

Traditional international law thus imposes two requirements on persistent objectors. First, its objection to the emerging custom must be made clear from an early stage in its development. To establish their defiance of the rule, persistent objector nations must declare their opposition expressly, vote against it, or openly behave in a manner inconsistent with it.[33] Second, persistent objectors must object *persistently*. That is, they cannot participate when the practice is convenient and object when it is

---

32 Although paradigmatic of the problem, the size of railroad gauges is unlikely to be the source of international litigation, and thus it is difficult to see it as hardening into binding CIL.

33 *See e.g.*, Mark E. Villiger, *Customary International Law and Treaties* (Boston, MA: Kluwer Academic Publishers, 1985), 15.

inconvenient. States are thus unable to 'game' the emergent custom with ambiguous behavior.[34]

There exists one exception to the first requirement: newly formed and newly independent states may gain persistent objector status after the rule has solidified if they object within a 'reasonable period of time'.[35] Obviously, this exception is meant to reconcile the need to respect the sovereignty of the newly formed state with the impossibility of objecting at a time predating its existence.

As to the second requirement, persistent objectors need not reject the emerging custom entirely for their objection to count as 'persistent'. They may, either by clear demonstration of intent or express articulation, 'partially object' to the practice, while agreeing to an attenuated version of it. For instance, a nation may reject an emerging customary duty to rescue foreign ships in distress which are within ten miles of its coast. However, it may be willing to participate in rescues that are five miles from its coast. So long as its objection is clear, and the objector behaves consistently, CIL will only impose a duty to rescue when distressed foreign ships are within five miles of its coast.

Consider now a party at t_0 (or alternatively, a party which has hitherto been a non-participant spectator), which chooses to opt out of an emerging custom. What would incentivize such withdrawal from the practice? We have already seen that parties to a nascent custom may experience heterogeneous incentives; let us now reconsider them in light of the persistent objector doctrine.

First, if the probability that the persistent objector would be an obligor is significantly greater than the probability that it would be a beneficiary, then its payoff function,

$$P(e)=\frac{1}{r}(pB(e)-qC(e)) \tag{6.14}$$

may simply fail to meet the participation constraint. Since all payoff functions in the present context will be for t_0, let subscript O denote the persistent objector, and subscript X denote any other participant in the custom. The condition that characterizes the persistent objector will be

---

[34] *See* Lynn Loschin, 'The Persistent Objector and Customary Human Rights Law: A Proposed Analytical Framework' 2 *U.C. Davis J. Int'l L. & Policy* 147–72 (1996).

[35] *See* Villiger, *supra* note 33, at 16–17.

$\frac{p_O}{q_O} < \frac{p_X}{q_X}$. Various facts may cause such a circumstance. For instance, the objector nation may simply have an enormous coastline; its waters may be especially treacherous; it may engage in comparatively little international shipping; or its ships may be more technologically advanced, better equipped, and less vulnerable to disasters. Whatever the reasons, if P_O is sufficiently low, then the objector may prefer the prospect:

$$\overline{P}(\overline{e}) = \frac{1}{r} p_O \left(B(\overline{e}) - \overline{C}(\overline{e})\right) \tag{6.15}$$

Here, the expected costs are not subject to the influence of probability function q. In the example of maritime rescue, this 'go it alone' approach means that the objector will bear the full cost of rescuing its own vessels. Correspondingly, $\overline{C}$ will differ from C, since the costs of rescuing its own ships will presumably impose different costs from rescuing foreign ships. If $\overline{P}(\overline{e}_O^{**}) > P^O(e_X^{**})$, then the objector nation will reject the emerging custom. However, if also $\overline{P}(\overline{e}_O^{**}) < P^O(e_O^{**})$, then the objector will choose only to partially object, setting its preferred obligation level to e_O^{**}. More precisely, the objector will fully object when $\frac{1}{\overline{a}} > \frac{p_O}{q_O a}$, partially otherwise.

Note, however, that states do not elect to be persistent objectors *only* when they prefer *lower* effort levels. It may sometimes be the case that a party desires a *higher* effort level than the emerging custom requires. Since the objector nation cannot unilaterally force other nations to adopt a higher effort level, it is again faced with the problem of whether a 'self help' alternative yields higher payoffs. The same inequality applies in this case: if $\overline{P}(\overline{e}_O^{**}) > P^O(e_X^{**})$ then the objector nation will reject the emerging custom. However, when the objector prefers a higher effort level, the best it can do is simply to accede to the effort level e_X^{**}. It cannot 'partially object' with a higher effort level. Though other nations may appreciate the extra effort exerted in the rescue of their ships, they will not reciprocate and will not be bound to do so.

Before moving to the subsequent objector doctrine, it is worth observing that the nations most likely to employ the persistent objector doctrine are those who tend to have a low $\frac{p}{q}$ ratio. In the case of maritime rescue, nations with long coastlines might plausibly fit this description. However, these are the nations whose participation would be most valuable to other participants in the emerging custom. Therefore, the defection of a high-cost party may decrease the expected benefits of the practice for other parties. Consequently, where the cost–benefit margins are close, the defection of a major cost-bearing nation may induce a chain reaction, which disrupts the formation of the CIL altogether.

Subsequent objectors

After a uniform practice solidifies into binding CIL, a party who failed to establish persistent objector status may still have a limited opportunity to opt out of the obligation under the subsequent objector doctrine.[36] The salient feature of the subsequent objector doctrine is that it applies bilaterally and requires the acquiescence of other nations (separately, not collectively).

Let us begin by assuming that the CIL emerged as between homogeneous parties, and that each state's private welfare more or less tracked the social welfare function, such that:

$$P_X = \frac{1}{r}(pB - qC) \qquad (6.16)$$

and that the parties' private optimum corresponded to efficient effort:

$$e^* = e_X^{**} = \frac{pb}{2aq} \qquad (6.17)$$

Now, the first reason why a state may wish to depart from the CIL obligation is because it has not hitherto been in the position of obligor. Thus, it has been 'free riding' on the custom until t_n, when it finds itself faced with the duty to rescue. Now faced with a present cost, the objector's private welfare P_O is described by formula (6.4) (with $\beta_n = 1$, and its optimal effort level $e_O^{**} < e_X^{**}$ is described by formula (6.6)).

Hence, the subsequent objector will propose to modify the CIL from e_X^{**} to e_O^{**}. Since spectator nations will continue to find e_X^{**} privately optimal, they will refuse to acquiesce to the objector's preferred effort

---

[36] There is another principle of customary law (also incorporated into treaty law in the Vienna Convention on the Law of Treaties, Art. 62), which allows nations to opt out after a CIL becomes recognized as a binding obligation. The *clausula rebus sic stantibus* permits nations, which have undergone fundamental changes since the time the CIL was formed, to subsequently reject the custom. *Rebus sic stantibus* requires, however, that the changes be genuinely uncontemplated during the time of accession of the CIL, and that the changes in circumstances be 'fundamental'. For instance, if a civil war caused the nation's boundaries to change, then obligations that were contingent on its geography may be voidable.

level. Moreover, the beneficiary nation's welfare will be described by:

$$P_B^{**} = \frac{1}{r}(pB - qC) + B \tag{6.18}$$

With optimal effort level:

$$e_B^{**} = \frac{(r+p)b}{2aq} \tag{6.19}$$

Since $e_O^{**} < e_X^{**} < e_B^{**}$, the beneficiary will undoubtedly reject the objector's proposal with particular disdain. And all the other parties having rejected the objector's proposal, the CIL remains unchanged.

Clearly then, in cases of strategically timed objections, the subsequent objector doctrine eliminates the ability of parties to renege on their obligations due to incident-to-incident changes in their cost–benefit functions, thereby preserving the stability of the CIL.

However, now consider what happens when a permanent (or nearly permanent) change in circumstances arises. World events may increase the cost of performing the obligation for *all* parties, decrease the value of being a beneficiary, increase the social discount rate, or alter the probabilities. In such a case, the social optimum may no longer be e^*, and the private optima for the parties will have certainly diverged from e_X^{**}. Let $\tilde{e}^{**}$ denote the changed effort levels of the parties.

Finding the changed circumstances suboptimal, the objector nation will propose a new standard $\tilde{e}_O^{**}$. Spectators, for whom this equals or exceeds the optimal effort level $\tilde{e}_O^{**} \geq \tilde{e}_X^{**}$, will acquiesce to the proposed reduction in CIL obligation. Spectators, for whom the objector's proposal represents an excessive adjustment $\tilde{e}_O^{**} < \tilde{e}_X^{**}$, will acquiesce as far as $\tilde{e}_X^{**}$. The beneficiary however may not be willing to depart from the old standard, because the new values $\tilde{B}$ and $\tilde{C}$ may not be offset by its present benefit (formula (6.18)). Thus, if $\tilde{e}_B^{**} \geq e_X^{**}$, then the beneficiary will not acquiesce to the change.

Ironically, unlike all of the previous scenarios we have discussed, where the obligor favored inefficient rules to escape present costs, in this case it is the beneficiary who represents an impediment to efficient CIL. Beneficiaries may therefore be obstacles to the evolution of CIL responding to global changes in circumstances. However, assuming role-reversibility, the beneficiary during a particular incident will eventually find itself in the position of obligor or spectator, at which stage it will likely either propose or acquiesce to a reduction in the effort level obligation.

In this way, CIL may reduce the burden of obligations to adapt to changed circumstances that affect all involved parties. However, this process creates two corollary effects, which are rather less desirable.

First, since each nation's decision to acquiesce, modify, or reject the objector's proposal only affects its obligations with respect to the objector, the consequence of this evolutionary process is a splintering of the uniform CIL into a series of idiosyncratic bilateral relationships. In an extreme case, it may be that the CIL no longer resembles a coherent 'law', in any meaningful sense. Ideally, the obligations under the fragmented bilateral relations will converge uniformly around a new $\tilde{e}^*$, generating a new (similar) CIL. However, whether this occurs is contingent on the nature of the change, which caused the departures from e^* in the first place.

Second, while the foregoing discussion reveals that CIL may adapt to changed circumstances with a reduction in the obligation e^*, later changed circumstances that increase the benefits of the practice cannot effect an *increase* in the requisite effort level. Consequently, the subsequent objector doctrine will have a downward ratcheting effect. The only antidote to the entropic effect is the formation of a new CIL. However, without the aid of something like the subsequent objector doctrine, the new custom will suffer all the formation obstacles discussed in the previous section. Moreover, the probability that other nations will follow the lead of initiators in a higher effort level is likely be attenuated due to the prior existence of a similar lower-commitment CIL.

IV. CONCLUSION

In this chapter, we briefly reviewed the prior literature on CIL. We then discussed the law and economics framework for CIL, taking as a starting point Goldsmith and Posner's insight that self-interest rather than *opinio juris* is the primary motivator of participation and primary determinant of effort level expenditures.

The model we presented identifies the relationships between the various elements affecting parties' incentives, and how these incentives can generate (or more often fail to generate) efficient customary norms. We also considered the two 'opt out' doctrines and their effect on the evolution of CIL, finding that the subsequent objector doctrine both preserved stability when departures were motivated by momentary opportunism, but suffered from potential entropic reduction in effort level obligations over time.

We did not consider the effect of reputational costs, which might plausibly 'correct' the disincentives that parties face when their 'turn' to play the part of obligor arises. Pulling in the opposite direction, reputational costs may also induce spectators and beneficiaries to acquiesce to objectors, facilitating more rapid entropy.

Additionally, free rider problems abound, because nations will in general be reluctant to unilaterally play the role of 'enforcer', when nations shirk their CIL responsibilities.

Finally, in general we found that the long formative process that antedates its recognition as binding law, the risk of unreciprocated compliance, and heterogeneous payoffs all tended to impede the formation of efficient CIL. Consequently, with the possible exception of coordination game scenarios, where first-movers define focal points, it seems plausible to suppose that treaty law may be a better vehicle for the generation of efficient rules.

PART III

Enforcement

7. Treaty enforcement

Paul B. Stephan

After a long history of neglect, both legal scholars and economists have studied treaty enforcement in recent years (Posner and Sykes 2011). Possible explanations for this methodological turn include the increase in number and salience of treaties that address subjects of long-standing interest to economists, including trade, investment and property rights (broadly conceived); innovative use of treaty claims in domestic litigation; and a general upswing in the use of economic tools by legal academics. Also significant is the growth within political science of rational choice analysis of international relations, including treaties. There exists substantial methodological congruence between rational choice approaches and positive economic analysis. As a result, a literature now exists that provides a foundation for both positive and normative assessment of treaty making and treaty enforcement, using the traditional economist's toolbox.

This chapter reviews the treatment in the scholarly literature of several positive questions: What mechanisms do states use to enforce treaties? What explains the choice of particular kinds of dispute resolution mechanisms? How does the choice of a treaty, rather than some other mechanism for creating a rule of international law, affect enforcement? Why do some, but not all, treaties invoke third-party dispute resolution as an enforcement mechanism? What explains the enforcement of treaties by domestic courts? It also examines research on the normative question of optimal treaty enforcement.

INTERNATIONAL LAW BACKGROUND

International law comprises treaties and custom. Treaties are formal agreements between or among states that create obligations that states generally regard as legally binding. The existence of a valid treaty is a prerequisite to any question of enforcement.

Treaty formation normally involves two stages, first a signing and then a ratification or accession. The bifurcation of the formation process reflects an assumption that negotiation of treaties unfolds among agents, who then must obtain the approval of their principals. In a pre-republican era, ministers would negotiate treaties on behalf of monarchs, who then would indicate their assent to the instrument. In the modern world, state representatives negotiate a text, and then the duly constituted domestic authorities decide whether to approve or not.

In the United States, the Constitution provides that approval of a treaty requires the consent of two-thirds of the Senate. A President probably retains the authority to withhold ratification even after obtaining Senate consent, although the issue is not free from doubt. In addition, since the dawn of the Republic Presidents have relied on legislative enactments as an alternative to Senate consent as a means of forming international agreements that, as a matter of international law, constitute treaties. Some scholars have questioned the legality of this practice, but no court has found occasion to interfere with this power.

Treaties generally do not address the question of how a state chooses to meet the obligations contained within the instrument, and in particular do not obligate states to use their domestic courts as enforcement agents. In many constitutional systems, especially those based on the so-called Westminster model, the head of state has the authority to ratify a treaty, but the act of ratification has no domestic legal effect. The legislature instead must implement the treaty, to the extent that compliance requires changes in domestic law. In these systems, domestic courts never enforce a treaty as such, but rather apply the relevant legislative enactment.

In the United States, the domestic enforcement issue is more complicated. The Supremacy Clause of the Constitution states that treaties to which the United States is a party operate as the law of the land and bind the states. The Supreme Court, however, has never interpreted this clause as automatically recruiting the domestic courts as enforcement agents of all treaty obligations that the United States has assumed. The criteria used by the Court to distinguish treaties that have direct effect in domestic law, in the sense that federal and state courts derive enforcement authority from them, are contentious and murky (Sloss, Ramsey and Dodge 2011).

An issue that presents some of the same problems as treaty formation is treaty interpretation. Treaties sometimes result from incomplete bargaining that elevates the production of an instrument above the resolution of questions about the content of the obligations created by the instrument. Incomplete agreements in turn can be seen as either truncated or as an implicit delegation to future decision makers to supply content as needed. In this situation, the process of treaty interpretation collapses into that of treaty formation (Stephan 2011).

Treaty interpretation can be, but need not always be, tied to treaty enforcement. Treaty parties may agree to submit disputes over interpretation to a body that does not have any direct authority to enforce its decisions. The Charter of the United Nations, for example, designates the Security Council as the body with the authority to compel compliance with decisions of the International Court of Justice (known colloquially as the World Court), thus implying that the Court itself lacks the capacity to compel compliance with its decisions. In other cases, an international tribunal or a domestic court has both the authority to interpret a treaty and normal judicial enforcement powers, such as the capacity to issue a money judgment (Scott and Stephan 2006: 128–41).

ENFORCEMENT MECHANISMS

With treaties, as with international law generally, one must distinguish between a state's exercise of power and influence in pursuit of its interests, on the one hand, and enforcement of a legal entitlement, on the other hand. Confusion between these two modes of behavior leads to exaggerated claims about the significance of international law, including treaty obligations (Goldsmith and Posner 2005: 27–8). The challenge for an inquiry into treaty enforcement is to identify mechanisms through which treaty obligations as such, rather than state interests, work to alter state behavior.

The purest example of a mechanism by which a treaty obligation operates as a quintessential legal interest, subject to the normal methods of private law enforcement, is a judicial proceeding in which private persons can assert the interest and obtain significant, material sanctions against a sovereign that violates it (or vice versa) (Scott and Stephan 2006: 4). Domestic courts deploy such a mechanism to the extent that they treat a treaty provision as equivalent to domestic enactments that create rules of decision applicable in litigation.

Some international tribunals operate in the same fashion as domestic courts. A few permanent bodies, for example, the Court of Justice of the European Union in Luxembourg and the European Court of Human Rights in Strasbourg, have the authority to issue rulings on behalf of or against private litigants that operate directly in domestic law. This mechanism means that at least some of the provisions of the various treaties constituting the European Community and the European Union, as well as the European Convention on Human Rights, are enforced formally and directly, much as a term in a private contract.

In addition, ad hoc tribunals established to hear commercial or investment disputes function much like domestic courts. Many modern bilateral investment treaties, for example, provide for enforcement under the Convention for the Settlement of Investment Disputes between States and Nationals of Other States. This process allows investors to bring claims before an arbitral body. Those bodies can issue monetary awards that function in domestic legal systems much as do private court judgments. Less often, states can enter into treaties that accept arbitration of disputes within the terms of the Convention on the Recognition and Enforcement of Foreign Arbitral Awards. The 1981 Algiers Accords between the United States and Iran, for example, submitted all outstanding commercial disputes between the two countries and their nationals to an arbitration mechanism. Courts in turn have recognized that the arbitral awards generated by this process constitute domestically enforceable legal obligations.

As contracts scholars have observed, however, formal enforcement through litigation is only one of many tools used to induce compliance with rules of conduct embodied in private agreements. This literature identifies informal enforcement mechanisms that substitute for formal enforcement. These mechanisms include: (1) reciprocity (behavior by one party to an agreement signaling an intention to behave cooperatively); (2) retaliation (behavior by a party to an agreement that punishes another party for behaving uncooperatively); (3) reputation (actions that signal a desire to be perceived by non-parties as cooperative); and (4) a preference for cooperative behavior (Scott 2003). International legal scholars have suggested that similar factors may induce states to comply with treaties (Scott and Stephan 2006: 84–109).

The analysis of reciprocity and retaliation as an informal means of inducing international cooperation goes back to the seminal (and Nobel-prize winning) work of Thomas Schelling (Schelling 1956; Schelling 1960). Schelling distinguished between frameworks in which each party could come out ahead if it defected while its counterparty cooperated (formalized as the prisoners' dilemma) and those in which everyone preferred cooperation to defection, but either were ignorant of the coordination point or preferred different points (coordination problems). Robert Axelrod explored the effect of iterative interactions on the dynamics of prisoners' dilemma games and identified a mixed approach of reciprocity and retaliation that would induce cooperation even in such games (Axelrod 1984). Axelrod in particular popularized the tit-for-tat strategy, in which actors in a two-person iterative prisoners' dilemma game would respond exactly symmetrically to the other's actions, as a means for inducing cooperation.

One policy area that had an enormous impact on this mode of analysis was the nuclear balance of terror and, later, arms control treaties. Schelling's work made an important contribution to the understanding of the incentives of adversaries, each of which possessed the capacity to render catastrophic injury on the other. The emergence of treaties in the 1960s as a means of managing nuclear capabilities, and in particular the Soviet–United States relationship, prompted further study of coordination problems and treaty enforcement (Abbott 1989). In essence, treaties specified norms that clarified whether behavior fell into the opportunistic or cooperative category. The inability of the parties to address all future states of the world means that these treaties are incomplete and thus subject to post hoc opportunism, but they do reduce the range of uncertainty about particular conduct. By clarifying the distinction between retaliation and opportunistic defection, a treaty can induce greater compliance.

International relations theorists built on this work to posit strong foundations for international cooperation, including treaty compliance, in the absence of formal enforcement. The amenability of a wide range of treaty regimes to an iterative games model invited this development (Setear 1997). Inevitably, a critical response arose. Mahoney and Sanchirico cautioned that the uncritical use of simple iterative game models risked misleading conclusions, in part because the international relations theorists had not stayed abreast of developments in economics. A first paper established that the spontaneous development of cooperative norms reinforced by tit-for-tat strategies requires that the actors not discount future payoffs relative to later ones. Drawing on evolutionary models developed by economists, they demonstrated that this condition limits the realistic use of the model (Mahoney and Sanchirico 2001). A later paper explored the paradox created by a defection from a previously observed cooperative equilibrium. The defection calls the existence of the norm into question and thereby undermines the incentives of third parties to sanction the defection. At least some formal legal intervention thus is needed to reassure observers about the content of the norm (Mahoney and Sanchirico 2003).

A formalist response to the criticisms raised by Mahoney and Sanchirico is that specification of a rule of behavior in a treaty (legalization, as political scientists would put it) solves both problems. A specified norm is not vulnerable to evolutionary changes or to uncertainty about the content of the rule. On reflection, however, this argument rests on strong assumptions about the expressive power of law in contexts where parties have powerful reasons to deviate from the stated rule. While clear definition of cooperative behavior helps parties who otherwise have incentives to let their behavior coalesce around a particular norm (such as driving on a specified side of the road, or portioning out the broadcast spectrum or geocentric orbits), it does not do much on its own to reinforce a norm in cases where everyone knows that the other actors would like to defect. In the latter case, formal legal sanctioning plays a larger role in reinforcing the credibility of the treaty norm. Recognizing this point, a number of scholars have concluded that reciprocity and retaliation function mostly as a solution to coordination problems, and not to collective actions situations where each party has an incentive to defect (Snidal 1985; Ginsburg and McAdams 2004).

In recent years attention has shifted to the reputational mechanism as a particular means of treaty enforcement (Guzman 2008). This work posits an informal model pursuant to which states monitor the actions of other states to assess whether they comply with their treaty obligations. States that fail to meet their commitments pay a price in terms of the unwillingness of other states to engage them in joint interest-maximization projects. States that manifest a commitment to meeting their obligations, even when doing so entails costs, are rewarded with more interest-maximization projects. A reputation for honoring treaty commitments thus functions in a manner somewhat analogous to human capital, i.e., an intangible capital asset that generates returns in proportion to the asset's size. This model is an extension of one that focuses only on reciprocity and retaliation but provides for third-party participation, inasmuch as third parties will act on reputational information only as opportunities arise in the future to engage in cooperative projects.

Because reputation implicates relations with all states, it is said to have greater significance than rewards and punishments imposed by states that are directly affected by treaty compliance. A breach of a trade obligation, for example, might induce direct retaliation only by the state that produces the goods affected by the breach. A reputation for non-compliance, by contrast, will affect all potential opportunities for interest-maximization with all states (Guzman 2008).

Critics have claimed that this argument overstates the role of reputation as a legal enforcement mechanism (Downs and Jones 2002; Brewster 2009a; Brewster 2009b; Scott and Stephan 2006: 118–22). They contend that it is implausible that reputation attaches to international law compliance as such, as opposed to behavior within specific issue areas. They also argue that a reputation for cooperativeness is not the same as one for compliance. The United States, by refusing to join the Statute of the International Criminal Court, acted completely within its international legal rights and transgressed no treaty obligations, but nevertheless garnered considerable criticism for its failure to support a project thought to be in the interest of international order. The lawfulness of the United States' decision did not insulate the state from some sort of reputational loss due to its failure to cooperate.

The criticism of the claimed effects of reputation as an enforcement mechanism can be generalized. With any informal mechanism, it is difficult to distinguish general state interests from legal entitlements. Put simply, compliance with treaty obligations is not exactly the same as cooperative behavior. A state may have opportunities to behave cooperatively or opportunistically in areas where no legal obligation exists. For example, one party to a bilateral arms control agreement might insist on a rigidly literal and narrow interpretation of the treaty so as to allow it to engage in a range of behavior that the other side might regard as opportunistic. Alternatively, a state might refuse to respond to an initiative to liberalize trade in a range of goods. Neither behavior would transgress a norm of treaty compliance, but both might signal an unwillingness to pursue joint interest-maximization projects. One can imagine a partner rewarding a state that responds affirmatively to proposals for deepening cooperation, and punishing rejections of such proposals, independent of any legal obligations.

Only recently have scholars considered the existence in the general population of a widespread but non-universal preference for cooperation as a complementary informal mechanism that induces compliance with obligations. Evidence that such a preference exists comes from a wide range of experiments conducted by economists. Contract theorists embraced this phenomenon as a means of extending the positive account for the persistence of informal enforcement mechanisms in the face of the limitations of the other explanations of informal enforcement (Scott 2003). International law scholars quickly realized the potential of this insight as a means of explaining compliance with international law (Scott and Stephan 2004).

The preference for cooperation significantly reinforces informal sanctions for non-compliance. It explains why actors would risk disappointment by behaving cooperatively, and invest in punishing defectors in cases where they derive no direct return, where less rich behavioral models would predict risk aversion or indifference. Rewarding behavior that benefits the group, and punishing opportunists, pleases a significant portion of the population. Knowing that people will expend some resources to indulge this preference, others, whether endowed with a matching preference or not, will honor commitments even when only informal sanctions apply.

Experimental evidence also reveals an important feature of the preference for cooperation: it has a rivalrous relationship with formal sanctions. Knowledge that a third party has been designated to sanction misbehavior discourages others from taking on the task themselves. Formal enforcement thus undermines informal sanctions, with consequences that will be discussed in the next section.

An important objection to the application of the preference for cooperation to treaty enforcement is the possible disanalogy between individuals, whom the experiments have studied, and states. That individuals might gain satisfaction from rewarding cooperation and punishing opportunism does not lead to the conclusion that public actors, operating within some collective decision-making structure, seek to maximize the same preference. A possible reply is that, although collective decision making may distort preference satisfaction, there is no reason to believe that this individual preference is intrinsically different than others that collective actors seek to meet. It is even possible to suppose that public acts, being subject to greater scrutiny than private actions, might respond even more to this preference. At present, however, the point remains open (Scott and Stephan 2006: 43–7, 106–8).

These observations do not mean that economic analysis leaves scholars without a coherent account of informal treaty enforcement. Rather, it suggests that models of informal enforcement need greater specification and, in particular, much greater validation through empirical and quantitative analysis than the field has seen to date. The models remain promising but have not yet fully delivered a convincing and comprehensive account of treaty compliance.

CHOICES OF ENFORCEMENT MECHANISMS

Recognition that treaties might employ either formal or informal enforcement mechanisms raises an obvious follow-on question: what explains the choice between these mechanisms? Some have depicted the question as one of risk aversion (Guzman 2002). States that regard the costs associated with formal enforcement by a third party as greater than the benefits that such enforcement will generate will either avoid an obligation altogether or elect for informal enforcement. This point, while indisputable, does not go very far to identify the factors that might lead states to prefer informal enforcement.

One study draws on contract theory to explain the use of informal enforcement of international treaties (Scott and Stephan 2006: 88–109). Contracts scholars have studied non-contractable terms, that is to say provisions that might be of value in a contractual relationship but which cannot be verified to a third party at an acceptable cost. If the parties to the contract can observe performance, even if they cannot prove to a third party whether the performance meets the desired standard, they might rely on informal sanctions to induce compliance.

A further insight of contracts literature is that, while the various informal mechanisms complement each other and thus strengthen informal enforcement as a whole, formal and informal sanctions seem to be substitutes rather than complements. As noted above, experimental economists have developed substantial evidence indicating that hardening the enforcement of a contractual term by making it subject to sanctions imposed by a third party reduces the willingness of the parties to invest in informal sanctions. Rather than rewarding cooperation or punishing defections themselves, the parties defer to the designated sanctioning body. This work has led to the somewhat counterintuitive insight that formal enforcement of some contractual provisions might reduce the gains from cooperation that parties might otherwise achieve. Formal sanctions will drive out informal enforcement in areas where informal sanctions would extend the range of contracting by solving non-contractability problems (Scott 2003).

The insights of contract theory can illuminate treaty practice (Scott and Stephan 2006). The analogy between states and firms as contracting entities is not perfect, but the fit is close enough to explain a wide range of state behavior. Many treaties address issues of great significance to the parties, but where the reduction of the quality of performance to a manageable standard poses significant problems. Treaties usually bar formal enforcement of such provisions. The absence of formal enforcement, however, is not the same as no enforcement.

A helpful illustration of limitation of enforcement mechanisms due to contractibility problems is the structure of national security exceptions in various treaties. In trade agreements, such as the General Agreement on Tariffs and Trade (GATT) or the North American Free Trade Agreement (NAFTA), one consistently finds a provision allowing a party to invoke national security as a ground for its failure to meet its obligation. Moreover, the validity of the invocation is, by the express terms of the agreement or by accepted practice, self-judging.

It seems plausible that, within the context of trade relations, states might regard the national security rule as subject to too many imponderables to invite third-party scrutiny. The United States has a long history of imposing trade sanctions on states that threaten its national interests. As a hegemon, the United States also has a broad conception of such threats, one that extends to systemic risks rather than direct attacks on its nationals or assets. During the 1980s, for example, the United States withdrew concessions from Nicaragua because its Sandinista regime sought to undermine regional stability, even though the impact of Nicaraguan behavior on the United States was indirect. The United States invoked the national security provision in the GATT to legitimize these sanctions, and then refused to accept GATT review of its determination. One can understand that states might regard the directness of a national security threat as not verifiable to an independent arbiter, even though the basic facts may be observable to all.

Designating a provision as subject to self-judging means that third-party tribunals lack the authority to look into the matter. It does not mean, however, that interested observers, including the state that suffers direct costs due to suspension of trade concessions, are unable to assess the claim. A state that invokes national security for pretextual reasons will invite retaliation and acquire a reputation for uncooperativeness. These factors constrain states from invoking national security whenever they wish to relieve themselves of a trade obligation. Indeed, states rarely invoke the national security exception to trade obligations.

The evident non-contractability of national security in trade law does not necessarily mean that all national security issues are dominated by non-verifiable issues. Contract law provides an analogy in *force majeure* clauses and the doctrine of impracticability of performance. Domestic courts traditionally have used these tools to determine when a party may suspend its obligations because of events such as war and upheaval. The treaty analog involves investment protection, where at least some arbitral tribunals have ruled that national security exceptions are not self-judging (Scott and Stephan 2006: 159–62).

A possible explanation of the different practice is that trade law involves an assessment of ongoing behavior, and dispute resolution has as its object the termination of non-compliant behavior. Investment law, by contrast, is a play-or-pay system, under which sovereigns remain free to undertake whatever policies they choose as long as they compensate victims. Past events are generally easier to verify than are ongoing and prospective risks.

More generally, parties can allow treaty bargains to extend to indefinite, and therefore non-contractable, future states by relying exclusively on informal sanctions (Horn, Maggi and Staiger 2010). Alternatively, parties can delegate to a third party the authority to devise rules that resolve problems arising in future states. The delegation normally takes the form of a vague standard (Scott and Triantis 2006; Scott and Stephan 2006: 72–5). Such delegations appear to take place less frequently in treaties than they do in private contracts, perhaps due to agency costs associated with third-party tribunals (Stephan 2002). Nonetheless, they do exist (Van Aaken 2009).

TREATIES AS AN ALTERNATIVE TO OTHER FORMS OF COOPERATION

A related area for further research is the connection between formalization of the expression of an international legal obligation and the effectiveness of informal enforcement mechanisms. Treaties, even with their interpretative baggage, tend to specify the content of an obligation more clearly than does unwritten custom. It seems plausible that the clarity of such a legal obligation may give it a greater independent impact on state behavior, in particular by inducing more effective informal sanctions to support compliance.

One difficulty with the existing literature is the tendency of some scholars to focus on the expression of the legal obligation only, rather than the range of sanctions used to enforce it. The result is not so much circularity as a failure to consider a significant variable, namely the role of sanctions in reinforcing an obligation.

To begin with, the literature invokes the concept of 'soft law' without an adequate definition of the subject. Rational-choice theorists have argued, for example, that soft law provides a useful alternative to binding legal obligations as a means of promoting international cooperation (Lipson 1991; Abbott and Snidal 2000). They argue that less definite international commitments provide a framework for joint interest-maximization activities while reducing the costs associated with the realization of regret contingencies (Guzman 2002; Guzman and Meyer 2009). This work, however, does not take into account enforcement mechanisms as such.

Abbott and Snidal understand soft law as that lacking in two elements: (1) the capacity to attain precision; and (2) subject to third-party adjudication. Guzman instead defines soft law as that not intended to impose a legal obligation. Neither approach ties the hardness of law to the consequences that flow from non-compliance.[1]

[1] In fairness to Abbot and Snidal, their definition was imposed on them by the organizers of the symposium in which they participated. For criticism of the decision by the organizers not to focus directly on enforcement mechanisms in building their concept of legalization, see Scott and Stephan 2006: 14; Goldsmith and Posner 2005: 17.

To illustrate why these definitions are unhelpful, some treaties impose very precise obligations but do not provide for third-party dispute resolution. The historic bilateral arms control treaties between the USSR and the United States provide a nice example. These agreements relied largely on reciprocity and retaliation, but for all that seem no less definite or binding than bilateral tax treaties or bilateral trade agreements in the pre-GATT era. Nor does the Guzman definition seem to work, as he apparently would regard as soft law treaties that rely on informal sanctions for enforcement. On balance, then, a distinction between treaties and soft law seems incoherent. Moreover, positing a distinction between hard and soft law, rather than analyzing differences in compliance sanctions, seems analytically unpromising.

These general points aside, the distinction between greater and less formality in the specification and enforcement of an international legal obligation has some value. A special case may be treaties that submit certain classes of disputes to third-party adjudication. Depending on the clarity of the terms of reference and the specific powers bestowed upon the tribunal, the obligation to comply with the resulting judgments may have high salience independent of the subject of the dispute. In particular, it seems plausible that states will exercise their control over the terms of reference of these tribunals to limit their competence to matters where the benefits from dispute resolution exceed the costs associated with an unfavorable outcome (Guzman 2002; Stephan 2002; Posner and Yoo 2005).

Extending this argument to its logical conclusion, a treaty-based obligation to determine a border or to pay a fixed sum of money might function independently of the underlying state interest from which the obligation is derived. International tribunals created by treaties appear to have the greatest effect on state behavior when they settle border disputes. Scholars have modeled these interactions as iterative coordination games, specifically a hawk-dove game. They attribute the general acceptance of tribunal resolutions of border disputes to the parties' incentive to accept the coordination solution supplied by a disinterested third party (Ginsburg and McAdams 2004). Similarly, compliance with a mandate to pay a sum of money, the normal outcome of an investment or commercial dispute submitted to ad hoc international arbitration, sends a less ambiguous signal than does compliance to do something where quality of performance is uncertain. Perhaps for this reason, states generally pay money judgments, even if the underlying dispute derives from sensitive policy areas such as a financial crisis (Scott and Stephan 2006: 161–2).

Conversely, tribunals that seek to adjudicate conflicts involving armed force have a far less impressive success rate. The World Court, for example, has an abysmal record with respect to exercises of its advisory opinion jurisdiction regarding issues of peace and security. The interested parties have no role in limiting the Court's advisory opinion jurisdiction. In several high-profile cases, including ones involving the Israeli security wall and the use of atomic weapons, the Court's edicts have produced profound indifference from the affected states. In other cases involving the use of force where the relevant party opposed the Court's jurisdiction, the result has been equally unimpressive. Following the Nicaragua decision, the United States blocked all efforts to implement the tribunal's judgment. The episode also led to the dissatisfied state's withdrawing its general *ex ante* consent to the Court's jurisdiction (Posner and Yoo 2005: 38–41).

THIRD PARTY DISPUTE RESOLUTION UNDER TREATIES

Political scientists as well as economists have studied the role of tribunals constituted by treaties to address disputes. Not all of the studies have paid close attention to variation in the character of these tribunals, however. Lumping together all third-party mechanisms misses important differences in enforcement mechanisms.

One significant distinction is between permanent tribunals that have *ex ante* jurisdiction over certain classes of disputes, on the one hand, and ad hoc bodies that may consider only those disputes that parties choose to refer to them (Posner and Yoo 2005). The latter in effect must compete for business, and thus have an incentive to generate decisions that future disputants will find useful. Tribunals that leave their composition as well as jurisdiction to the selection of the parties, as is true generally in investment and commercial arbitration, represent an extreme manifestation of this process. Some institutions have a mix of mandatory and ad hoc jurisdiction. The World Court, for example, has some jurisdiction based on binding treaties, but also can entertain disputes referred to it by the affected states on an ad hoc basis.

Some empirical evidence indicates that ad hoc tribunals enjoy greater success in demand for their services and in compliance with their decisions than do permanent tribunals (Posner and Yoo 2005). The issue is clouded somewhat by the recent tendency of states to create new permanent tribunals with mandatory jurisdiction, especially on a regional basis (Helfer and Slaughter 2005). The available evidence does suggest that, whatever the reasons for states to create new tribunals, the permanent–ad hoc distinction does have some explanatory power with respect to state compliance with tribunal decisions. The intuition behind this may seem self-evident: the less say a state has in choosing the venue for dispute resolution, *ceteris paribus*, the less likely it is to accept the outcome of the process.

It is plausible that the creation of new tribunals might reflect political economy, rather than welfare maximization, factors. The new regional tribunals generate rents for certain elites and seem to do very little work. One might surmise that these bodies exist mostly as infrastructure projects that benefit the providers of inputs (judges, litigants, service staff, the builders of their offices) and that retain funding by not doing anything that would threaten the interests of the states that fund them. Further research is needed to confirm this hypothesis, however.

A second dimension for classifying various international tribunals is sanctioning capacity. At one extreme along a sanctioning continuum, a treaty might give a tribunal the authority to determine the issue in dispute but not to attach any consequences to its decision. At the other, a tribunal might have the power to impose monetary penalties or even criminal punishments that function exactly as do those issued by a domestic court. The existence of tribunals that fall across the entire continuum suggests that a mix of factors drive choices about the design of sanctions. On the one hand, endowing a tribunal with meaningful sanctioning authority over which it has exclusive control sends a strong signal about the importance of compliance with the tribunal's decisions. On the other hand, the existence of powerful and independent tribunals might weaken the incentive of states to make *ex ante* commitments to submit to their jurisdiction.

One awaits a systematic review of the evidence, but an informal review of international tribunals suggests that both of these conjectures have some explanatory power. Tribunals with strong sanctioning power tend to be those that take only disputes that parties refer to them. A classic example is investment and commercial arbitration tribunals. Conversely, tribunals with mandatory jurisdiction tend to employ only weak sanctions. The Court of Justice of the European Union in Luxembourg received the authority to impose fines for non-compliance with its judgments only late in its history, and rarely has exercised this power. The willingness of particular states to disregard its orders is notorious. As for the European Court of Human Rights in Strasbourg, it levies only modest fines, functionally equivalent to parking tickets. States that have little interest in complying with its decisions, such as Russia and Turkey, pay these fines but do not address the underlying human rights determinations.

An interesting, as well as important, example of intermediate sanctioning is the World Trade Organization (WTO) Dispute Settlement Body (DSB). The DSB has three tiers – an initial ad hoc arbitral panel, a permanent appellate body, and a committee of the whole of WTO members. The highest tier can alter appellate body decisions only by consensus. The DSB may authorize complaining states to retaliate against a state that fails to comply with its determinations. Retaliation is limited to an amount of trade preferences approved by the DSB and may not exceed the ongoing injury caused by non-compliance with the DSB decision (Brewster 2011). In other words, the sanction does not include compensation for past injury caused by a violation of WTO law, only the injured state can invoke the sanction, and it is not obliged to do so.

Several scholars have argued that this sanctioning structure reflects the rational interests of the states that created it. Schwartz and Sykes argue that, by limiting compensation to the amount of ongoing harm from non-compliance, the regime encourage efficient breaches of trade commitments. A state can adjust to changed conditions by defecting from its WTO obligations, and will do so if the benefit of the adjustment exceeds the cost of the sanction (Schwartz and Sykes 2002). A drawback of their analysis, however, is their assumption that the DSB's sanction fully compensates the state that suffers due to the adjustment. They wrote relatively early in the history of the WTO DSB. Its practice now makes clear that authorized sanctions will not account for injuries suffered before a DSB's determination of the illegality of a particular practice. This limitation arguably encourages opportunistic, rather than efficient, breaches.

Brewster analyzes the WTO's choice of an under-compensatory standard for retaliatory sanctions (Brewster 2011). She notes that it gives states an incentive to engage in temporary breaches of their trade obligations. Because states suffer no punishment for breaches that are cured at the end of the DSB process, states have no reason not to prolong the dispute resolution process. As long as the political benefits to the government from protecting the industry in question exceed the costs of participating in the dispute resolution process, states will refuse to settle. The likelihood of ultimate victory would have little impact on this calculus. Consistent with this conjecture, the rate of settlement of WTO disputes is remarkably low.

Sykes analyzes a separate feature of WTO dispute resolution, namely the limitation to states of standing to bring a dispute (Sykes 2005). This limitation used to be universal in international dispute resolution and still applies to tribunals such as the World Court. Sykes contrasts the states-only standing rule for trade law violations with the extension to private investors of the right to initiate claims under modern investment protection treaties.

A state monopoly over standing enables a treaty party to waive international law violations in return for offsetting concessions in other areas by the violator. Private standing allows vindication of the treaty right even in situations where the overall national interest might benefit from its surrender (Scott and Stephan 2006: 138). Sykes argues that the stronger protection of investor rights indicates the relatively greater strength of investor interests and the lack of domestic constituencies that directly compete with that group. In the case of trade liberalization, by contrast, home states constantly confront distributional tradeoffs between exporter groups who benefit from the liberal WTO regime and domestic producers who seek protection from foreign competition. The state monopoly over standing means that WTO parties can incorporate these tradeoffs into the calculus as to whether to vindicate WTO rights.

Sykes's argument draws on positive political economy and is not meant to reach any normative conclusions. Later, this chapter will address proposals to permit private enforcement of WTO rights as part of a general welfare analysis of treaty enforcement. The political economy literature has developed substantial evidence indicating that legacy domestic producers enjoy success in procuring protection even where their benefits are dwarfed by the costs borne by prospective exporters, as well as by (politically ineffectual) consumers forced to pay higher prices. In light of this political reality, a hard rule requiring private standing to enforce trade rules might deter governments from entering into welfare-increasing trade agreements. The government might regard the loss of the capacity to balance the interests of the nominal beneficiaries of trade rules and the domestic groups threatened by them as too high a price to pay for such an agreement.

DOMESTIC LITIGATION AS AN ENFORCEMENT MECHANISM

Treaties normally impose obligations on states, but do not bind states as to the domestic mechanisms that they must employ to honor those obligations. A multilateral treaty such as the Convention against Torture and other Cruel, Inhuman or Degrading Treatment or Punishment, for example, requires a state to abolish a certain set of practices. But it does not stipulate what sanctions should apply to persons who violate the obligation and in particular does not address the issue of whether a state should provide private lawsuits to compensate victims. This agnosticism about domestic enforcement stems from a recognition that national legal systems vary widely in terms of the structure of the criminal justice process (inquisitorial versus adversarial) and the means for compensating persons injured by wrongful acts, as well as critical secondary issues such as the scope and content of accessory liability.

Domestic legal systems respond to this agnosticism in different ways. As noted above, most countries that trace their constitutions to the British model regard treaties as completely outside the domestic legal order. In these systems, domestic courts will apply the legal rules found in treaties only when instructed to do so by an act of the legislature. Although superficially clear cut, this approach in many instances packs the question of domestic treaty enforcement into issues of statutory interpretation. Courts eager to invoke treaty rules can read legislation liberally to find an authorization to use the treaty, while those hostile to treaties can read legislation narrowly.

A handful of countries go to the opposite extreme by allowing their courts generally to apply treaty rules. Where it exists, this power raises a secondary question, namely the reconciliation of conflicts between treaties and domestic legislation. A very few states assign a higher priority to treaties than to domestic legislation. A more common approach is the last-in-time rule, which applies the last adopted legal obligation. The United States in particular follows this model. Even under the last-in-time rule, however, courts retain some discretion to determine whether a conflict between a treaty and domestic law exists. By creative reading of either the treaty or the statute, a court either can find a wide range of conflict, or none.

Where it operates, domestic litigation can have a significant impact on the enforcement of a treaty. Compared to international tribunals, domestic courts generally extend standing to sue to a broader class of persons. To the extent private enforcement entails monetary compensation, victims have a direct monetary incentive to bring their claims. All things being equal, opening up treaty rights to domestic litigation should lead to more enforcement of the treaty in question.

The extent of the impact of domestic litigation will depend to some degree on the nature of civil adjudication in any particular country. The United States, for example, employs a range of mechanisms in its civil litigation that, most believe, increase incentives to bring claims. These include the American rule for attorneys' fees, the allowance of contingency fee arrangements, the class action device, liberal pretrial discovery, the availability of jury trials, and the possibility of punitive damages. These features, of course, apply to all categories of claims, private as well as public, but seem especially salient in the international context. No other legal system has this combination of features, each of which seems on balance to enhance the value of filed claims.

A related issue is the choice of mechanism to determine what treaty obligations qualify for domestic judicial enforcement. No legal system enlists its courts in sanctioning violations of all treaty obligations. Instead, some combination of standing doctrine and domestic constitutional law determines when courts have a license to apply treaty norms (Nollkaemper 2011). During the last thirty years, the United States increasingly has addressed this question expressly at the time it has acceded to a treaty. In the case of multilateral human rights agreements, the Senate habitually has included a statement indicating that the treaty would not have any effect on the domestic legal order. In the case of trade agreements, implementing legislation invariably limits domestic enforcement to suits brought by the United States government for injunctive relief.

Complicating the incentive effect of domestic enforcement of treaties is the difficulty of collecting money judgments against sovereign actors. While the United States and many other countries have rejected absolute sovereign immunity, almost all countries do recognize immunity from civil suits for foreign states not involved in commercial operations or not committing torts on another state's territory. Even when a treaty (such as one protecting foreign investors) provides for binding third-party adjudication, courts normally look for a separate legal basis, such as another treaty commitment, before they will enforce monetary awards resulting from such arbitration. And separate, typically broader concepts of sovereign immunity limit the kinds of state-owned assets that can be attached by a domestic court to enforce a judgment.

Even where immunity does not exist, asset partition can frustrate enforcement of civil judgments. Many states take advantage of limited liability of legal entities, which both protects assets belonging to the entity's owner from serving as a means of satisfying the entity's obligations and frees an entity's assets from the obligation to satisfy the owner's debts. States can put property that is located in foreign jurisdictions, such as aircraft or ships, in separate companies. Absent a corporate-veil-piercing rule, these assets cannot be used to satisfy liability that attaches to the state, as distinguished from the state entity that owns and operates the assets.

More uncertainty exists about the liability of government officials, as distinct from the state itself, for treaty violations. In the United States, foreign official immunity is in a state of flux. A recent Supreme Court decision ruled that the existing legislation does not apply to physical, as opposed to legal, persons, but that some common-law immunity doubtlessly exists. The lower courts have just begun to consider the scope and basis of such immunity. The issue matters because, while the vast majority of foreign government officials are judgment-proof, a handful have significant assets located outside their native country. Moreover, even judgment-proof officials might regard an outstanding claim as grounds for avoiding travel to the United States.

Looming in the background are questions of domestic liability of private actors for treaty violations. To date, the question has arisen only in the United States, where the case law reveals a deep division among courts. Most of the litigation has involved violations of international custom rather than of treaties, but the possibility of a private actor being found liable as an accessory for treaty violations does exist.

As a practical matter, the question of accessory liability becomes one of suing multinational corporations. These entities tend to be both susceptible to suit in the United States and possess attachable assets. Proponents of liberal accessory liability argue that litigation will induce firms to internalize the costs suffered by victims of treaty violations. Critics argue both that liability should rest on clear legislative choices, rather than general common law, and that holding firms subject to United States judicial jurisdiction to different standards than those applicable to the rest of the world creates a welfare-reducing trade barrier.

WELFARE EFFECTS OF TREATY ENFORCEMENT

The welfare consequences of the enlistment of domestic litigation to enforce a treaty are difficult to assess in the abstract. Attaching greater and stronger sanctions to a rule expressed in a treaty normally should increase treaty compliance. Whether the overall instrumental consequences of this incentive will be positive or negative is complicated.

The general literature of law enforcement teaches that maximal enforcement normally does not constitute optimal enforcement (Shavell 1993; Ehrlich and Posner 1974). In many instances, the proscribed behavior bears some resemblance to socially desirable behavior. The greater the sanctions attached to the proscribed behavior, the greater the chances that actors will be deterred from desirable conduct that might be confused with the proscribed behavior. Optimal deterrence involves a comparison of the benefits from discouraging unwanted conduct and the costs of discouraging wanted conduct.

This insight applies to international law as much as to any other legal regime (Posner and Sykes 2011). In some cases, compliance with a treaty obligation may entail more costs than benefits. In others, changed circumstances may render the obligation generally irrational. To maximize welfare, the international law of remedies should ensure that sanctions do not discourage welfare-increasing breaches.

An example from trade law illustrates the distinction between optimal sanctions and maximal sanctions. Several scholars have argued for changing the enforcement regime for WTO law as a means of maximizing the value of trade concessions. Proposals include allowing private actors to invoke this law either in international tribunals or domestic courts, requiring cash compensation, and extending compensation to injuries suffered from the onset of the violation (Guzman 2008; Shaffer 2003; Trachtman and Moremen 2003). They argue credibly that these reforms would increase compliance with WTO obligations. One also might suppose that opposition by homogenous, well-organized interest groups, such as legacy domestic producers, block states from agreeing to enforcement measures that would increase global welfare.

But unless one somehow could ban interest groups from participating in domestic politics, stripping them of the power to limit remedies for trade law violations may have negative consequences. Insisting on powerful enforcement mechanisms would discourage states from committing to extensive WTO commitments in the first place. Arguably, the benefits from broad obligations informally enforced are greater than those from narrow obligations formally enforced (Nzelibe 2008).

Sykes argues more generally that private enforcement of treaty rules, like private enforcement of other regulatory regimes, may result in welfare-diminishing trade barriers (Sykes 2008). Private enforcement by its nature is local, in that the victim must pursue a wrongdoer in a jurisdiction where it can be located. Private enforcement of treaty rules only in a jurisdiction where civil litigation entails significant costs to potential defendants, such as the United States, may induce firms with ties to the United States to avoid doing business in jurisdictions where treaty violations are likely to occur, and deter firms that operate in such jurisdictions from developing ties to the United States. If the firm deterred from entering a market because of exposure to liability risk otherwise were the least-cost producer of the goods in question, efficiency would suffer.

Some have proposed to work around the problem of localism by adopting a principle of universal jurisdiction over certain core obligations that are said to be owed to all humanity. Were every state to commit to enforcement of such norms, and if enforcement entailed roughly the same sanctions in every jurisdiction, then all regulated actors would have to internalize the costs of their actions no matter where they act or where their attachable assets were located. The treaty obligations regarding torture and grave violations of the laws of war are said to exemplify such obligations. But, under realistic assumptions about state behavior, universal jurisdiction is more likely to result in opportunistic litigation that may impose sanctions well in excess of the costs of the regulated behavior (Kontorovich 2008).

An issue that only recently has received focused attention is the mechanism for determining how to sanction treaty violations. Enforcement mechanisms can either be selected at the time of creation of a treaty obligation or left to later determination by some agent, either an international body or a domestic court. Uncertainty about whether the agent will adopt formal enforcement, or instead allow informal enforcement to proceed unimpaired, results in a net welfare loss (Stephan 2011). On pure welfare grounds, then, both tribunals and domestic courts should refuse to provide formal enforcement of treaties without a clear *ex ante* direction to do so, and fully enforce those treaty provisions where they have received such a direction.

CONCLUSION

Focused analysis of treaty enforcement, bolstered by the economist's conventional tools, has unfolded mostly in the last decade. At present, the field has generated important insights into current practice and proposed interesting hypotheses about state behavior. At present, however, scholars have relied mostly on anecdotal evidence, rather than systematic quantitative analysis, to test these theories. One hopes that, as the theoretical groundwork becomes more fully developed, we will see more rigorous efforts at validation.

(This manuscript was submitted in August 2011 and was current as of that date. It does not take into account later publications).

REFERENCES

Abbott, Kenneth W. 1989. 'Modern International Relations Theory: A Prospectus for International Lawyers' 14 *Yale Journal of International Law* 335–411.

Abbott, Kenneth W. and Duncan Snidal. 2000. 'Hard and Soft Law in International Governance' 54 *International Organization* 421–56.

Axelrod, Robert. 1984. *The Evolution of Cooperation*. New York, NY: Basic Books.

Brewster, Rachel. 2011. 'The Remedy Gap: Institutional Design, Retaliation, and Trade Law Enforcement' 79 *George Washington Law Review* 102–58.

Brewster, Rachel. 2009a. 'Unpacking the State's Reputation' 50 *Harvard International Law Journal* 231–69.

Brewster, Rachel. 2009b. 'The Limits of Reputation on Compliance' 1 *International Theory* 323–33.

Downs, George, and Michael Jones. 2002. 'Reputation, Compliance, and International Law' 31 *Journal of Legal Studies* S95–114.

Ehrlich, Isaac and Richard A. Posner. 1974. 'An Economic Analysis of Legal Rulemaking' 3 *Journal of Legal Studies* 257–86.

Ginsburg, Tom and Richard H. McAdams. 2004. 'Adjudicating in Anarchy: An Expressive Theory of International Dispute Resolution' 45 *William and Mary Law Review* 1229–1339.

Goldsmith, Jack L. and Eric A. Posner. 2005. *The Limits of International Law*. Oxford: Oxford University Press.

Guzman, Andrew T. 2008. *How International Law Works: A Rational Choice Theory*. Oxford: Oxford University Press.

Guzman, Andrew T. 2002. 'The Cost of Credibility: Explaining Resistance to Interstate Dispute Resolution Mechanisms' 31 *Journal of Legal Studies* 303–26.

Guzman, Andrew T. and Timothy L. Meyer. 2009. 'International Common Law: The Soft Law of International Tribunals' 9 *Chicago Journal of International Law* 515–35.

Helfer, Laurence R. and Anne-Marie Slaughter. 2005. 'Why States Create International Tribunals: A Response to Professors Posner and Yoo' 93 *California Law Review* 899–956.

Horn, Hendrik, Giovanni Maggi and Robert W. Staiger. 2010. 'Trade Agreements as Endogenously Incomplete Contracts' 100 *American Economic Review* 394–419.

Kontorovich, Eugene. 2008. 'The Inefficiency of Universal Jurisdiction' 2008 *University of Illinois Law Review* 389–418.

Lipson, Charles. 1991. 'Why Are Some International Agreements Informal?' 45 *International Organization* 495–538.

Mahoney, Paul G. and Chris William Sanchirico. 2003. 'Norms, Repeated Games, and the Role of Law' 91 *California Law Review* 1281–1329.

Mahoney, Paul G. and Chris William Sanchirico. 2001. 'Norms, Competing Norms and Social Evolution: Is the Fittest Norm Efficient?' 149 *University of Pennsylvania Law Review* 2027–62.

Nollkaemper, Andre. 2011. *National Courts and the International Rule of Law*. Oxford: Oxford University Press.

Nzelibe, Jide. 2008. 'The Case Against Reforming the WTO Enforcement Mechanism' 2008 *Illinois Law Review* 319–57.

Posner, Eric A. and Alan O. Sykes. 2011. 'Efficient Breach of International Law: Optimal Remedies, Legalized Noncompliance and Related Issues' 110 *Michigan Law Review* 243.

Posner, Eric A. and John C. Yoo. 2005. 'Judicial Independence in International Tribunals' 93 *California Law Review* 1–74.

Schwartz, Warren F. and Alan O. Sykes. 2002. 'The Economic Structure of Renegotiation and Dispute Resolution in the World Trade Organization' 31 *Journal of Legal Studies* S179–204.

Schelling, Thomas C. 1960. *The Strategy of Conflict*. Cambridge, MA: Harvard University Press.

Schelling, Thomas C. 1956. 'An Essay on Bargaining' 46 *American Economics Review* 281–306.

Scott, Robert E. 2003. 'A Theory of Self-Enforcing Indefinite Agreements, 103 *Columbia Law Review* 1641–99.

Scott, Robert E. and Paul B. Stephan. 2006. *The Limits of Leviathan: Contract Theory and the Enforcement of International Law*. Cambridge: Cambridge University Press.

Scott, Robert E. and Paul B. Stephan. 2004. 'Self-Enforcing International Agreements and the Limits of Coercion' 2004 *Wisconsin Law Review* 551–629.

Scott, Robert E. and George G. Triantis. 2006. 'Anticipating Litigation by Contract Design' 115 *Yale Law Journal* 814–79.

Setear, John K. 1997. 'Responses to Breach of a Treaty and Rationalist International Relations Theory: The Rules of Release and Remediation in the Law of Treaties and the Law of State Responsibility' 83 *Virginia Law Review* 1–126.

Shaffer, Gregory. 2003. *Defending Interests: Public–Private Partnerships in WTO Litigation*. Washington, DC: Brookings Institution Press.

Shavell, Steven. 1993. 'The Optimal Structure of Law Enforcement' 36 *Journal of Law and Economics* 255–87.

Sloss, David L., Michael D. Ramsey and William S. Dodge, eds. 2011. *The U.S. Supreme Court and International Law: Continuity and Change*. Cambridge: Cambridge University Press.

Snidal, Duncan. 1985. 'Coordination versus Prisoners' Dilemma: Implications for International Cooperation and Regimes' 79 *American Political Science Review* 923–42.

Stephan, Paul B. 2011. 'Privatizing International Law' 97 *Virginia Law Review* 1573.

Stephan, Paul B. 2002. 'Courts, Tribunals and Legal Unification – The Agency Problem' 3 *Chicago Journal of International Law* 333–52.

Sykes, Alan O. 2008. 'Transnational Tort Litigation as a Trade and Investment Issue' 37 *Journal of Legal Studies* 339–78.

Sykes, Alan O. 2005. 'Public versus Private Enforcement of International Economic Law: Standing and Remedy' 34 *Journal of Legal Studies* 631–66.

Trachtman, Joel P. and Philip M. Moremen. 2003. 'Costs and Benefits of Private Participation in WTO Dispute Settlement: Whose Right Is It Anyway?' 44 *Harvard International Law Journal* 221–50.

Van Aaken, Anne. 2009. 'International Investment Law between Commitment and Flexibility: A Contract Theory Analysis' 12 *Journal of International Economic Law* 507–38.

8. The interaction between domestic and international law

Tom Ginsburg

INTRODUCTION

The relationship between domestic and international law has been a favorite topic of international lawyers for over a century, and is of increasing political and legal salience (Nijman and Nollkaemper 2007). Yet it has been oddly neglected in much economic scholarship on international law. In part this is because of the enduring legacy of political science realism and its natural affinity with rational choice theory. Realism treated the state as a 'billiard ball' with unitary preferences that were then the subject of negotiation and interaction with other states on the international plane. The leading works on the economics of international law also tend to adopt a simple assumption of a unitary state actor (Goldsmith and Posner 2005; Guzman 2007: 19; Scott and Stephan 2006; Trachtman 2008:18).

While appropriate for many modeling purposes, this approach misses many interesting dynamics that would benefit from more rigorous economic analysis. It is also in tension with the increasing recognition that compliance with international legal norms is typically driven in large part by domestic interests and institutions (Trachtman 2008: 20–1; Simmons 2009). State preferences on the international plane are in part the product of domestic politics and institutions, so that to fully understand international behavior, one must understand domestic structures and preferences. The reverse is also true. As transnational interest groups arise it makes less sense to speak of preferences as wholly domestically constituted. And international institutions can alter the structure of domestic institutions. For example, article 8(a) of the Agreement on Trade-Related Aspects of Intellectual Property Rights (TRIPS) requires nations to create patent filing offices; and article X(3)(b) of the World Trade Organization (WTO) Agreement requires the establishment of 'judicial, arbitral or administrative tribunals or procedures' to review administrative action related to customs matters. These institutions can have domestic spillovers.

This increasingly complex and dense set of interactions calls out for rigorous analysis. Yet we have relatively little work in law and economics that tackles the problem of interactions among multiple levels of law-making authority and enforcement at the international level. Voigt and Salzberger (2002), in a foundational contribution, argued for treating international and domestic delegation in the same framework, but few others have followed their line of work. This chapter surveys the literature and provides some examples of the way in which considering both the international and domestic legal levels in the same framework can provide analytic payoff.

The chapter is organized as follows. Part I introduces the idea of nested jurisdictions as a framework for understanding the interaction of domestic and international law. It considers the functions of domestic and international law in providing public goods, resolving commitment problems and dealing with agency costs. Part II discusses whether international and domestic institutions play complementary or substitute roles, and describes domestic norm convergence as a product of international interaction. Part III considers the impact of international norms on domestic political structures. The conclusion brings the two strands together under the rubric of nested jurisdictions.

I. NESTED JURISDICTIONS, COMMITMENT AND AGENCY COSTS

The interaction between domestic and international law can be considered part of a general species of problems of nested jurisdictions. The old paradigm of international law was one of intergovernmentalism, in which a discrete number of state actors concluded agreements for limited purposes of mutual benefit. In the increasingly integrated world, every jurisdiction is embedded in many broader regimes or orders through treaty commitments, membership in international organizations, and interactions with allies and other states. In this sense the relationship between a nation state and international structures bears a qualitative similarity to that of a sub-state in a federalism, except that each state on the international plane has an individually tailored set of commitments.

Problems of nested jurisdictions vary along certain dimensions, chief among them scope and depth. In some cases the superior jurisdiction will be multi-dimensional, in other cases it might concern only a single purpose. We call this the dimension of scope. Contrast, for example, the European Union regime, which covers a broad range of topics in a linked set of agreements, with a single-purpose convention such as the Land Mines treaty or a bilateral investment treaty. Another dimension is depth: in some cases the superior jurisdiction may reach deeply into the legal order of the inferior jurisdiction, while in others it will be shallow. The United Nations Charter preserves an explicitly dualist structure, without directly affecting local actors. In contrast, the less high-profile International Centre for Settlement of Investment Disputes (ICSID) regime displaces domestic legal jurisdiction over an important class of disputes. Table 8.1 illustrates the possible configurations

Table 8.1 Possible configurations

	Broad	Narrow
Shallow	United Nations Treaty	Land Mines Convention
Deep	European Union treaty; sub-state in a federalism; WTO	Bilateral investment treaty regime; ICSID

What determines the particular set of commitments of a state? There are three core economic functions that might be played by the allocation of powers to different levels of government: the generation of public goods at the appropriate level to benefit from economies of scale; the resolution of commitment problems; and the reduction of agency costs.

A. Public Goods

One economic perspective on these issues is to treat the hierarchy of jurisdictions as resulting from a process of exchange to generate public goods for citizens. Traditional international law conceives of sovereignty as a unitary quality of states, which they either have or do not have. But in fact, all states have a spectrum of sovereign control, exercising more practical autonomy in some areas and less in others. Weak states may be happy to delegate aspects of their governmental function to other states or to international regimes in order to provide public goods for their citizens and to compensate for internal weaknesses. Military alliances supplement purely local provision of national defense and help ensure territorial integrity; and trade agreements provide market access for domestic goods and services. A state that does not fully control the means of coercion, the provision of infrastructure, or the generation of information for its own use will have an incentive to turn to the international plane to contract for these services.

Beyond these local public goods, there may be particular public goods that are produced at the bilateral, regional or even global levels. The need for environmental protection, for example, does not typically correspond to state borders. Neighboring states may have an incentive to produce negative externalities that lead to the demand for more international cooperation. Because states vary in their preferences for public goods and their ability to generate them through international cooperation, they will have different propensities to cooperate. However, we should generally expect a trend toward demand for deeper cooperation as global interdependence increases. There may be network effects associated with particular regimes, so that the benefits rise with the number of members: trade is an obvious example here. Furthermore, there may be a reduction in the transaction costs of negotiating agreements as states interact more frequently. Ideally, we would have a perfectly functional allocation of institutional structures to produce the optimal bundle of public goods, though of course free-rider problems among states and agency problems among government officials may not produce this configuration in reality.

B. Commitment

A second function of allocating powers to different levels is commitment. Because international law binds states, rather than governments, and limits the options of policymakers, it can serve as a commitment device, even for the generation of purely local public goods. One can view the delegation of lawmaking to the international community as a device in which politicians entrench their particular policies against domestic preference shifts. From this perspective, demand for international delegation will itself be a product, in part, of internal constitutional arrangements that incentivize politicians (Scott and Stephan 2006). We might imagine, for example, that democracies would have greater demand for international cooperation than dictatorships because of the need for credibility, given that democratic leaders will certainly leave power after some time.

Of course, a long tradition has analyzed domestic constitutional arrangements, including the separation of powers, as commitment devices (Holmes 1995: 135; Sunstein 2001: 241; von Hayek 1960: 179; Pritchard and Zywicki 1999: 447–9; Boudreaux and Pritchard 1993). When Congress and the President must cooperate to make new law, over-turning prior outcomes is difficult, enhancing the value of those earlier bargains. Commitment can also be obtained through assignment of power to internal actors such as bureaucrats or an independent judiciary. By delegating authority to insulated actors, such as to a central bank or independent regulatory agencies, the legislature and executive can ensure that their policies will be safe from partisan tinkering long after the particular parties to the original bargain are out of office.

From a commitment perspective, international delegation would seem to have significant advantages relative to assigning powers to an independent judiciary, or specialized independent regulatory agencies. Independent regulatory commissions and national judiciaries are well and good, but a party cannot credibly promise *never* to interfere with them. A party that wins overwhelming support in a national political process over an extended period of time will be able to influence the composition of independent regulators and courts. In contrast, international agencies are more difficult for any single nation to control. Only a handful of countries are in a position to unilaterally influence outcomes on any issue at all, and no country, even the United States, can *dictate* outcomes confidently, consistently or cheaply. Thus international delegations may have more value in signaling commitment.

In addition, international delegations *may* be more enduring. Because international commitments are made by states rather than governments, embodying obligations in treaties is one way to ensure their survival past the current government. Indeed, the doctrine of state succession means that commitments may outlast not only the current government, but even the dissolution of the state itself.[1] Endurance should enhance credibility, and international delegation should enhance endurance. To be sure, the point about endurance is not certain. International delegation requires ongoing consent of the state-principal doing the delegating. As a formal matter, states are nearly always free to withdraw delegations they made at an earlier period. Most international obligations are still based in the theory of state consent, and consent, of course, can be withdrawn at any time. This means that, so long as withdrawal costs are not too high, exit is possible. So long as they do not formally withdraw, the obligations will be quite enduring. But states may have a difficult time committing not to withdraw (Epstein and O'Halloran 2008). We have several prominent examples of states exiting international arrangements (Helfer 2002;

---

1 *Gabcikovo-Nagymaros Project* (*Hung.* v. *Slov.*), 1997 I.C.J. 7 (September 25).

2005).[2] Furthermore, the possibility of simply ignoring the international obligation is always present. Though such behavior may have some costs, it may also be beneficial in terms of the domestic political calculus.

Consider the contrast with domestic delegation. Once a government sets up an agency, it will likely incentivize the development of regime-specific interest groups that will fight to maintain the regulatory status quo. But history is also littered with 'exited' international organizations. North Korea exited the Nuclear Non-Proliferation Treaty when it was unhappy with inspections; the United States and France exited from the compulsory jurisdiction of the International Court of Justice when faced with unfavorable decisions. To be sure, some international delegations such as the WTO are effectively irreversible, where the network benefits of the international organization essentially lock in the delegation of power (Guzman and Landsidle 2008). But even some organizations once thought to be impossible to exit, like the European Union, now appear a little less secure.

Exit is thus easier in the international arena, as a general matter, than on the domestic plane. This is appropriate, in part because exogenous change is more likely at the international level, in which persistent uncertainty is the only constant. The variation in conditions over time means that it is difficult to determine in advance the costs that will be associated from violating an international obligation. Some of these costs depend on other states voluntarily punishing the violating state through bilateral retaliation or third-party reputational sanctions. These decisions will be made in accordance with the particular political situation of the potential enforcer at the time of violation, as well as the relative power of the violator. From the point of view of a domestic interest group seeking to entrench its policies in international obligations, this reduces the certainty of an externally imposed cost.

---

[2] Indonesia withdrew from the United Nations in 1965 in response to the seating of Malaysia in the Security Council, rejoining some 15 months later. The United States and United Kingdom withdrew from UNESCO in 1984, rejoining in 2002 and 1997 respectively after reforms to the organization (Helfer 2005). Caribbean nations withdrew from the jurisdiction of the Privy Council in response to decisions on the death penalty (Helfer 2002). The United States withdrew from optional clause jurisdiction of the International Court of Justice after the adverse decision in the *Nicaragua* Case. See *United States: Statement on the U.S. Withdrawal from the Proceedings Initiated by Nicaragua in the International Court of Justice*, January 18, 1995, 24 I.L.M. 246. More recently, it withdrew from the Optional Protocol to the Vienna Convention on Consular Relations concerning the Compulsory Settlement of Disputes, 596 U.N.T.S. 487 (1963).

Still, exit may not be practicable in every instance. As Brewster (2004) points out, exit is an all-or-nothing proposition. Complex multilateral treaties involve lots of different issues, so that withdrawal will affect many different groups and impose many costs. Network effects may also put exit out of reach as a practical matter. The multi-sectoral, networked nature of the WTO, for example, likely prevents exit from being a real threat. For some international delegations, then, there will be conditions that prevent exit and enhance entrenchment, even if exit on the international plane is easier on the whole.

Available empirical evidence is consistent with the idea that international delegation provides effective commitment in some areas. Dreher and Voigt (2008) show that countries which are members of more international organizations have better risk ratings than those with less. He suggests that the key factor is that international organizations provide increased credibility, relative to domestic commitment devices. Assuming for the moment that all countries have the same domestic commitment technologies available to them, more or less, credibility is enhanced chiefly by international delegation. Ginsburg (2006) shows that new democracies, which may be in particular need of effective commitment devices, are particularly willing to delegate the lawmaking function to the international community as a constitutional matter, for example by incorporating specific treaties or customary international law into the domestic constitution.

Commitment is a standard explanation for international trade agreements. For example, Maggi and Rodríguez-Clare (2007) argue that governments sign trade agreements in order to make credible commitments vis-à-vis domestic interest groups. Trade agreements tie the hands of governments, thus helping them to avoid protectionist demands from particular interest groups. This enhances overall national welfare. Some empirical evidence supports this view (Maggi and Rodríguez-Clare 2007: 1374).

Note that states are differently situated in their ability to make commitments, as well as their demand for commitment. Martin (2005) points out that the relative difficulty of making treaties in the United States implies that the obligations, once entered into, are likely to be seen as very strong signals of future policy. Many actors must agree to ensure the passage of a treaty. Countries with easier treaty-making processes in contrast will have less difficulty entering into international agreements, but the signal of their commitment will be correspondingly less strong. Understanding the tradeoff between strength and frequency of commitments is an area for further inquiry.

C. Agency Costs

A third economic function of international law from the point of view of a national sovereign is the reduction of agency costs. Agency costs arise whenever an official hired to undertake a particular task fails to exert full effort to achieve it, or instead acts on her own behalf. While domestic structures such as an independent judiciary and a vigorous administrative law regime can reduce agency costs, international organizations can also provide monitoring and discipline of domestic agents. One might think of the international human rights machinery, for example, as a device to ensure that government agents do not abuse their citizens. The international institutions can both incentivize better behavior on the part of state actors through carrots and sticks, as well as provide information about the quality of state actors for domestic actors to utilize in their own enforcement efforts.

To be sure, international delegation raises new agency problems. International delegation has commitment value precisely *because* agents will be insulated from the immediate control of the principal. Agency costs are the flip side of commitment and can dominate the benefits of credibility in some cases. International bodies by definition have multiple principals, a feature associated with greater slack in principal–agent theory (McCubbins, Noll and Weingast 1987; 1989). More generally, the chain of delegation is by definition longer to the international sphere than to the domestic one. In the domestic sphere, citizen-principals delegate to politician-agents, who in turn delegate to expert bureaucracies and courts. In the international sphere, citizen-principals delegate to politician-agents who delegate to an association of states parties who in turn assign tasks to international bureaucrats. In other instances, the delegation to an international organization is conducted by domestic bureaucrats. In either case, there is at least one extra step in the chain of delegations; *ceteris paribus*, longer delegation chains mean greater agency problems.

Another consideration is the presence of third parties to monitor *international* agency slack. In the domestic sphere, interest groups organize around agencies to monitor their behavior and provide information to legislative principals. It seems likely that as a general matter, there are fewer third parties willing and able to monitor international agents, for the costs of doing so may be higher and the organization of such monitors is subject to complex cross-border collective action problems.

D. Summary

In short, international legal arrangements can help to provide for public goods at an appropriate level. They can also serve to reduce agency costs and to serve as effective commitment devices. But there are tradeoffs across domestic and international delegation. International delegation generally involves a greater release of control, enhancing commitment, but also generating new agency costs. These features directly affect the value of the delegation as a commitment device. On the other hand, the costs of exit on the international plane may in fact be lower, depending on the issue area and network quality of the public goods created through the delegation. On the whole, internationalization involves tradeoffs, but has significant potential to help states obtain political goods that are unavailable domestically.

II. INTERACTIONS: SUBSTITUTES, COMPLEMENTS AND DUPLICATES

So far we have examined features of the two levels of delegation as being essentially substitutes, so that adoption of a rule or institution at the international level would reduce or obviate the need to adopt it at another level. This could be because such adoption at a second level would be redundant or unnecessary. Consider, for example, the regulation of foreign investment (Ginsburg 2005). When domestic law and courts are seen as potentially biased, foreign investors demand that investment be regulated by stand-alone bilateral investment treaties (see Guzman 1998). If investors are satisfied with the international machinery, they will not be concerned with domestic structures.

One might alternatively imagine that international delegation plays a largely *complementary* role for national level actors. For example, international instruments may specify goals with greater precision than local law; they may provide for supplementary enforcement beyond the boundary of the nation state, by actors less likely to be locally captured or influenced; and they may communicate a kind of authority to convince skeptical local actors that rights are indeed universal. International norms may also constitute a signal to the international (and domestic) community that the state is indeed a 'good type' likely to comply with limits on its power. For these functions, the national level reinforces an international obligation by promising domestic articulation and enforcement of norms.

In the context of human rights, Gardbaum (2008) argues that the international level can provide gap-filling and supplementary rules for the domestic constitutional level. These supplements can be substantive in character; they may be geographic (reaching parts of the territory not obviously covered by domestic regulation, such as Guantanamo); or they may be personal, in the sense of providing coverage to those who might not otherwise be protected domestically, such as immigrants and aliens. Supplements might be institutional as well. International bodies can provide precise definitions of rights violations for domestic actors, particularly in new states or new democracies without much experience in rights enforcement. Also, international agreements provide an easy way to 'modernize' a state's own rights infrastructure without the sometimes steep costs of undergoing constitutional revision. To the extent that rights serve as signals, enshrining them in both international and domestic instruments might influence the intensity of the signal, and so the two levels would supplement each other.

Another role that international instruments can play is one of coordination (Goldsmith and Posner 2005). Suppose states agree in general that a particular norm is important, but are unlikely to agree on the definition of the norm, and thus unable to cooperate. International instruments can play a role in communicating information to national actors about the perceptions of *other* states in this regard.

Another possible relationship between international and domestic law is duplication. Here, a state might be willing to accede to an international instrument because it entails no further obligations than already incurred under the domestic legal order. The international agreement becomes a kind of cheap talk. Alternatively, a state that is party to an international covenant might add a similar set of rights to the domestic constitution because it is not very costly to do so. Theories of human rights accession that assert that ratification is costless seem to imply that duplication is one possible outcome (Hathaway 2002; but see Simmons 2009).

The game theoretic notion of a pooling equilibrium captures the idea that all players have an incentive to send the same signal. This may be particularly true in the case of costless signals, or cheap talk. In the context of international human rights agreements, for example, we might expect most or all states to seek to accede, and we do of course have examples of nearly universal treaties, such as that on the Rights of the Child. These treaties, with relatively weak enforcement provisions, produce nominal convergence at the level of norms, if not practice.

A signaling theory of law (Ahdieh 2004) also implies convergence of domestic norms under some conditions. We thus might expect that there would be convergence of norms both within levels of jurisdictions, as well as across jurisdictions if players have incentives to send the signal through multiple channels simultaneously. This notion relies on an assumption that more channels indicates more serious commitment. A large literature on policy diffusion has documented the possibility of norm cascades, in which states converge on a set of norms. The international level can play a critical role as a transmission device for diffusion of norms (Elkins, Ginsburg and Simmons, 2013).

Another complementary function of the two levels is of enforcement. A growing number of empirical studies have begun to document how, if at all, the globalization of legal norms has affected actual practices on the ground. On the one hand, some studies have been skeptical that constitutional rights (Keith 2002) or the ratification of human rights treaties (Hathaway 2002; Hafner-Burton and Tsutsui 2005) translate directly into better human rights practices. On the other hand, new research suggests that treaties are quite effective instruments for rights improvements when there is the opportunity for political and or legal mobilization to demand effective implementation (Simmons 2009). Sandholtz (2012) finds that international treaty ratification has a positive impact on rights protection when it is accompanied by judicial independence of the domestic courts.

To summarize, from an economic perspective international and domestic delegation serve to resolve similar problems for governments. They both facilitate the generation of public goods. They both provide for mechanisms to make credible commitments and to reduce agency costs. But they have different features that might make them more or less desirable in particular contexts, for particular kinds of countries. While the configuration of institutions within nested jurisdictions is complicated, economic theory provides a way of making some sense of it.

III. INTERACTIONS: SHIFTS IN INTERNAL SEPARATION OF POWERS

We have hinted that internal state constitutional structure can affect a state's need for and ability to accede to international obligations. It is worth considering the reverse relationship as well. The availability of international devices can have an impact on the internal balance of powers domestically. International delegation may at times be utilized strategically by particular actors seeking to escape domestic constraints on their power.

The most obvious way in which the availability of international options can affect the internal balance of powers is through agenda setting. It is typically the executive that has the power to set the agenda for negotiating international obligations, and this allows the executive to gain leverage vis-à-vis the domestic legislature and other branches. Indeed, in some areas, the executive may have unilateral ability to bind the state, which of course provides a good deal of leverage over other actors (Moe and Howell 1999). In a similar vein, Slaughter (2003) has argued that transnational networks of bureaucrats are able to gain policymaking power through their interaction.

International commitment devices also allow national actors to bypass internal constraints of a federal nature. In the famous case of *Missouri v. Holland,* the US Supreme Court held that the federal government could conclude a treaty with Canada and Britain regulating the hunting of migratory birds.[3] Previously, Congress had attempted to pass similar rules by statute, only to be told by a lower court that it had no power to do so under the enumerated powers of the Constitution. Congress then authorized the conclusion of a treaty accomplishing virtually the same policy, and the US Supreme Court upheld it, holding that the federal government can accomplish by treaty what it cannot by statute, and that such treaties will bind states under the Supremacy Clause (Spiro 2000; Bradley 1998; Golove 2000).

It is not only the national government that can leverage international norms to enhance its power. Local and state level governments, as well, have the ability to implement international norms, rely on unratified treaties, and engage in international exchanges that effectively enhance their power and flexibility (Wexler 2006).

The literature is somewhat divided on the effect of international delegation on judicial power in liberal democracies. On the one hand, international delegation may lead courts to be more deferential if they have adopted notions of executive supremacy in foreign affairs.[4] On the other hand, Eyal Benvenisti and George Downs (2009) interpret the recent trend in democracies toward judicial constraint of executives in foreign affairs matters in light of the broader context of inter-judicial cooperation and globalization. Many scholars have asserted that judges are increasingly reading each other's opinions, and some have argued that judges are more likely to cite international law. If true, these judges are producing a new, transnationally generated corpus of material to justify particular outcomes. Benvenisti and Downs argue that courts are increasingly using transnational communication to coordinate across borders to

---

3 252 U.S. 416 (1920).

4 *US v. Curtiss-Wright*, 299 U.S. 304 (1936).

constrain their national executives. This requires resolution of a transnational collective action problem among judges. Transnational dialogue and globalization, in their view, empowers courts over executives. This view, however, assumes that judges have enough interest in their epistemic community to engage in such collective action. Moreover, the mechanism by which 'dialogue' genuinely constrains is unclear (Ginsburg 2010).

In short, the availability of the 'outside options' afforded by international law changes the structure of government within states. This might involve a shift of power from the local to the center, or vice-versa; it generally empowers the executive; and its effect on judicial power is quite contested. What is beyond dispute, however, is that the structure of domestic law is affected by the international level.

CONCLUSION

The nesting of jurisdictions implies interaction between multiple levels of government. While traditional nesting relationships could be divided into two basic types, a deep integration of national federalism and a shallow integration of international law, that dichotomy makes less sense as the number and depth of international commitments expand dramatically. Even a state that purports to guard its national sovereignty jealously will have many areas of law that are beyond its effective control. The content of norms increasingly comes from abroad, even as the international norms themselves sometimes reflect the influence of particular powerful states.

From the point of view of a nation state, international delegation makes a good deal of sense, both as a substitute for domestic delegation, but also as a complement. International delegation has certain features, including longer time horizons, possible network effects, and relatively disinterested actors that may make it particularly attractive as a commitment device for certain kinds of problems. At the same time, it has certain weaknesses that may exacerbate agency costs. Stipulating the tradeoffs among these various considerations may get us closer to a theory of the observed interaction of domestic and international law.

REFERENCES

Ahdieh, Robert B. 2004. 'Law's Signal: A Cueing Theory of Law in Market Transition' 77 *Southern California Law Review* 215.

Benvenisti, Eyal and George Downs. 2009. 'National Courts, Domestic Democracy, and the Evolution of International Law' 20 *European Journal of International Law* 59.

Bourdreaux, Donald J. and Adam C. Pritchard. 1993. 'Rewriting the Constitution: An Economic Analysis of the Constitutional Amendment Process' 62 *Fordham Law Review* 111.

Bradley, Curtis A. 1998. 'The Treaty Power and American Federalism' 97 *Michigan Law Review* 390.

Brewster, Rachel. 2004. 'The Domestic Origins of International Agreements' 44 *Virginia Journal of International Law* 501–44.

Dreher, Axel and Stefan Voigt. 2008. 'Does Membership in International Organizations Increase Governments' Credibility? Testing the Effects of Delegating Powers' CESifo Working Paper Series 2285, CESifo Group Munich.

Elkins, Zachary, Tom Ginsburg and Beth Simmons. 2013. 'Getting to Rights: Treaty Ratification, Constitutional Convergence, and Human Rights Practice' 54 *Harvard International Law Journal* 61–94.

Epstein, David L. and Sharyn O'Halloran. 2008. 'The Paradox of Retrogression in the New VRA: Comment on Persily' 117 *Yale Law Journal Pocket Part* 245.

Gardbaum, Stephen. 2008. 'Human Rights as International Constitutional Rights' 19:4 *European of Journal International Law* 749–68.

Ginsburg, Tom. 2010. 'National Courts, Domestic Democracy, and the Evolution of International Law: A Reply to Eyal Benvenisti and George Downs' 20:4 *European Journal of International Law* 1021–6.

Ginsburg, Tom. 2006. 'Locking in Democracy: Constitutions, Commitment and International Law' 38 *NYU Journal of International Law and Politics* 707–59.

Ginsbury. Tom. 2005. 'The Regulation of Regulation' in Eddy Wymersch, Hideki Kanda, Harald Baum and Klaus Hopt. (eds.). *Corporate Governance in Context: Corporations, States and Markets in Europe, Japan and the U.S.* Oxford: Oxford University Press, 321–38.

Goldsmith, Jack and Eric Posner. 2005. *The Limits of International Law.* New York, NY: Oxford University Press.

Golove, David M. 2000. 'Treaty-Making and the Nation: The Historical Foundations of the Nationalist Conception of the Treaty Power' 98 *Michigan Law Review* 1075.

Guzman, Andrew T. 2007. *How International Law Works: A Rational Choice Theory.* New York, NY: Oxford University Press.

Guzman, Andrew T. 1998. 'Why LDCs Sign Treaties That Hurt Them: Explaining the Popularity of Bilateral Investment Treaties' 38 *Virginia Journal of International Law* 639.

Guzman, Andrew T. and Jennifer Landsidle. 2008. 'The Myth of International Delegation' 96 *California Law Review* 1693.

Hafner-Burton, Emilie M. and Kiyoteru Tsutsui. 2005. 'Human Rights in a Globalizing World: The Paradox of Empty Promises' 110:5 (March) *American Journal of Sociology* 1373–1411.

Hathaway, Oona. 2002. 'Do Human Rights Treaties Make a Difference?' 111:8 *Yale Law Journal* 1935–2042.

Helfer, Laurence R. 2005. 'Exiting Treaties' 91 *Virginia Law Review* 1579.

Helfer, Laurence R. 2002. 'Overlegalizing Human Rights: International Relations Theory and the Commonwealth Caribbean Backlash Against Human Rights Regimes' 102 *Columbia Law Review* 1832.

Holmes, Stephen. 1995. *Passion and Constraint: On the Theory of Liberal Democracy.* Chicago, IL: Chicago University Press.

Keith, Linda Camp. 2002. 'Constitutional Provisions for Individual Human Rights (1977–1996): Are They More Than Mere "Window Dressing?"' 55:1 *Political Research Quarterly* 111–43.

Maggi, Giovanni and Andrés Rodríguez-Clare. 2007. 'A Political-Economy Theory of Trade Agreements' 97 *American Economic Review* 1374.

Martin, Lisa L. 2005. 'The United States and International Commitments: Treaties as Signaling Devices' 35 *Presidential Studies Quarterly* 440.

McCubbins. M. D., R. G. Noll and B. R. Weingast. 1989. 'Structure and Process, Politics and Policy' 75 *Virginia Law Review*, 431–82.

McCubbins, M. D., R. G. Noll and B. R. Weingast. 1987. 'Administrative Procedures as Instruments of Political Control' 3 *Journal of Law, Economics, and Organization*, 243–77.

Moe, Terry M. and William G. Howell. 1999. 'The Presidential Power of Unilateral Action' 15 *Journal of Law, Economics and Organization* 132.

Nijman, Janne, and André Nollkaemper (eds.). 2007. *New Perspectives on the Divide Between National and International Law.* Oxford: Oxford University Press.

Pritchard, Adam C., and Todd J. Zywicki. 1999. 'Finding the Constitution: An Economic Analysis of Tradition's Role in Constitutional Interpretation' 77:2 *North Carolina Law Review* 409–521.

Sandholtz, Wayne. 2012. 'Treaties, Constitutions, Courts, and Human Rights', 11:1 *Journal of Human Rights* 1732.

Scott, Robert E. and Paul B. Stephan. 2006. *The Limits of Leviathan: Contract Theory and the Enforcement of International Law.* Cambridge: Cambridge University Press.

Simmons, Beth A. 2009. *Mobilizing for Human Rights: International Law in Domestic Politics.* Cambridge: Cambridge University Press.

Slaughter, Anne Marie. 2003. *The New World Order.* Princeton, NJ: Princeton University Press.

Spiro, Peter. 2000. 'Missouri v. Holland: Besides the Point?' 19 *American Society for International Law Proceedings* 140.

Sunstein, Cass R. 2001. *Republic.com.* Princeton, NJ: Princeton University Press.

Trachtman, Joel P. 2008. 'International Economic Law Research: A Taxonomy', in Colin Picker, Isabella Bunn and Douglas W. Arner (eds.). *International Economic Law: The State and Future of the Discipline*. Oxford: Hart Publishing.

Voigt, Stefan and Eli Salzberger. 2002. 'Choosing Not to Choose: When Politicians Choose to Delegate Powers' 55 *Kyklos* 281–310.

von Hayek, Friederich A. 1960. *The Constitution of Liberty.* Chicago, IL: Chicago University Press.

Wexler, Lesley. 2006. 'Take the Long Way Home: Sub-Federal Integration of Unratified and Non-Self-Executing Treaty Law' 28 *Michigan Journal of International Law* 1.

PART IV

Applications and Extensions

9. Atrocity, policy, and the laws of war: what does political science have to say to law?

James D. Morrow*

Over the last decade and a half, political scientists have turned their attention to the study of the progress of war as a political event. States at war change their strategies to improve their chances of winning. The outcomes of battles shift the bargaining power of the warring parties and whether they are willing to continue fighting. Failing efforts on the battlefield can lead countries to change leaders. Third parties intervene in ongoing wars in an effort to shift the course of the war. And, relevant to international law, states sometimes engage in atrocities in their efforts to win.

When do states, their militaries, and rebel groups engage in acts that violate international agreements to restrict the scope of violence during wartime? I develop two primary arguments: one concerning the strategic advantages gained through atrocities or restraint, and two, how militaries develop internal mechanisms of discipline and control. The first argument concerns how the leadership of states and rebel groups view the consequences of violations for their efforts to prevail in battle and realize their war aims. The second argument addresses how that leadership controls their soldiers on the battlefield, whether they seek to limit atrocities or encourage them. Of course, these two causes of atrocious violence can be linked in practice: an army that wishes to use atrocities to intimidate its opponents may encourage them by failing to discipline soldiers that commit crimes.

Law shapes both of these arguments. Law can define what acts are violations and the consequences of those acts. It aids leaders in anticipating how those they are at war with will respond to possible violations.

* I would like to thank John Ciorciari, Monica Hakimi, Eugene Kontorovich, Steve Ratner and Allan Stam for their comments on a draft of this chapter.

Law provides guidance in developing codes of conduct for soldiers in addition to specifying the rights and responsibilities of the combatant on the battlefield.

This chapter develops these two arguments, and how law can influence warring parties away from atrocities and toward restraint, in interstate and civil wars. The two causes of atrocities, strategic advantage and lack of control, occur in different forms in these different types of wars. The two types of wars also pose different issues for restraint in combat. States at war with one another have a wider range of weapons, including those deemed as outside the bounds of decency, than most rebel groups.

Political scientists think about the issues posed by the laws of war differently than lawyers do. Law focuses first on how the principles of law are applied to individual cases and then what those principles should be. Political science focuses on state policy, how those policies affect whether violations occur, and what drives those choices of policy. Political science is less concerned with individual violations and more on patterns of violations. The difference between the two approaches to the subject are less stark than I am drawing them: certainly, lawyers care about state policy and broad patterns of compliance and violation of law, and political scientists care about the law of war because of the human suffering caused by violations of it. Further, some in both fields work in the area between the two. Indeed, one of the central questions I explore here is how treaty law shapes state behavior, which requires understanding the principles of the law and how they apply during wartime.

INTERSTATE WARS

Political scientists who study war have focused more of their attention on interstate wars – those between two recognized states – than other types of wars. Interstate wars are easier to study as a clear difference between war and peace is easier to find in most interstate conflicts, the parties are easier to identify, and it is easier to collect information on them. Civil wars are often chaotic with violence that rises then recedes, with rebel groups that grow then fracture and whose exact strength is difficult to determine. Other forms of war, such as the colonial wars fought by the European states first to build their empires in the nineteenth century and then to retain them in the middle of the twentieth century, pose the same problems for study that civil wars do. Additionally, the nature of combat between interstate wars and those fought against non-state parties often differs. Interstate wars are generally fought between formed armies with recognized and limited combat zones, such as a front line, even though the combat zone may move. Other wars are often fought by irregulars, who move among a civilian population and spread the combat zone to wide areas where combat is possible at any time. Of course, there are contrary examples to these generalities, guerrilla interstate wars and conventional civil wars. Both of these features of interstate wars simplify the problem of controlling violence in accord with the laws of war. Additionally, the status of the law in the conflict can be determined from whether the warring states have ratified the relevant treaties.

A first view of the question of state conduct during war is that nothing binds states from doing whatever it takes to win. Arreguín-Toft (2001; 2005) argues that states use barbarism – by which he defines as 'the deliberate or systematic harm of non-combatants in pursuit of a military or political objective' (Arreguín-Toft 2005: 31) to prevail in asymmetric conflicts. When weak parties face militarily powerful states, they cannot hope to win a direct, conventional conflict. Instead, they need to turn to guerrilla strategies where they can frustrate the military advantages of the stronger party. If the stronger, conventional state tries to fight a guerrilla war with a conventional strategy by seeking to defeat the enemy forces in combat, the weaker side has a better chance of winning. Each side has a direct strategy aimed at the enemy forces and an indirect strategy aimed at defeating the will of the enemy (Arreguín-Toft 2005 does recognize that other strategies are possible). When those strategies match – direct attack against conventional defense or barbarism versus guerrilla war – the strength of the larger party prevails. When they differ, the weak party can compensate for its strength disadvantage and win. Barbarism is the winning strategy when a weaker defender will not stand up and fight. Legal restraint under those circumstances is a fool's game.

Beyond moral objections, this argument is less than convincing. Arreguín-Toft (2001; 2005) presents a comparison across many wars and several case studies to support his argument. The definition of barbarism is flexible, with little idea how extensive violations must be to qualify as barbarism. His comparison across wars includes interstate, colonial and civil wars but excludes symmetric wars such as the World Wars if the weaker side was at least one-fifth the strength of the stronger. It is unclear how he judged the colonial and civil wars as asymmetric because the Correlates of War data on war he used does not give the military capabilities of non-state groups. The deeper problem here is conceptual: if matching strategies is better for the stronger side, why does the stronger side ever adopt a direct, conventional strategy against a weaker opponent using a guerrilla strategy? Arreguín-Toft offers some plausible explanations, such as imitation of successful direct strategies in more even wars or unwillingness to engage in barbarism. Further, if the choice of strategy is a matching problem, where the stronger side wishes to match while the weaker wishes to ensure they adopt different strategies, the sides should change strategies frequently in an effort to produce the combination that favors them. Arreguín-Toft's case study of Vietnam shows both sides changing strategies, but only once each over the period of years. Later in the section on civil wars, I return to the question of whether restraint helps or hinders efforts to defeat an insurgency.

Interstate wars are generally fought conventionally rather than with guerrilla tactics, except for partisan warfare in zones controlled by the enemy. Some of these conventional campaigns end quickly, while others turn into indecisive, protracted wars. Protracted wars could provide the reason to break the rules. Raise the other side's costs of continuing the fight, and you may be able to break their will. Downes (2007; 2008) argues that states adopt policies that kill enemy civilians either to end a protracted war or to clear territory which the state wishes to annex. The costs of protracted war encourage the killing of enemy civilians to limit one's own losses. Provocatively, Downes argues that democracies are more likely to adopt policies that deliberately kill enemy civilians than autocracies. The human costs of war weigh more heavily in a democracy because their leaders eventually must answer to their voters, whose sons, brothers, and husbands may be dying in an endless, bloody war. Downes collected data on numbers of civilians killed during interstate wars, showing that democracies kill more enemy civilians on average, particularly when they are fighting a war of attrition. He supports these statistical results with case studies of the British blockade of Germany during World War I and the Allied bombings of Germany and Japan as well as shorter studies of cases where civilians were not victimized, particularly the Gulf War in 1991. Valentino et al. (2006) similarly argue and find that the strategic conditions of the war drives levels of deliberate killing of civilians. They also find that neither democracy, ratification of the Hague or Geneva Conventions, depending on time period, nor the combination of the two have a statistically discernable effect on the numbers of civilians killed. Similar to Arreguín-Toft's argument about the instrumental uses of barbarism, these arguments claim that the necessities of war drive states to adopt policies that kill civilians. Perhaps crime pays.

Others focus on how normative restraint could arise. Price (1997) argues that a taboo has grown up around the use of chemical weapons, making it impossible to imagine using them. Price's primary concern is how people came to understand that it was unthinkable to use chemical weapons, at least by the leading countries in the international system. He is less concerned with the cases where such weapons were used.

The explanations examined so far do not address how militaries might be able to control their own soldiers, they assert that violations result directly from state policy. Legro (1995) focuses on how the ways armies think they should fight influence their willingness to follow norms of good conduct when they fight. Military culture is the organizational culture of a military. Organizations have cultures that explain how they are run inside and how they deal with outside forces. Culture is a set of shared beliefs across the members of the organization that defines what an organization should do and how it should do it. Although these beliefs help the organization coordinate the efforts of their members, they may not be efficient in the sense that organizations facing the same external environment could have different cultures. Militaries as organizations need these beliefs about how they should fight to prepare for combat through training and planning. Military culture persists in part because it is valuable to the organization and in part because even war produces mixed signals about the most effective ways to fight (Legro 1995: 17–29).

Military culture, in this view, determines whether states comply with norms of restraint in combat. When those norms accord with their culture, a military will follow the prescriptions of the norms to the best of their ability. When they clash, a military will follow their culture and violate the norms. Legro examines the issues of submarine warfare, strategic bombing, and chemical weapons and concludes that military culture accounts for compliance or the lack thereof between Germany and Britain on these three issues. Germany, for example, was reluctant to escalate to strategic bombing against Britain because the military culture of the Luftwaffe emphasized close support rather than strategic bombing; and Britain escalated because the Royal Air Force saw strategic bombing as the way it could contribute to winning the war (Legro 1995: 94–143).

Law plays little direct role in any of these explanations for atrocities during wartime. Law does not restrain barbarism according to Arreguín-Toft, nor does it limit the willingness of states to kill enemy civilians according to Downes. For Price and Legro, normative restraint rather than law is key. Consequently, none of these authors examines treaty language or whether the states in question were bound to observe those treaties through ratification. Valentino et al. (2006) assess legal obligations under the Hague Conventions as joint ratification because those treaties bound only when both sides had ratified, while the 1949 Geneva Conventions are unilaterally binding, obligating ratifying states regardless of what the other side does. Valentino et al.'s (2006) coefficients for treaty status and regime type are not statistically significant, but their estimated substantive effects are large.[1] Further, these studies do not attempt the difficult task of assessing whether the policies that killed civilians could be legally justified through military necessity or proportionality. On this line, these studies do not assess whether killing civilians works, whether it leads to victory, shortens wars, or limits the casualties of the side doing the killing. Finding the effects of law on state behavior requires understanding where to look for its effects.

Morrow (2002; 2007; 2014) presents a theory of the laws of war and tests it against the record of compliance with it during interstate wars of the twentieth century. The two views of state violations – strategic advantage and normative restraint – are both incomplete. Each focuses on one half of the considerations states face in the control of violence at the expense of the other. Law combines the two views into one where calculations of self-interest depend in part on the reactions of other states and those reactions depend in part on shared standards of appropriate conduct. Norms and self-interest work together in law. Norms as codified in treaty law help actors understand what conduct is acceptable and the likely responses to unacceptable conduct. In turn, self-interest undergirds shared standards of normative conduct. Law reinforces this logic in two ways. One, treaty law specifies more clearly what acts are violations, supplying the precision that norms lack. There are acts deemed legal that violate the norms underlying and motivating that law. Two, states accept their treaty obligations publicly through ratification, which accepts a specific text as binding. They know when the other side has accepted such obligations and can judge whether specific acts violate those obligations, both of which aid in the formation of their own policy and their response to the acts of their opponents.

---

[1] Their model is multiplicative, so the effect of treaty status is to shrink civilian deaths to a percentage of the base. From their Table 1 (Valentino et al., 2006: 804, 366), the estimated effects are as follows:

Treaty status (joint ratification for the Hague Convention and unilateral ratification for the Geneva Convention) alone (from Model 1) = 41.6% of base rate (i.e. a 60% reduction in civilian casualties)

Treaty status and democracy (from Model 3) = 28.6% of base rate (almost a three-quarters reduction)

Treaty status and democracy and maneuver strategy (from Model 4) = 10.4% of base rate (90% reduction!)

The variables they focus on – strategy, war aims, and duration of the war – have larger substantive effects than treaty status and regime type.

None of this, of course, guarantees that states will live up to their legal obligations, but it does shape their conduct during wartime. Some states will seek to live up to their legal obligations because they see compliance with the law as in their interest. Humane treatment of prisoners taken may encourage enemy soldiers to surrender, while poor treatment induces them to fight to the death. Other states see full compliance as costly and a restraint on their forces in the field. They may seek to project the image of legality while they skirt the spirit of those rules, such as the British blockade of Germany during World War I. Still, other states believe that limits on violence during wartime are a hindrance in their efforts to win and so do not wish to obey any legal limit on their actions. The reactions of other states and their soldiers are the only mechanism for restraint in the latter cases.

These differences in how states view whether restraint is in their interest provide another reason for treaty law: ratification serves as a screen to separate those who do not intend to follow that law from those who may. States that see little interest in restraint have no reason to ratify treaties. When they do not ratify a treaty, then other states can infer their intent to violate the standards of that treaty. By setting a fixed standard which states can opt in or out off, the laws of war help states and their militaries anticipate what may happen when war breaks out. Joint ratification of a treaty in a particular issue-area creates a shared anticipation of efforts to comply with the standard of that treaty.

The anticipations of compliance created when both sides ratify a treaty also aid in the enforcement of that standard. Violations after a public acceptance of a treaty often lead to responses in kind. Sometimes, this reciprocity is direct, targeted, and proportionate, such as in the Shackling Crisis over prisoners of war between Britain and Germany in 1942. Other times, the reciprocal response comes through a general deterioration of conduct. The logic of war can drive states to adopt measures they would not have considered beforehand, in accord with Downes' view detailed earlier. Reciprocity also occurs on the battlefield. Some areas of the laws of war lie within the control of state policy, while others rest in how soldiers of both sides conduct themselves on the battlefield. The treatment of prisoners once they reach collection points behind enemy lines is an example of the former, while the risks of abuse or execution from the time they signal their intent to surrender to the moment when they enter a collection point exemplifies the latter. States and their militaries attempt to influence how their soldiers conduct themselves on the battlefield through training and discipline, yet the logic of combat can override those efforts. Atrocities provoke responses, which even the best discipline cannot eliminate. These responses on the battlefield provide a form of reciprocity outside the direct state control, a further possible consequence of systematic violations. Some states, particularly those that favor an unrestrained battlefield, choose to provoke such responses.

The scope for these violations by individual soldiers beyond state policy varies with the issue in question. It is smallest when violations can only be committed when authorized by central military and civilian authorities. Individual soldiers, for instance, lack the ability to use chemical weapons if their military does not provide them. The scope is largest for issues where each individual soldier on the battlefield has the ability to commit violations on his own initiative, such as treatment of civilians or prisoners. Other issues fall inbetween these extremes. For issues where the scope for individual violations exists, training beforehand and military discipline afterwards are the only tools available for command authorities that wish their troops to exert restraint. Each side then seeks to control its own soldiers in a parallel logic to that in Fearon and Laitin (1996), where each group punishes violators within its own members in order to prevent their violations from causing a breakdown into violence between the two groups.

This view of how the laws of war work in practice leads to the following conclusions about when states and their soldiers comply. First, joint ratification strengthens reciprocity and improves compliance, although it may not work perfectly. We should expect that the behavior of both sides is more likely to match, compliance for compliance, violations in response to violations, because both have accepted a common standard of conduct and can judge when that standard has been violated. Second, compliance on average should be lower for issues which provide a wider scope for violations by individuals.

Morrow (2007; 2014) provides systematic tests of these conclusions and other patterns in compliance with the laws of war during interstate wars of the twentieth century (Morrow and Jo 2006 provide a full description of the data set.) Each war was broken into warring directed dyads, accounting for those parties that fought under joint command. Compliance was coded for eight issues – aerial bombing, armistices and ceasefires, chemical and biological weapons, protection of civilians, protection of cultural property, conduct on the high seas, prisoners of war, and treatment of enemy wounded – in terms of the frequency and magnitude of violations. Each observation reports the conduct of one side toward the other on a specific issue. The two scores of violations are combined to create a four-level measure of compliance, from full, through high and low, to non-compliance: these four levels can be clearly distinguished in a way that is consistent across cases and issues. The compliance data is matched with data on treaty ratification, judged by the most recent treaty for the particular war, and a variety of other variables, such as whether the country in question is a democracy and the relative power of the two sides.

The statistical patterns of compliance support the argument laid out above (Morrow 2007; 2014). Joint ratification increases reciprocity and produces higher levels of compliance compared to dyads where at least one side has not ratified the most recent treaty. Average compliance deteriorates across issues as the scope for individual violations rises. Relative power makes little difference in compliance, although more intense wars have lower compliance when we measure intensity by the battle deaths as a percentage of prewar population. Democracies are more likely to comply when they have ratified the relevant treaty but their opponent has not, but they have the worst record of compliance when they have not ratified the relevant treaty. This pattern suggests democracies take their legal obligations seriously even when their opponent is not bound to observe the same restraint. Unfortunately, unilateral ratification leads to the lowest level of reciprocity and the worst record of compliance across the two warring parties. Clear legal violations trigger stronger reciprocal responses as one would expect if they clarify what conduct is unacceptable. The evidence, however, is weak because most violations clearly break the relevant treaty standard rather than fall into legal grey areas. States respond more strongly to violations committed by individuals compared to those that are clearly state policy, perhaps because there is some hope of inducing the other side to bring their troops under control in the former case but not the latter.

Further results support and flesh out this picture (Morrow 2014). First, violations tend to come early in wars, suggesting that states violate treaties because they see a clear strategic advantage in doing so. Reciprocal responses also come very quickly after those first violations, most within the first month afterward. There is no evidence of systematic retaliation across issues, such as punishing the prisoners taken from a side that uses chemical weapons.

Together, these results support the argument that public acceptance of treaty law shapes how states and their soldiers will act during wartime. Compliance with law is not straightforward, however, because of the variation in the scope for individual violations across issues and the difficulties such violations create for reciprocal enforcement. The acceptance of normative restraint combines with the strategic logic of war and the battlefield to make compliance with the laws of war more or less likely.

Comparison with Other Results and Arguments

How can we reconcile the results of others with this argument about treaty law and the incentives of war? All of the other arguments capture part of how law and strategic interest produce compliance or violations, but all of them are also incomplete. None of these studies, with the exception of Valentino et al. (2006) seeks to test the effect of law by assessing when states are bound by law and what those commitments entail. The research designs of Arreguín-Toft (2005), Downes (2008), and Valentino et al. (2006) focus on the country at war as the unit of analysis, making it difficult to test for dyadic relationships such as reciprocity and joint ratification. These designs do not directly test for reciprocity or how reciprocity varies with legal obligation through joint ratification. Both Downes (2008) and Valentino et al. (2006) examine how the character of the war influences civilian fatalities. Because the character of the war is common to both sides, these studies capture one element of the strategic interactions between the two. Legro (1995) also uses the warring state as the unit of analysis, although his case studies do examine the question of reciprocity in order to compare that logic to his argument about military culture. In short, these studies do not seek to test for the bilateral obligations of the laws of war, and so miss its effects.

These studies also do not find that democracies kill fewer enemy civilians during wartime, contrary to Morrow's (2007; 2014) finding that democracies are more likely to comply when they have ratified the most recent treaty on the issue in question. There is an important element of truth in their results: democracies have done some horrible things during their wars. They have used a variety of strategies in their efforts to win that have killed hundreds of thousands of enemy civilians. Democratic leaders answer to their own people, and their primary responsibility is to preserve the lives of their own citizens, including those inducted into the army as soldiers. Put bluntly, enemy civilians do not vote in their elections. But the observation that democracies kill as many enemy civilians as autocracies does not directly address whether democracies are more likely to comply with the legal obligations they have accepted through treaty ratification.

The picture is more complicated once we look closer. Both Downes (2008) and Valentino et al. (2006) treat all policies which kill civilians as the same even when they fall under different portions of the law of war. The British blockade during World War I may have violated the naval rules in the Hague Conventions, but it did not violate the provisions to protect civilians. The aerial bombing campaigns of World War II probably violated the provisions of the Hague Conventions concerning bombardment, but there was no treaty regulating aerial bombardment directly. Relatively few of the policies that kill large numbers of enemy civilians fall under the issue of treatment of civilians. Legal compliance has to be assessed against the relevant treaty standard, not just a general norm not to kill enemy civilians. Actions that violate a norm to not kill civilians are not necessarily legal violations.

Even though democracies adopt policies that kill civilians, they do not do so as openly as autocracies do. They seek to obscure the consequences of their policies for enemy civilians. The British government denied in the House of Commons that it was intercepting food shipments bound for Germany in February 1915, even though it had begun to do so (Downes 2008: 93). The blockade was also popular with the British public: the primary constraint was the possible reactions of neutral countries (Downes 2008: 96–8). Autocratic Germany, in contrast, was open about its use of unrestricted submarine war, again only constrained by the reactions of neutrals such as the United States (US).

Democratic leaders also often invoke retaliation to the violations of the other side and point to legal ambiguities to justify these acts. US leaders persisted in describing their strategic bombing of Germany during World War II as 'precision' when it was anything but that. The British defended their blockade during World War I as allowed under the law, including its expansion to cover food. All of these acts were popular with British and US citizens, in part because they were seen as retribution against an enemy that committed its own atrocities. When democracies kill civilians, their leaders describe it as a response justified by the violations of the enemy.

When democracies kill enemy civilians, they do not do so in clear violation of their legal obligations and commonly offer a legal justification to cover their acts, even when that justification may be a strained interpretation of the laws of war.

Protracted wars may provide the motivation to break the rules, but law and regime type shape how they do so. This is how law differs from norms. Norms prescribe broad standards of conduct without the detail necessary to judge which specific acts violate those standards. Law sets such standards subject to interpretation and application of those standards to specific cases. Further, law renders some acts legal as well as ruling some out as illegal. Strategic bombing that targeted the war industry could be argued to be legal even when its effect was indiscriminate city bombing. Parties can also interpret law in their own favor to justify their own acts. For the gas attack at Ypres, Germany could interpret the standards in the Hague Conventions opportunistically to claim that attack was allowed within the law. Finally, law cannot prevent those who will violate no matter what the sanction is. The law of war limits violations in some cases, but it cannot prevent all of them, much as the law of murder does not ensure a society free from homicide.

Legro's (1995) argument about military culture determining whether states comply also captures part but not all of the legal compliance argument. How a military prepares for war influences how it fights. Large organizations do not change quickly, so prewar judgments about how to organize and fight persist during wartime. Military culture affects compliance because it favors some strategies over others. Countries which invested in heavy bombers or submarines were in a better position to use those weapons, and break the norms that sought to limit them, than those that did not.

A broader view, however, reveals a more complex picture. The Luftwaffe engaged in terror bombing of the cities of countries that could not retaliate against German cities. Its culture of close tactical support did not foreclose this option. The British Navy may not have had a doctrine of unrestricted submarine war, but it was willing to breach the rules of conduct on the high seas after Germany unleashed its U-boats. The US Army Air Corps' doctrine emphasized precision daylight strategic bombing, but it abandoned that doctrine in favor of night attacks with firebombs on Japan's cities. Military culture shapes how militaries fight, but they can and do change how they fight during wartime.

Military culture is a product of decisions about how a military should fight. States accept limitations on how they fight because they think they benefit from them, particularly when they induce restraint from their opponents. Countries are more likely to ratify treaties that fit with how they would like to fight during wartime, and those countries will also create a military culture that fits with how it would like to fight. Some see restraint as favorable and develop the training and discipline needed to restrain their forces, others prefer an unrestrained battlefield, create a military designed to fight an unrestrained war, and refuse to ratify relevant treaties. States incorporate their ideas of how they should fight into military doctrine and culture in part to meet those commitments. Germany rejected limits on submarines and adopted a doctrine of unrestricted submarine warfare even though Hitler preferred restraint at the outbreak of the war. Britain wanted submarines outlawed but failed in that effort; it adopted a doctrine which used submarines in support of the battle fleet rather than attacking merchant shipping.

Once fighting begins, these commitments can shift. Violations by the other side, even those outside the control of central military authorities, provoke responses. The absence of clear legal agreement on what the standard is and the mutual public acceptance of it make misunderstandings and misinterpretations of what the other side is doing, and so how to respond, more likely. When military culture incorporates restraint and backs it up with military discipline, compliance by that military is more likely. Military culture matters for compliance because it reflects the commitment of a state and its military to follow the rules. Even with institutional restraints, compliance is not guaranteed in the face of an unrestrained opponent and an unclear standard.

The treaties of the laws of war aid states in restraining violence during war when they believe that restraint is in their interest. Treaty ratification acts as a screen to separate out those states that have no interest in following those rules. Ratification by both sides in a war creates a shared anticipation that both will attempt to fight in accord with the restraints of the treaty in question. Even with those anticipations and a clear standard, compliance is complicated by strategic calculations of advantage at the national level and reciprocity between soldiers on the battlefield. States can limit violations on the battlefield through training in the laws of war backed up by military discipline. Still, full compliance is problematic for the issues where soldiers have wide scope to commit violations on their own, such as protection of civilians. Treaty law assists those states that would like to comply to do so by creating a shared anticipation of efforts to comply and a shared understanding of what compliance means.

CIVIL WARS

Civil wars pose a variety of issues for the regulation of violence. Civilians generally are a larger proportion of casualties in civil wars than in interstate wars. Irregular warfare, where small units of combatants operate surreptitiously through a wide range of territory, fighting only when they choose to, is more common in civil wars. Even civil wars that are fought conventionally between formed armies in the field generate some irregular war, as the American Civil War did in Kansas and Missouri. Rebel groups may not be as well trained or disciplined as regular armies. Both sides may wish to target the supporters of the other side. The disruption of civil war may also degrade the rule of law and the authority structures that support and carry it out, leading to a rise in lawlessness. The key observation here is that violence and atrocities are used for strategic effect during civil wars; they are not 'wanton and senseless' acts (Kalyvas 1999).

Civil wars are fought over the legitimacy of the government; the rebels reject it in some form, contesting either control over the central government or the right of that government to rule in some portion of its territory, and assert their right to use force to end that control. The government views the rebellion as treason. Both of these complicate the application of law to violence during civil war.

Rebels often use irregular tactics and conduct guerrilla war to compensate for the difference in military power between government forces and themselves. Irregular warfare spreads fighting around the country and implicates civilians in it. In the famous analogy of Mao Zedong, the guerrilla is the fish that moves in the ocean of the people (Mao 1937). Guerrillas draw support from the people, indoctrinate them, recruit among them, and use them as their eyes and ears; they are the native element of the guerrilla. If the rebels are successful in living off the population or a segment of it, government forces may come to see that population as complicit in the rebellion and so a target for military action. Valentino et al. (2004) describe this as 'draining the sea'; denying the rebels the support of a potentially sympathetic population by killing them. They examine 147 cases of states at war, including civil, interstate and anti-colonial wars, from 1945 to 2000 for patterns of when states engage in 'mass killing', killing at least 50,000 in five years or less. These killings cover both direct action to kill and indirect actions that will result in civilian deaths, such as forced relocations with inadequate support, but exclude civilian deaths from the general chaos of war or collateral damage from legitimate military operations. They find that guerrilla warfare, conflicts based on issues of identity such as ethnic conflicts, duration of the war, and population that could be targeted all increase the likelihood of mass killing. Democracies were less likely to commit mass killings. Among the guerrilla wars alone, widespread civilian support for the guerrillas and the size of the guerrilla forces increased the likelihood of mass killing, while democracies were much less likely to fight guerrilla movements with mass killings. The increases in the likelihood of mass killing from irregular wars is massive; rebels who fight irregular wars with widespread civilian support are among 20 times more likely to provoke mass killing by government forces as conventional wars. Mass killing in their data is rare in interstate and conventional civil wars, while it is common in the guerrilla wars in their data. Mass killing in their view is the strategy of a desperate government faced with a resilient and widely supported rebel guerrilla movement. However, they do not examine whether mass killing aids the government in defeating such a robust rebel movement. Nor do they examine mass killing by rebel groups. It also does not explain how the killing occurs, simply when government forces are more likely to commit mass killing.

The nature of irregular warfare drives how and why both sides kill civilians in many civil wars (Kalyvas 2006). Guerrillas operate in small bands, moving about the countryside and regularly visiting villages in areas they control or contest. Some guerrillas live in the villages they control, farming when government troops are not around and taking up their arms only when they are. Because government forces cannot be everywhere all the time, they too patrol regions, moving from village to village looking for guerrilla forces in their effort to destroy them as an effective fighting force. Because the rebels do not operate openly, government forces require informants to help them locate the guerrillas when they patrol. These civilian informants may volunteer information or government troops may coerce information out of them, just as the rebels may receive material support like food and shelter from the civilian population either voluntarily or through coercion, such as 'revolutionary taxation'. Rebels in turn will seek to identify and punish government informers and reward supporters, both after government forces have left the immediate area and before they arrive. This war for information is waged most fiercely in the regions that both sides contest. The presence of both government patrols and guerrillas is frequent, and each side seeks to secure full control of the territory by driving the forces of the other side out.

Civilians are not passive actors in the war for information. Some sympathize with the government or the rebels and volunteer information and support to their preferred side. Others cooperate out of fear that they will be coerced if they do not. Still others will be coerced if patrols cannot get what they want from the population. Civilians then could be sympathizers of either side, supporters who shift sides based on which side is stronger at that time, or those who simply wish to be left in peace. Each side would like to target the hard core supporters of the other side, both to win the war of information and secure their control over the loyalty of the local population. The problem is determining who they are. Government officials are obvious targets for the rebels, but the hard core supporters of either side do not identify themselves when the soldiers of the other side pass through. Patrols have to rely on what the locals tell them, but can they trust who claims to support them and what those informants tell them? An informant could be a loyal supporter, an opportunist who wants to curry favor with them, or even one who wishes to use them to carry out a personal vendetta. Because they have to patrol across a wide area, soldiers are unlikely to know the allegiance of everyone in every village they visit. Further, civilians have good reason to conceal their true loyalties or change them as patrols of both sides come and go, so even prior experience may not be a reliable guide. Because civilians are the essential sources in the war for information, the battlefield logic of kill-or-be-killed often extends to include them. The war of information breaks down the barrier between combatants and civilians by implicating civilians in the use of violence.

The war for information often leads to atrocities. Those singled out as supporters of the other side may be executed, those who know where the other side is may be tortured for that information, and supplies may be stolen. This bloody business of killing on a small scale can accumulate to a heavy toll. That toll rests heaviest when control of an area is contested between the government and rebel forces. Both sides will be patrolling the area and pushing to distinguish their supporters from their opponents among the local population. Encounters with civilians will be frequent, and civilians will have contact with patrols of both sides, often within days, sometimes the same day. Talking to the rebels in the morning could lead to death at the hands of the government forces in the afternoon. Killing, when it occurs, seeks to discriminate and target the hard core supporters of the other side, subject to the difficulty of identifying them during a patrol. Still, these killings can lead to a substantial death toll if the area is contested over a long period of time.

When one side dominates an area, the soldiers of the other have little opportunity to move among the populace. The supporters of the other side will keep low to avoid detection. Atrocities will be rare. The side not in control of the area may engage in indiscriminate violence, such as massacres or bombings of public places. Government forces may conduct sweeps of rebel-held areas that lead to massacres of civilians in those areas. Terror bombings in cities or of gatherings also fall into this category. The key is that the attackers make no effort to identify supporters of the enemy and instead attack the general population thought to support the other side. These attacks seek to demonstrate that the side in control cannot protect their supporters from violence. The other side may have to concentrate its forces to protect their supporters, forcing them to move troops away from contested regions. Although these indiscriminate attacks may not be as frequent as acts of violence in contested areas, they too can produce a heavy toll among civilians.

Guerrillas typically operate in small groups, gathering together into larger units only for occasional planned attacks on government bases and towns. Government patrols seeking guerrillas also typically operate in small units. The low-level warfare increases the risk of individual soldiers or small units committing atrocities and war crimes on their own initiative. Control of these violations through military discipline becomes more difficult as the primary witnesses are those in the unit suspected of committing the atrocities. Mao (1937) saw the control of guerrillas as a central part of the strategy of guerrilla war. Guerrillas should pay for their supplies and treat civilians and prisoners fairly. Only volunteers should be accepted into the guerrilla army, and they must be trained in military and political matters fully to ensure their obedience, loyalty and restraint. Because low-level officers and ordinary soldiers will have great power compared to civilians, restraint can only come from within their ranks.

Irregular armies are organizations, and as such they need to recruit, train and discipline soldiers to their mission. Weinstein (2007) argues there are two polar models of what can be termed the industrial organization of rebel groups. One, call it the constraint model, is Mao's model of careful recruitment to select only volunteers, political indoctrination to ensure that recruits understand their purpose and the need for restraint, and control through military justice to deter those who might seek to abuse their position. The second model, call it the criminal model, accepts anyone, trains them primarily in how to fight, and allows them to do as they wish in the field. The extreme example of the criminal model is the Lord's Resistance Army which kidnaps and impresses boys to be soldiers and girls to be sex slaves for the fighters. Recruitment and training are essential to weed out those who seek to join the irregular forces for the power being armed brings. Again, internal control is the most effective tool for limiting violations by individual soldiers. Each model has its advantages and disadvantages. The criminal model makes it easier to generate and sustain an army at the cost of its discipline and the support it can attract from the civilian population. Outside support or local resources that generate profits, such as illegal drugs or alluvial diamonds, make the criminal model easier to follow because recruits can be paid and less cooperation is needed from the local population to secure supplies. The restraint model is also difficult to carry out when the local population is hostile to the rebels to begin with, such as for ethnically based rebel movements when they operate on the territory of other ethnic groups. The criminal model may also be more robust to changes in the political and combat environment because its appeal to recruits remains the same. On the other hand, the restraint model creates greater loyalty to the movement in its soldiers, which can aid when a rebel army faces a major challenge, such as the Long March was for Mao's army in the 1930s.

The two models imply different military strategies. The restraint model is, well, restrained in its governance of areas it controls and its use of violence. They may seek to explain their actions to local populations and involve them in local governance, even while asserting their authority. The criminal model gives license to combatants to do as they wish in the field, both in how they handle others and how they run the areas under their control. Both of these models are extreme types, and rebel groups can occupy the full spectrum between these two ideal types.

Both of these arguments address rebel groups that use irregular tactics, but not all civil wars are guerrilla wars, just as not all guerrilla wars are civil wars. Conventional civil wars, like many interstate wars, have front lines that define the territory that each side controls (Balcells 2010; 2011). There are no zones of contested control that give rise to the war of information. Within the area that either side controls, there can by sympathizers of the other, but they are likely to keep their allegiances to themselves. Those partisans of the other side that have acted publicly in favor of them are at risk of being targeted by the full range of violence. Partisans of the side in control of an area may use the opportunity to target their local opponents by denouncing them to the army in control. Violence against civilians by the side in control of the area where they live will be targeted on the opponents of that side. Those who support the side in control will be safe provided that the other side lacks the ability to harm them. Even when a warring party does not control an area, it may be able to attack civilians in the area through bombing, either from the air or through long-range bombardment of a city. It could also cut off supplies to the region through blockade, killing civilians through deprivation. Sieges of cities often combine these two forms of indirect killing of civilians. Parallel to the logic of indiscriminate violence in irregular war, indirect violence in conventional civil wars seeks to attack civilian support for the other side, to attack the control of the other side and to deny it the resources to conduct the war. The logic of targeting civilians in conventional civil wars parallels that of irregular ones, once we account for the differences in control and access to supporters of the other side.

Although both of these arguments about when violence is used in civil war contend that violence against civilians is often targeted and limited rather than random or indiscriminate, they do not imply such violence observes the boundaries of the law. Revolutionary justice rarely meets the standard of due process. Summary executions, where the victims are identified as enemies of the men with the guns, are the primary form of targeted killings. Public denunciation rather than a legal procedure determines the fate of the victims. If there is even a show trial, it serves to advance the propaganda cause of the killers, such as when rebels 'try' government officials before executing them, or when they seek to implicate the witnesses in the killing in the effort to hold their loyalty.

These public killings intimidate civilians while instilling a need to identify with the killers if only to avoid the possibility of retaliation should the forces of the victim return to the area.

Evidence on these Arguments about Insurgency

The evidence supporting these arguments is limited. Both arguments focus on micro-processes, those that happen on the level of the village or the small unit of rebel or government soldiers. Consequently, the tests of these arguments examine the details of particular cases where researchers have been able to collect those details. Kalyvas (2006) draws on the ethnographic literature of many rebellions for illustrations of his argument about the war of information and then tests his argument against patterns of killings during the partisan war in part of Greece during World War II. Weinstein (2007) conducts two matched case studies of pairs of rebel groups: the National Resistance Army in Uganda, Renamo in Mozambique, and the Shining Path in Peru, where the branch of the movement in the Upper Huallaga Valley adopted the criminal model because of that location's importance to the drug trade as opposed to the restraint model in the other regions of Peru. The key question of inference facing these micro-level studies is whether their conclusions are general of the process of violence in civil war or specific to the conflicts in question. Kalyvas (2007) criticizes Weinstein (2007) on this issue among others. Both books attempt to examine whether their arguments generalize, but a definitive study would require detailed study of a large number of conflicts, a study that would take many years.

The war of information makes targeting killing of irregular rebels difficult because they are hard to identify. Kalyvas and Kocher (2007) analyze those killed by the Phoenix Program, which sought to kill key members of the National Liberation Front (NLF, commonly known in the US as the Viet Cong) during the latter period of the US involvement in the Vietnam War. Potential targets were classified by the number of sources identifying a target as a member of the NLF and how reliable the information was. Kalyvas and Kocher show that those weakly identified as NLF members were much more likely to be killed than those who were strongly identified as such, using multiple sources with reliable information. This pattern suggests that the Phoenix Program killed large numbers of innocent or weak partisans as opposed to the hard core members it sought to target. The inability to target just the strong partisans of a rebel movement produces a perverse effect; because the risk of being killed if one is not involved in a rebel movement may be as high or higher than being involved, recruitment of rebels is easier. Many (beginning with Tullock 1971) argue that rebel movements face a collective action problem when they recruit new members. All share in the benefit of the revolution if it succeeds, but only the rebel fighters bear the risk of being killed during the struggle, according to this argument. But if uninvolved civilians face substantial risks of being killed, there is no added risk for joining a rebel movement, and the collective action problem disappears. This logic provides a reason for restraint by counterinsurgent forces.

The recruitment of co-ethnics or others with local knowledge by the counterinsurgent forces could help address the war of information. If the inability to distinguish rebel supporters from uncommitted civilians is the fundamental problem facing a counterinsurgent, those with local knowledge might be better able to extract that information from the local population. Lyall (2010) examines whether co-ethnic soldiers are more effective than soldiers lacking such knowledge when they conduct sweeps for insurgents. During the Second Chechen War from 2000 to 2005, the Russian army recruited Chechens and conducted sweeps with Russian, Chechen, and mixed units. These sweeps were often reported, particularly when the soldiers abused Chechen civilians. Lyall compares the frequency of rebel attacks after these sweeps, finding that those by Chechen units led to lower levels of rebel attacks afterwards. This difference may not result from greater restraint because Chechen sweeps were more likely to result in the kidnapping of a local than those conducted by other units. The ability to target the supporters of insurgents, particularly their families, could increase crimes, such as taking hostages to pressure insurgents in the field. Again, even well-targeted violence in the war of information often leads to abuses.

Abuse could also be part of a deliberate strategy to intimidate sympathizers or the potentially sympathetic population from which the rebels recruit. Leiby (2009) studied sexual violence during the civil wars in Guatemala and Peru using the records of their truth commissions. In both cases, government forces were more likely to use sexual violence, which includes humiliation, mutilation, and rape of women and men. In Guatemala, Leiby finds that sexual violence was generally used indiscriminately and publicly against many in villages believed to support the rebels. In Peru, sexual violence was more often targeted against individuals in government control who were either suspected rebels or could provide specific information under interrogation. In both cases, Leiby believes that the crimes were common enough that military leaders must have known of them and, at best, turned a blind eye to them. These two cases are an example of how military and political leaders could use the uncertainty produced by the possibility of individual violations to cover systematic policies of violations.

Bhavani et al. (2011) extend the logic of the war of information to multiple rebel factions where the government forces are stronger than either rebel faction and the factions control different areas. They test this argument on the three-sided violence between Israel, Fatah, and Hamas. Selective killings by the government should be greatest in areas of weak rebel control, such as those where Israel and Fatah share security responsibilities, with indiscriminate killings most likely in areas of clear rebel control, namely Gaza under Hamas control. The patterns during the period 2006 to 2008 support their argument; selective killings are most frequent in areas of shared control, while indiscriminate killings are most common in Gaza.

Balcells (2010; 2011) examines patterns of killings of civilians in Aragon and Catalonia during the Spanish Civil War. She finds that in areas under the control of one side, killings of those sympathetic to the other were heavier in districts where the parties representing the two sides had been even in their strength in prewar elections. Balcells (2011) also finds that Nationalist forces were more likely to conduct lethal aerial bombardments of cities under Republican control if the Republican parties were stronger in those cities before the war. In contrast, Herreros and Criado (2009) examine the number of civilians killed by both the Nationalist and the Republicans during the Spanish Civil War by provinces. They find that the Nationalists killed strategically to increase their control over areas, while killings increased in provinces when the Republic lost control over society in the regions they controlled. The latter killings were not driven by the political authorities, but rather by revenge or other motives.

Who Commits Atrocities?

Humphreys and Weinstein (2006) studied when combatants committed atrocities during the civil war in Sierra Leone. They surveyed participants after the war was over about the behavior they witnessed when they were combatants. This approach seeks to address the problem that few may be willing to admit to their own misdeeds by having them discuss what others did. From eight questions, they construct an index of abuse by the group that the respondents fought for, measured for both the rebel faction they fought with and the location where they fought. They found that abuse increased for factions that used material incentives to recruit fighters, that lacked strong internal military discipline, and that recruited across more ethnic groups, which they argue decreases solidarity within fighting units. Conversely, the local conditions of the region where rebel factions operated – its wealth relative to other districts, whether the group was operated in its home region, either in terms of geography or ethnicity of its fighters – had the effects we would expect, but those effects were small and were not statistically significant. Degree of local control – whether the district or region was contested – had little effect as well. This evidence is contrary to the argument about the war of information; to be careful, the scale in Humphreys and Weinstein (2006) measures how bad the conduct of the rebel faction was, not the intensity of killing.

Does Restraint Pay?

Both arguments, the war of information and institutional control, assert that restraint improves the chance of success in irregular war, particularly for counterinsurgents. If true, this would be a powerful argument in favor of restraint in guerrilla wars. Lyall and Wilson (2009) examined what factors lead to success in irregular war across 286 insurgencies since 1815 and concluded that mechanization of counterinsurgent forces decreases their chance of winning. This result could hold because mechanized forces might lack the local knowledge needed to use a strategy of discriminate violence. Their evidence about whether restraint aids the quest for victory is indirect as they cannot assess whether mechanized forces are incapable of using forces discriminately.

Kocher et al. (2011) provide detailed evidence of the harm of indiscriminate violence in their study of the aerial bombing conducted by the US during the Vietnam War. They combine detailed data of bombing sorties conducted by US forces with data on control of villages collected by the US Army during the war to examine whether aerial bombing led to an improvement or a deterioration of control over villages. The US conducted aerial bombing in support of ground troops during engagements with insurgents. Much of the bombing was indiscriminate because the munitions were not guided and heavy bombers, such as the B-52, carried out a significant fraction of the sorties. From the point of view of civilians in the neighborhood of these bombings, there was substantial risk of collateral damage and the simple terror induced by many of these attacks. They find that bombings during September 1969 shifted control away from the government of South Vietnam and in favor of the NLF as measured from July 1969 to December 1969. Bombing both weakened government control over villages within their control, and it strengthened insurgent control over those villages they controlled. Kocher et al. conduct their comparisons in a variety of way to address threats, drawing the inference that bombing hurts counterinsurgent control, such as the possibility that bombing is conducted only in areas that are already slipping out of government control. This is a specific, but important, piece of evidence that a lack of restraint hurts counterinsurgents.

A contrary view is found in Lyall's (2009) close study of indiscriminate shelling by Russian forces in Chechnya from 2000 to 2005. The Russian army had two bases in Chechnya that engaged in indiscriminate shelling of villages in lieu of close patrols and to disrupt insurgent activity. Unpredictability of the shelling, some caused by the drunkenness of the soldiers in question, made the shelling effectively a random treatment. Lyall compared villages that had been shelled to those that had not to see if insurgent attacks increased afterwards, after using statistical matching to secure the closest comparison between the two. This research strategy seeks to ensure that whether the village was shelled is the only difference between the two groups. Surprisingly, indiscriminate shelling reduced insurgent attacks in the two months following the attack. Further, shelling did not raise the chance of attacks in neighboring villages, countering the possibility that it provoked insurgents to attack elsewhere. This disturbing result suggests that indiscriminate violence succeeds in at least some cases. Indiscriminate violence by counterinsurgents could have two effects, one which aids the insurgents by making recruiting easier, and a second which hurts them by hindering their operations. It could be that the civilian population in Chechnya was already alienated from the Russian government through the earlier periods of the war so that the added provocation of indiscriminate shelling did not create more insurgents nor radicalize them further. Indiscriminate violence works in this case because only the second effect of hindering rebel operations matters.

Collateral damage provides another test of whether restraint is an advantage in irregular war. Civilians killed inadvertently are as dead as those deliberately targeted, and often it is impossible for witnesses to tell if reassurances that a death was an unintended mistake are sincere. Rules of engagement influence the frequency of collateral deaths by restricting how freely troops may use their weapons. Of course, this restraint may be costly if it limits the ability of troops to defend themselves in combat. Condra and Shapiro (2012) examine the pattern of insurgent attacks during the insurgency in Iraq from 2003 to 2009 to see if attacks increase after collateral deaths caused by the insurgents and counterinsurgent forces. They use the collection of death from the Iraq Body Count and separate out civilian deaths that are the result of collateral damage as opposed to sectarian killings or those where the perpetrator could not be determined. The collateral deaths caused by both sides are used to predict insurgent attacks at the district level (typically in the 100,000s of people in a district) in the following weeks. They find that collateral deaths caused by the counterinsurgent forces lead to a higher level of attacks, while those caused by the insurgents lead to lower levels of attacks, after controlling for the effects of different districts over time (such as the Anbar Awakening) and the tendency of the level of attacks within a district to be correlated from week to week. They attribute this pattern to the willingness of civilians to provide information to the counterinsurgent forces, allowing them to target insurgents more effectively. This pattern is strong in mixed districts, suggesting that the residents of such districts are not turning to ethnic militias for protection; if they did, collateral deaths by the insurgents would not lead to a decrease in attacks. The effects are stronger in Sunni districts and collateral deaths by the counterinsurgent forces do not increase insurgent attacks in Shia and Kurdish districts, which is consistent with the information argument, but none of these effects are statistically distinguishable from 0. Community engagement in the form of emergency response projects and funds do not affect the level of attacks. Condra and Shapiro ascribe this pattern as resulting from the war for information. Civilians are more willing to cooperate with the counterinsurgents when they see evidence that the counterinsurgent forces are concerned about their welfare. Limiting collateral damage is one way to demonstrate that concern. Insurgent killings may lead civilians to inform on insurgents, both to protect themselves from further risk of fatalities and to punish the killers. To be careful, they do not have direct evidence that collateral deaths lead to changes in the flow of tips to the counterinsurgents from the population. Restraint through cautious rules of engagement can carry significant rewards.

Does Law Matter?

As mentioned earlier, law plays little role in these studies of civil war. Legal obligations are rarely considered, nor the thorny problems of when rebel groups are legally bound and whether the lack of such an obligation undercuts reciprocity by the government, even when it is bound by Protocol I of the Geneva Conventions. Simmons and Danner (2010) argue that ratification of the Rome Statute serves as a commitment device that governments can use to reassure rebels that the ratifying state will not abuse them if they lay down their arms. They first show that democracies that have not faced a recent civil war and unaccountable autocracies that have faced a recent civil war both ratify the Rome Statute more quickly than other countries. Further, democracies that have faced a recent civil war ratify the treaty even more slowly than autocracies that have not. Their interpretation is that democracies take their treaty ratification seriously, so democracies that fear they may commit abuses if the civil war renews do not commit themselves to being subject to the jurisdiction of the International Criminal Court. Autocracies faced with a rebellion can use treaty ratification to commit themselves to limiting abuses in the future, a commitment needed to reassure current and future rebels. Simmons and Danner further show that treaty ratification by autocracies increases the chance that an active civil war ends, but not ratification by more open political systems. Ratification also makes the resulting peace more durable, evidence that the commitment reassures former rebels so they do not restart the rebellion out of fear of government abuse. This evidence is indirect but consistent with the position that legal commitments in hand with self-interest can help parties limit the risk of atrocities and the conflict the fear of that risk could produce.

CONCLUSION

The laws of war face two main threats to compliance, that warring parties will choose to violate them to secure an advantage and that they may fail to control their agents from committing violations. These two threats are often intertwined in practice as neglect of control can have the same effect as encouragement to kill and plunder. This chapter traces the contribution of the literature in political science on how and when violence is limited during interstate and civil wars. These two types of wars pose different challenges for limiting violence from the differences in centralized control of forces, whether the law has been publicly accepted by all parties in civil wars, and the higher rates of irregular warfare in civil wars. These differences contribute to worse conduct in civil wars than interstate wars, but compliance is problematic in the latter as well.

The research divides into studies that compare across many conflicts and those that look at the detailed record of specific ones. The former paint the big picture, while the latter are better at showing the causal processes underlying those patterns in a specific case. These studies, however, leave important questions unanswered. For example, do the laws of war reduce the costs of war, as Posner (2003) argues? Does compliance contribute to victory? Even Kalyvas (2006) and Weinstein (2007), two exemplary studies, focus on the conduct of violence during civil war at the expense of the two key questions of how civil wars start and what we can do to end them.

These studies also have little to say about the design of international law to limit violence during wartime. Instead, they focus on why warring parties commit atrocities. Surely the two are linked, but those links have not been drawn clearly. Perhaps attention should be focused on better ways to implement existing law rather than promoting new treaties or international bodies to enforce. Given that atrocities appear to be more common in civil wars, more attention could be focused on the compliance of rebel groups in such wars. Public scrutiny could help identify those groups who are more attentive to controlling their soldiers and limiting the worst violence. The International Committee of the Red Cross has sought to instruct armed groups in their obligations and rights under international humanitarian law. Encouraging rebel groups to create the structures of control that might limit violence might reduce atrocities committed by government forces in response. Still, any such effort still faces the difficulty that many parties still see atrocities as an attractive strategy during wartime.

REFERENCES

Arreguín-Toft, Ivan. 2005. *How the Weak Win Wars: A Theory of Asymmetric Conflict*, New York, NY: Cambridge University Press.

Arreguín-Toft, Ivan. 2001. 'How the Weak Win Wars: A Theory of Asymmetric Conflict' *International Security* 26, 93–128.

Balcells, Laia. 2011. 'Continuation of Politics by Two Means: Direct and Indirect Violence in Civil War' *Journal of Conflict Resolution* 55, 397–422.

Bacalls, Laia. 2010. 'Rivalry and Revenge: Violence against Civilians in Conventional Civil Wars' *International Studies Quarterly* 54, 291–313.

Bhavnani, Ravi, Dan Miodownik and Hyun Jin Choi. 2011. 'Three Two Tango: Territorial Control and Selective Violence in Israel, the West Bank, and Gaza' *Journal of Conflict Resolution* 55, 133–58.

Condra, Luke N. and Jacob N. Shapiro. 2012. 'Who Takes the Blame? The Strategic Effects of Collateral Damage' *American Journal of Political Science* 56, 167–87.

Downes, Alexander B. 2008. *Targeting Civilians in War*, Ithaca, NY: Cornell University Press.

Downes, Alexander B. 2007. 'Restraint or Propellant? Democracy and Civilian Fatalities in Interstate Wars' *Journal of Conflict Resolution* 51, 872–904.

Fearon, James D. and David D. Laitin. 1996. 'Explaining Interethnic Cooperation' *American Political Science Review* 90, 715–35.

Herreros, Francisco and Henar Criado. 2009. 'Pre-emptive or Arbitrary: Two Forms of Lethal Violence in a Civil War' *Journal of Conflict Resolution* 53, 419–45.

Humphreys, Macartan and Jeremy M. Weinstein. 2006. 'Handling and Manhandling Civilians in Civil War' *American Political Science Review* 100, 429–47.

Kalyvas, Stathis N. 2007. 'Review of Weinstein, *Inside Rebellion*'. *Comparative Political Studies* 40, 1146–51.
Kalyvas, Stathis N. 2006. *The Logic of Violence in Civil War*, New York, NY: Cambridge University Press.
Kalyvas, Stathis N. 1999. 'Wanton and Senseless? The Logic of Massacres in Algeria' *Rationality and Society* 11, 243–85.
Kalyvas, Stathis N. and Matthew Adam Kocher. 2007. 'How "Free" is Free Riding in Civil Wars? Violence, Insurgency, and the Collective Action Problem' *World Politics* 59, 177–216.
Kocher, Matthew Adam, Thomas B. Pepinsky and Stathis N. Kalyvas. 2011. 'Aerial Bombing and Counterinsurgency in the Vietnam War' *American Journal of Political Science* 55, 201–18.
Legro, Jeffrey W. 1995. *Cooperation under Fire: Anglo-German Restraint during World War II*, Ithaca, NY: Cornell University Press.
Leiby, Michele L. 2009. 'Wartime Sexual Violence in Guatemala and Peru' *International Studies Quarterly* 53, 445–68.
Lyall, Jason. 2010. 'Are Co-ethnics More Effective Counterinsurgents? Evidence from the Second Chechen War' *American Political Science Review* 104, 1–20.
Lyall, Jason. 2009. 'Does Indiscriminate Violence Incite Insurgent Attacks?: Evidence from Chechnya' *Journal of Conflict Resolution* 53, 331–62.
Lyall, Jason, and Isaiah Wilson. 2009. 'Rage Against the Machines: Explaining Outcomes in Counterinsurgency Wars' *International Organization* 63, 67–106.
Mao Zedong. 1937. *On Guerrilla Warfare*. Available at www.marxists.org/reference/archive/mao/works/1937/guerrilla-warfare/.
Morrow, James D. 2007. 'When do States Follow the Laws of War?' *American Political Science Review* 101, 559–72.
Morrow, James D. 2002. 'The Laws of War, Common Conjectures, and Legal Systems in International Politics' *Journal of Legal Studies* 31, S41–S60.
Morrow, James D. 2014. *Order within Anarchy: The Laws of War as an International Institution*. New York, NY: Cambridge University Press.
Morrow, James D. and Hyeran Jo. 2006. 'Compliance with the Laws of War: Dataset and Coding Rules' *Conflict Management and Peace Science* 23, 93–113.
Posner, Eric A. 2003. 'A Theory of the Laws of War' *The University of Chicago Law Review* 70(1), 297–317.
Price, Richard M. 1997. *The Chemical Weapons Taboo*, Ithaca, NY: Cornell University Press.
Simmons, Beth A., and Allison Danner. 2010. 'Credible Commitments and the International Criminal Court' *International Organization* 64, 225–56.
Tullock, Gordon. 1971. 'The Paradox of Revolution' *Public Choice* 11, 89–99.
Valentino, Benjamin, Paul Huth and Dylan Balch-Lindsay. 2004. '"Draining the Sea": Mass Killing and Guerrilla Warfare' *International Organization* 58, 375–407.
Valentino, Benjamin A., Paul. K. Huth and Sarah E. Croco. 2006. 'Covenants without the Sword: International Law and the Protection of Civilians in Times of War' *World Politics* 58, 339–77.

Weinstein, Jeremy M. 2007. *Inside Rebellion: The Politics of Insurgent Violence*. New York, NY: Cambridge University Press.

10. Behavioral economic analysis of international law*

Anne van Aaken and Tomer Broude

I. INTRODUCTION

Over the last decade or so, numerous compelling analyses of a broad range of questions relating to international law and institutions have built on particular assumptions of what may be termed 'perfect' rationality, roughly conforming to Rational Choice (RC) theory. This is the growing field of economic analysis of public international law,[1] to which the majority of contributions in the present book squarely belong. In many other areas of legal scholarship, however, the value and validity of applying such forms of RC theory to legal and societal questions – generally referred to as 'Law and Economics' (L&E) – has no less recently been questioned and contested by empirically grounded streams of cognitive psychology and behavioral economics (Colin 1999; Rabin 1998). These alternative approaches focus on observable, systematic, divergences from the perfect rationality assumed by standard RC (Ulen and Korobkin 2000; Zamir and Teichman 2014). Surprisingly, with very few exceptions,[2] these approaches have not been applied to international legal issues, and no comprehensive methodological framework has been provided for such international research.[3] In this chapter, we explore the

---

* This chapter builds substantially on the authors' respective writings in the field, primarily (Aaken 2014) and (Broude 2015). The authors thank Katherine Caballero for diligent research assistance.

[1] Any bibliographical list would risk injury by omission. For a partial literature survey see Sykes 2007. Important examples can be found in the 2002, 'Symposium on Rational Choice and International Law,' 31 *Journal of Legal Studies*; and in 2008, *University of Illinois Law Review*. Central treatises on the topic are Posner and Sykes 2013; Trachtman 2008; Guzman 2008; and Goldsmith and Posner 2005. For an overview, see Aaken 2012.

[2] For notable examples, see footnotes below.

[3] See contributions Aaken 2014; Broude 2015; and Aaken and Broude 2017.

potential for the applicability of such behavioral economic analyses to international law.

Generally, we contend that a behavioral economic approach, if employed properly and subject to appropriate methodological safeguards, can greatly contribute to international legal research, both by raising interesting hypotheses and theoretical applications relating to problems in international law and by providing frameworks for experimental and empirical testing, with significant explanatory and normative implications. A behavioral economic approach considerably augments, and in some cases supplants, the now common, if not necessarily commonly accepted, RC analyses of international law. In our view, behavioral analysis must be added to the international legal research toolbox of methodologies. The success of this approach will be measured in three ways: by its design and application; by the empirical and experimental work that will test the hypotheses it generates; and, ultimately, by the light it will cast on our understanding of international legal process and substance.

In making the case for behavioral economic analysis of international law, this chapter shall proceed as follows. In Section II, we will briefly explain the chief differences between standard RC approaches to international law and international politics, on the one hand, and behavioral economic analysis of international law, on the other hand. We will then advocate the need for the latter. Subsequently, in Section III, we will address several theoretical and methodological challenges to the application of behavioral economics to international law, suggesting a viable research framework that engages with these challenges and overcomes them. Section IV provides schematic applications of behavioral economics to selected issues in international treaty law, an area to which L&E has been extensively applied.[4] Section V concludes with general observations.

II. RATIONALIST AND BEHAVIORAL APPROACHES OF INTERNATIONAL LAW CONTRASTED

A. Rational Choice and its Discontents

What is a behavioral approach to international law, why is it necessary and how does it stand in relation to the L&E of international law? To

4 See, e.g., Parisi and Pi, Chapter 4 in this book.

address these questions, let us revisit the basic tenets of the L&E of international law. The most imperative of these is a fundamental set of assumptions regarding the rationality of states and other actors under international law. Studies employing standard RC in the analysis of international legal problems and systems typically adhere to conventional assumptions about human rationality and apply them *en banc* to states.[5] A classical definition of rationality, used by economists as well as L&E scholars, is given by Gary Becker: '[a]ll human behavior can be viewed as involving participants who [1] maximize their utility [2] from a stable set of preferences and [3] accumulate an optimal amount of information and other inputs in a variety of markets' (Becker 1976). The central precepts are therefore utility maximization, stable preferences, rational expectations and optimal processing of information. In traditional L&E of international law, these assumptions have been transferred without much ado to collective actors, such as states or international organizations.

Rarely are these assumptions qualified. The possibility of miscalculation by rational actors might be conceded by some rational choice analyses of international law, though not inconsistently with traditionally expected utility theory. Only decisions that are haphazard, arbitrary, random or otherwise a priori inutile are removed from the model. The latter cases are, of course, symptoms of irrationality, not of qualified rationality – divergences from perfect rationality are considered mistakes, not behavioral patterns.

Another halfway house example of a qualification of perfect rationality is the application of 'thin' rationality.[6] This is where states are deemed rational in their behavior, pursuing self-interest within a certain set of preferences, but those preferences are acknowledged as idiosyncratic and in accordance with their own emotional, cultural and historical charges, not by somehow 'objective' standards of utility or efficiency. This is a contextualization of state behavior that would appear obvious to traditional, regionalist or otherwise specialist scholars and analysts of international politics, but it is an important modifier to conservative economic analysis. Moreover, within the broader international legal research context, it stumbles upon the can of worms of cultural relativism, thereby making it highly contingent on specific assumptions about individual

[5] See e.g., Guzman 2005: 586: 'This Article assumes that states are rational beings; that they act in their own self-interest, at least as that interest is defined by the political leaders of the state; and that states are aware of the impact of their actions on the behavior of other states.'

[6] On 'thin' rationality, see Green and Shapiro, 1994: 17–19.

state or societal preferences and utility functions. However, thin rationality ultimately only calls into question what it is that rational actors seek to maximize, not the rationality of their decision-making with respect to it.

What, then, is wrong or problematic with the perfect rationality model of international law and politics? First and foremost, it is empirically unsubstantiated in two ways: concerning the preferences of states, on the one hand, and cognitive errors, on the other hand. Are states and other international legal actors perfectly 'rational' in reality, when they interact with each other in practice while making, abiding by, violating or enforcing international law? More precisely, one might ask, what is the *nature* of their rationality? Here behavioral economics can provide us with some answers.

B. Enter Behavioral Economics

Rationality studies have gradually evolved into the establishment of a behavioral school of economics that challenges basic assumptions of human rational choice, judgement and decision-making with alternative, empirically based observations on cognitive psychology. This is something public policy debates cannot ignore. Allowing these insights 'to bring new and more accurate understandings of behavior and choice to bear' (Sunstein 2000: 1) for international law is the current challenge. With a long scholarly tradition, cognitive psychology has led to analyses of domestic legal systems. These efforts are not without flaws, but they do hold great potential. It would be analytically and discursively productive to now merge them into a research area of behavioral economic analysis of international law.

Simplified, the central concept underlying research in this field is first of all, the recognition that human cognitive capabilities are not perfect or infinite, our rationality is 'bounded'. Second, the preferences of human actors are more complex. The human brain makes shortcuts in judgement and decision-making that diverge from expected utility theory. Limiting aspects of bounded rationality and the shortcuts taken to overcome them – generally known as biases and heuristics – inevitably cause human decisions that would be regarded as erroneous if compared with theoretically/perfectly rational decisions and outcomes. This should at least give pause to standard RC approaches to law in general and international law in particular, whose assumptions about the rationality of states and other actors are often distant from behavioral realities.

Momentarily setting this caveat of contingency aside, perhaps the single most important insight of behavioral psychology vis-à-vis economic analysis derives from Prospect Theory (Kahneman and Tversky 1979). Prospect Theory questions the validity of the Coase Theorem, which both expresses and relies upon the idea of perfect rationality. In Coasean economics, in the absence of transaction costs, the initial assignment of resources or entitlements is not determinative on their ultimate allocation. Cost-benefit bargaining between rational actors will assign the entitlements efficiently to the actor to whom they hold the most value, regardless of the starting point (Coase 1960). The Coase Theorem is elemental for classical economic analysis of law because it neutralizes the psychological contexts of human interactions. Indeed, it is the basis of L&E's overarching parsimony. However, experimental observations have shown repeatedly, in varying circumstances, that initial assignments of entitlements do matter significantly, in that they influence actor's decisions, and in particular, their willingness to part with their entitlement. In Coasian terms, $10 (or any other thing of value: in international affairs this could be territory, resources or other assets of political or symbolic importance) have equal worth, whether gained or lost or compared to rags or to riches. Yet in real life, people do not regard losses and gains of equal size indifferently. For example, they will often invest more in the prevention of loss than in the generation of gains of the same amount. This is the logic that underlies a variety of related terms that derive or are otherwise related to the ideas of Prospect Theory, such as loss aversion,[7] the endowment effect (Kahneman, Knetsch and Thaler 1990; Sunstein 2000: 211)[8] and framing effects.[9] Those phenomena might impede consent and cooperation, not only in contract law but also in international law.

There are additional psychological kinks in rationality that are systematically substantiated by scientific experiments in cognitive psychology. For example, under the availability bias, 'people tend to think that risks

---

[7] For the most comprehensive and thought provoking study of loss aversion in legal contexts, see Zamir, 2012.

[8] The endowment effect is also related to the phenomenon known as 'status quo bias', see Korobkin, 2000: 117.

[9] Framing effects arise when alternative descriptions of the same decision problem give rise to different preferences. Thus, in one classic example, people who have lost $10 on the way to the theatre will tend nonetheless to purchase a ticket, but people who have lost a pre-purchased ticket to the theatre worth $10 will not even go, though in expected utility terms, the rational decision should be the same. See examples in Tversky and Kahneman 1981 and 1986.

are more serious when an incident is readily called to mind' (Sunstein 2000: 5). Under the so-called hindsight bias, people tend to overestimate *ex ante* predictions they had made 'concerning the likelihood of an event's occurring after learning that it actually did occur' (Ulen 2005: 410; Fischhoff 1975). 'Probability matching' is a proven tendency of human subjects to make choices that match the relative frequency of events, instead of utility-maximizing choices that would presuppose the occurrence of the most probable (for example, when faced with a 6-sided die with 4 red sides and 2 white sides and asked repeatedly to guess the color that would be rolled, people choose red two-thirds of the time instead of the utility-maximizing solution that would choose red all the time) (West and Stanovich 2003).

Like Prospect Theory in general, the availability bias, hindsight bias, probability matching and other biases and heuristics hold important lessons for the design of law and legal process in a variety of areas. For example, it has been argued that the availability bias, compounded by social and political processes, makes risk regulators vulnerable to inefficient decisions (Kuran and Sunstein 1999), and that hindsight bias, in conjunction with other biases, means that increased tort liability for drivers will not reduce traffic accidents (Ulen 2005). Others have argued that probability matching supports employing a risk-based rather than a harm-based liability scheme in tort law, inducing individuals to behave more like maximizers than 'probability matchers' (Guttel and Harel 2005). Similar lessons exist for international law, for example in security decisions or negotiations (McDermott 2004).

These expressions of bounded rationality show that individuals are in many situations incapable of rational utility-maximization because of the way the human mind handles information and reacts to particular circumstances. In many cases, heuristics can provide very effective ways of reducing costs in decision-making, yet at the same time, they may lead to systematic and repeated errors.

Finally, to complete the picture, in contrast to RC's assumptions of self-interest, people sometimes deliberately act contrary to their own interests in the name of fairness in order to benefit or punish others. Evidently, in many cases, the human utility function includes values relating to the utility of others. In the literature, this aspect of human behavior is sometimes referred to as 'bounded self-interest'. The calculus of fairness in actual rationality also includes the expectation of fair treatment from others. Both of these aspects of fairness considerations can be demonstrated through consistent experimental results in 'ultimatum games', in which subjects regularly make offers and responses that diverge from the rational economic prediction. These results are preserved even when agents do not know each other and possible reputational effects or social contexts are controlled for, suggesting that fairness is not (only) a social phenomenon but one that is embedded in human rationality.[10] Furthermore, experiments have shown that individuals punish others even though at their own cost, especially in public good games or commons. This is highly relevant for international law and its enforcement and leads to more optimistic predictions concerning the compliance mechanisms of reciprocity and retaliation (Fehr and Schmidt 1999; Ostrom 1990; 1998) in comparison with the RC approach in public good and commons constellations.

C. Caveats and the Research Record So Far

Having said all this, it is important to understand that behavioral economics does not aspire to replace one ideal-type decision-maker (a perfectly rational one) with another (boundedly rational) one. Rather, the behavioral research agenda aims to explore the characteristics of real decision-making processes of different types of actors under different circumstances. So far various important generalizable characteristics have been identified, but behavioralists do not claim that they exist equally among all decision-makers in all cases and under all conditions. The importance of a behavioral approach to international legal research, therefore, lies mainly – but not exclusively – in its enhancement of the 'empirical turn' (Shaffer and Ginsburg 2012) in international law. Louis Henkin once asked 'how nations behave' (Henkin 1979). Hypotheses and methods from behavioral science can help in answering this question and others affecting the operation of international law (Chilton and Tingley 2013).

Behavioral research has already entered the domain of international law, employed by both legal scholars and political scientists. These include applications of prospect theory to international trade disputes (Elms 2004), discussions of psychological effects on reactions to mass atrocities (Slovic, et al. 2011) and applications of the behavioral availability bias to bilateral investment treaties (Poulsen and Aisbett 2013). A study of treaty design by Jean Galbraith (2013), ongoing experimental work by Emilie Hafner-Burton, David Victor and others at the University of California, San Diego (Hafner-Burton, et al. 2011), and an analysis of

[10] Respectively, discussing the role of society and culture in the development of behavioral biases and heuristics, see Mellers, et al. 2001 and Henrich, et al. 2001.

opt-in and opt-out 'negotiated choice architecture' in complex trade talks (Broude and Moses, 2016), all focus on behavioral traits of decision-makers. Legal theories about the development of customary international law has been tested by Christoph Engel and David Kurschilgen (Engel and Kurschilgen 2013). A forthcoming experimental and survey-based study regarding the ability of judicial decision-makers and treaty-interpreters to ignore information that should not formally influence them, such as *travaux preparatoires*, provides significant input on the impact of international legal expertise (Shereshevsky and Noah 2016).

Third, perhaps most importantly, though closely related to the former observation, behavioral international law is not, and should not be considered, a normative theory of law. Examining the way states, collectives and individuals engage within legal frameworks is first and foremost an empirical, descriptive, exercise. What we do with that knowledge may become normative (Broude 2015; Aaken 2016).

D. Meanwhile, in the Parallel Universe of International Relations Scholarship

When considering the current scholarship in the L&E of international law, it is important to recall that social scientists studying International Relations (IR) have utilized the same assumptions and similar methods of RC for over 50 years,[11] while international law scholarship mostly occupied distant methodological universes of doctrinaire positivism, 'natural' law idealization or intuitive 'policy-oriented' prescriptiveness.[12] After the Cold War, however, international legal scholars turned to IR theory for international law (Abbott 1989; Slaughter 1993; Slaughter et al. 1998),[13] and today, RC and economic analysis of international law are very much in vogue.[14]

---

[11] The 'realist' school that launched the disciplinary study of IR in the late 1940s in a Hobbesian tradition employed rudimentary concepts of rational choice by emphasizing the role of national interest in the determination of state behavior and state sensitivity to incentives presented by power relations; see Morgenthau 1948. Neo-Liberal IR theory built on the rationality of states and added layers of strategic thinking to state behavior through the use of game theory; see e.g., Morrow 1994; Snidal 1985a and 1985b.

[12] For a non-critical but comprehensive survey of traditional doctrines of international law, see Dixon 2004.

[13] For current evaluations of the IR/international law interface, see Dunoff and Pollack 2013 and Hafner-Burton, et. al. 2011: 51.

[14] See references given *supra* note 1.

Moreover, in the realm of behavioral analysis, IR theory has been using behavioral economics for a while under the heading of political psychology. In handbooks of IR, there is often an entry on the psychology of IR (Goldgeier and Tetlock 2008; Gross Stein 2002), and the beginning of this line of research is usually ascribed to a seminal article by Robert Jervis (Jervis 1976). Political psychologists in IR challenge realist theories which assume that states maximize power or security, as well as institutionalist theories, which assume that states maximize wealth or utility. They also engage with constructivism,[15] usually assuming that a lot depends on how human beings construct their world and their normative understanding (Wendt, 1995: 73). However, they presume that at a foundational level constructivism is more compatible with political psychology (Goldgeier and Tetlock 2001: 83). The call for 'behavioral IR' is well articulated (Mintz 2007).

Political psychologists in IR take the cognitive biases described above into account, arguing that bounded rationality, emotions, as well as procedural and distributive justice should be included and tested in IR theories (Goldgeier and Tetlock 2001: 68). They also test whether they have better explanations than either realists or institutionalists, both of which use the RC paradigm. The defining characteristic of the political psychology approach is the focus on the individual level (Jervis 1976), i.e., on central or elite decision-makers. They stress the contextual effects: history, development and learning, which are assumed to be important to dynamic political processes (McDermott 2004). Uniqueness of situations and the condition and contextual aspects of a particular decision-maker with a unique history in a specific situation is the subject of analysis. Explanation, rather than prediction, is the goal of the exercise.

---

[15] Constructivists stress ideas, norms and the management of the norms as well as the perception of fairness and legitimacy. For an overview see Adler 2002. Extensively, Wendt 1995. Critical IR 'theory', however, is not a single theory. It is a family of theories that includes postmodernists (Ashley, Walker), constructivists (such as Adler, Kratochwil, Ruggie, Katzenstein and Wendt), neo-Marxists (Cox, Gill), feminists (Peterson, Sylvester) and others. What unites them is a concern with how world politics is 'socially constructed', which involves two basic claims: (1) that the fundamental structures of international politics are social rather than strictly material (a claim that opposes materialism); and (2) that these structures shape actors' identities and interests rather than just their behavior (a claim that opposes rationalism).

As IR researchers are retreating from the analytical strictures of perfect RC (Mercer 2005; Rabin 2002), international legal scholars are discovering it. But rearguing intellectual debates subsequently settled in the IR discipline should be avoided, and L&E's venture into international law (although generating interesting hypotheses) has not always been backed up by empirical substantiation. Granted, hypotheses are advanced, but they have been rarely tested beyond anecdotal evidence. In this respect, economic analysis of international law can and should be salvaged by developing a more rigorous empirical dimension.

III. CHALLENGES AND METHODOLOGIES FOR BEHAVIORAL ANALYSIS OF INTERNATIONAL LAW

A. Key Difficulties in Applying Behavioral Theory to International Law

Several theoretical and methodological objections to a behavioral approach to international law can be raised. First, cognitive psychology and behavioral economics concern individuals whereas international law consists of collective entities: states. Second, cognitive psychology strengths are difficult to replicate in international law due to empirical observations from human subjects. Third, traditional rational choice analyses of international interactions are superior to that of bounded rationality. Though legitimate objections, they are not sufficient to reject the project of the design of research methodologies that incorporate behavioral insights in the analysis of international law. We deal with each of these objections in turn below.

B. The Individual Focus of Behavioral Theory

A behavioral approach to international law could be faulted if it made a simple leap from 'methodological individualism',[16] on which behavioral theory and research are premised, to 'methodological statism'.[17] There

[16] The term is used here loosely to refer to cognitive psychology's focus on the individual, without any statement about the theoretical framing of the relationship between the individual and society in the social sciences. For a comprehensive survey and discussion of this grand debate, see Udehn 2001.

[17] See e.g., the objection to the application of prospect theory to decision-making of states, in Shafir, 1992: 313–14. Notwithstanding the objection, for

are, however, three levels of analysis to behavioral economic analysis of international law that address this concern in different ways: (1) the state as a unitary actor; (2) decision-making collectives in international law; and (3) the individual as a decision-maker in international law.

(i) The state as unitary actor

This is perhaps the most difficult objection, but it does not hold. First, is a state any more perfectly rational than individuals? If the general rules of human behavior are captured by bounded rationality, the assumption that states conduct themselves within perfect rationality would be an exception to that rule. Indeed, there are good reasons to think that states are, in certain circumstances, less rational than individuals. If the unit of analysis is supposed to be the state per se, methodologies become more complicated.

Looking *beyond* the state, the argument against applying behavioral economic analysis to states shows that even if they naturally acted according to bounded and not ideal rationality, the international environment in which states act would somehow have a corrective effect, thereby becoming more perfectly rational. By being imperfectly rational, states would adjust their behavior accordingly.

When applying behavioral international law to states, an important methodological qualification is to seek systematic diversions from rationality in state behavior without assuming that those biases and heuristics found in individuals are replicated by states. States cannot simply reproduce particular individual behavioral traits. Thus, a behavioral approach to international law could focus on examining the decisions made by states from a behavioral perspective and not simply apply individual behavioral theory. Secondly, looking *within* the state, a state's behavior within international law consists of intricate social, political, administrative and legislative processes, yet this does not negate the subsequent treatment of the state as an actor with individually observable behavioral traits. A note of caution is necessary: most research does not take into account different institutional features of different states. This makes cross-country comparisons more difficult but also generates very interesting research questions.

Arguably, for bounded rationality to manifest itself, international biases and heuristics must be factored in at the domestic level. There is a

---

such theoretical applications in specific international contexts, see e.g., Levy 1996 and McDermott 1992, both of which apply prospect theory to state leaders and small decision-making groups, rather than to states as unitary actors.

substantial body of research and scholarship on the role of bounded rationality in domestic political processes (Simon 1985; Bendor 2010), as well as public policy and administration (Jones 2003). Domestic bounded rationality might play a part in the production of bounded rationality at the international level, but it is not essential for international behavioral analysis, for it does not necessarily reflect upon the overall rationality of the state as an actor in pursuit of those preferences in the international environment. In principle, states can be domestically imperfectly rational yet internationally perfectly rational. Conversely, bounded rationality might simply carry over to the international plane in other ways. How bounded rationalities interact with each other at different levels is not really known. For this reason, behavioral analysis of international law should be encouraged.

(ii) Decision-making collectives in international law

A second response to the objection based on individual behavioral analysis would look at behavioral collective decision-making within states that leads to outcomes in international law, thereby avoiding state-level analysis. Here, it is recognized that people or groups of people do make decisions relating to international law, not states.

There are debates surrounding the existence and effects of 'group-think',[18] and Prospect Theory[19] has also been applied to group decisions, foreign policy decisions and bureaucracies (McDermott 1998). Moreover, studies have shown decision-making biases in extremely large decision-making collectives, such as the United States (US) electorate (Berinsky and Lewis 2007). In short, there is room to seriously engage in the study of the rationality of choices pertaining to international law at the decision-making group level of analysis.

The state or other collective units interacting with international law could encompass behavioral traits observable at the individual level,

---

[18] A phenomenon where group decisions suffer 'a deterioration of mental efficiency, reality testing, and moral judgment that results from in-group pressures'; see Janis 1982; Hart 1990; and Whyte 1998.

[19] Prospect theory posits that under certain conditions, decision-makers are either more or less willing to take risky decisions: small probabilities of failure are treated as equivalent to zero, high probability of success is treated as certain, and losses are felt more heavily than gains. When states are in the domain of losses (e.g., Serbia 'losing' Kosovo), they are more likely to take an irredentist approach (i.e. they are taking more risk). When they are in the domain of gains (e.g., when Serbia is offered membership in the European Union), they are more likely to accept the status quo (Goldgeier and Tetlock 2001: 70 et seq.).

which might 'wash away' at the collective level. Possibly, internal decision-making settings have a corrective effect on individual bounded rationality which may lead to more perfect rationality at the leadership level. If selection effects of parliamentary politics or military command could be shown, implications understanding the rationality of group decisions in international law might have a relatively low level of biases and heuristics, thereby showing that decision-making groups are more rational than individuals. However, applying behavioral approaches to collective decision-making is not simple. The important point here is that behavioral research on international law can be analyzed at this level, thereby setting aside the 'individual methodology' objection to a behavioral approach to international law.

(iii) The individual as a subject and decision-maker in international law

A third response to the individualist methodological objection would be to focus on individual decision-making that relates to international law because individuals are increasingly direct addressees and beneficiaries of international law. However, application of *individual* decisions to international law faces problems, for behavioral decisions are directly relevant to situations where an individual makes choices among several external alternatives. Experiments in the lab, where the psychological insights into decision-making were first developed, are highly structured, and very few of those conditions that are present in the lab are present in the real world of IR (Levy 1992: 285). In classical international law, individual actions may be attributed, of course, to the state, giving rise to state responsibility under various circumstances (Crawford 2002), so analyzing individual behavior is important for understanding state behavior. Many cases of compliance or non-compliance with international law are ultimately made by individuals: for example, soldiers in the field, immigration officers, customs officials, legal advisors. Furthermore, individual decision-making in international courts and tribunals is of relevance.

In any case, it is clear that behavioral analysis of international law is not restricted to 'unitary' state behavior. There is a rich field of international legal issues that can be examined at the level of individual behavioral economics at state and group decision-making levels.

C. The Empirical Foundations of Behavioral Theory

Another objection surrounding a behavioral approach to international law is that the empirical and experimental approaches of behavioral analysis are difficult, if not impossible, to apply to international law. There are methodological difficulties in applying an experimental empirical approach to international law, accessibility being a main hindrance. The state cannot be put into a lab, and most researchers have limited access to the decision-making groups. Even if achieved, designing experiments that replicate the real-life environment of decision-making would be difficult. However, this objection merely underscores the non-empirical basis of most international legal research. There is a growing faction of legal scholars applying quantitative and qualitative empirical research methods to international law.[20]

A number of ways in which behavioral analysis could be applied to international law are based upon empirical findings, for a behavioral approach to international law is no different than general behavioral legal research. Following Tor's useful menu for research (Tor 2008: 272–91), behavioral insights on the law can be gained through three complementary channels: (1) theoretical applications; (2) experimental research; and (3) field studies (for a more detailed application and analysis, see Broude 2013). The strengths and weaknesses of each methodology should be recognized, but each retains an empirical basis and could be applied to different international legal puzzles, thereby showing that this objection is definitely not one that can stop behavioral analysis of international law at the threshold. There is no a priori reason to discard the idea of conducting empirical behavioral research in international law, for such research can be conducted in all three methodological streams in meaningful ways.

D. The Parsimony of Traditional Concepts of State Rationality

The final general objection to a behavioral approach to international law surrounds its high degree of contingency making it unparsimonious, in contrast to the parsimony that characterizes 'traditional' economic or rational choice analyses. This is true, but experimental literature has discovered many cognitive biases, which creates a danger in making generalizations in research. This critique would not, however, be unique to international behavioral analysis, and the response provided by behavioralists would also apply here. The parsimony achieved through rational choice theory comes at the expense of empirical accuracy and predictive power. Ideally, one should have both parsimony and accuracy. However, a

---

[20] See e.g., (a truly partial selection): Hathaway 2007; Franck 2008; Busch and Pelc 2011; and Pelc 2013; for an overview, see Shaffer and Ginsburg 2012.

behavioral approach to international law would be an addition to the arsenal of methodologies of international law. Therefore, the risk of a lower degree of parsimony in behavioral analysis is a methodological constraint to keep in mind in the design of research, but it is not a barrier to it.

IV. BEHAVIORAL APPROACHES TO TREATY LAW: AN OUTLINE

Rationalist approaches to international law often[21] use economic contract theory[22] when analyzing international treaties (Scott and Stephan 2006; Trachtman 2008: 120 et seq.; and Posner and Sykes 2013: 24).[23] Generally speaking, it is assumed that states will participate in treaties only if the expected costs of constraining their (regulatory) sovereignty do not exceed their expected net benefits from cooperation. Parties would write a '[p]areto-efficient complete contingent contract' (Shavell 1980), if there were no contracting imperfections, such as bounded rationality and unforeseeability, no transaction costs, and no enforcement costs. Such contracts would assign risks, rights and responsibilities in every possible state of the world. The context of the contract would be free of market imperfections, unforeseen developments and opportunistic behavior. In such a counterfactual situation, parties would, under rationalist assumptions, maximize their *ex ante* commitment, because there are no assurance problems. There are thus two essential questions. First, when will states enter into treaties in the first place? Second, if yes, how should treaties be drafted? In both instances, the rationalist answer is modified by behavioral insights. We will deal with both questions in turn.[24]

---

[21] But see Parisi and Pi, Chapter 4 in this book, who warn about the analogy between treaty law and contract law. Efficient breach is well known in international relations (in spite of the principle *pacta sunt servanda*). Furthermore, we believe that treaties are better analogized to contracts than to letters of intent – there are also behavioral reasons for that, e.g. the expressive function of law; see Cooter 1998 and McAdams 2000.

[22] For a short overview of incomplete contracting in a commercial law setting, see Scott 2006.

[23] For an application to World Trade Organization (WTO) law, see Schropp 2009; for an application to investment law, see Aaken 2009.

[24] For more detailed accounts, see Aaken 2014 and Broude 2015.

A. Consent to Treaties

The first question has a straightforward answer in RC, derived from more general theory on contract negotiation: states enter treaties if their participation constraint is met; that is, whenever they assume that the gains from cooperation are higher than the costs from non-cooperation (Korobkin and Guthrie 2004). Guzman argues, from a standard RC perspective, that the strict requirement of consent to multilateral treaties often makes agreement difficult to reach and therefore more forms of non-consensual international law-making should be used (Guzman 2012). As he explains, under the consent requirement of treaty law, a Pareto-efficient improvement in treaty law (whether reforms to an existing treaty regime, or the launch of a new one) would entail that at least some parties gain from it, but none are made worse off by it (in comparison to the prevailing legal situation prior to the change). In contrast, a Kaldor-Hicks-efficient treaty improvement would be such that the benefit granted to some states from the change would be greater than the disadvantage caused to other states; in other words, aggregate utility is increased, although there are winners and loser in a distributive sense (Guzman 2012: 758).

Guzman's compelling analysis 'against consent' assumes first that states will, as a rule, agree to changes in treaty law if they benefit from them or at the very least do not suffer from them (Pareto-efficient treaty reform); or if they are counted among the 'winners' from a Kaldor-Hicks efficient treaty change. In the face of these rationality-based assumptions, cognitive psychology provides a startling insight: all things considered, people actually have a tendency to prefer an existing state of affairs over alternatives that might leave them better off. This is the behavioral status quo bias. Experiments with individuals show that they disproportionately prefer the status quo over alternatives when making decisions: 'faced with new options, decision-makers often stick with the status quo alternative, for example, to follow customary company policy, to elect an incumbent to still another term in office, to purchase the same product brands, or to stay in the same job' (Samuelson and Zeckhauser 1988). This phenomenon is conceptually related to the endowment effect, in the sense that people view the existing state of affairs as an endowment that they value more than possibly improved conditions that they associate with risk and uncertainty.

What might this mean for treaty negotiation and adoption? What does it imply for the RC critique of the efficiency of the strict consent requirement in treaty-making? Generally, it suggests that contracts will tend to be inherently 'sticky', and inefficient, because agents prefer to keep the law as it is, lagging behind changes in their otherwise rational interests and preferences about the way the law should be, even in the face of personal, commercial or other developments.[25] The immediate implication is that states might regularly be withholding consent from new treaty regimes and treaty reforms, not (or not only) because they believe these regimes and reforms run counter to their best interests, but because of an embedded behavioral aversion to change.

Thus, where Guzman sees the consent requirement as the *cause* for an *observed* 'status quo bias' in international treaty law,[26] it might be that the 'excessive commitment to consent' that he decries (Guzman 2012: 749) is in fact the formal *result* of a *behavioral* status quo bias. States preserve the constraints of the consent requirement, because it enables them to pursue their (imperfectly rational) preference for status quo.

Many other cognitive aspects may be at play in the negotiation of international treaties, providing additional obstacles to the achievement of consent, beyond the rationalist Paretian framework that Guzman and most traditional RC analysts employ. Thus, from a behavioral perspective, Korobkin and Guthrie (2004: 789), in a study not focused on international law, find that some common heuristics are likely to influence a negotiator's decision-making processes in reciprocal bargaining. They discuss anchoring and adjustment, availability, self-serving evaluations, framing, the status quo bias, contrast effects, and reactive devaluation, all present in negotiators (Korobkin and Guthrie 2004). If the concession aversion is added to the list, this makes for a forceful argument for Guzman's suggestion – consent or the lack thereof may not be based solely on objective judgement and choice of negotiators but might be blurred, leading to bargaining impasse.[27] Behavioral approaches thus open up venues for new negotiation design and different forms of finding consensus, rather than cutting against the consent requirement.

B. Treaty Design

Let us now turn to how treaties are written and how they ought to be written. Since we do not live in a Panglossian world, complete contracts

---

[25] For a survey of evidence of status quo bias and an application to contract law, see Korobkin 1998.

[26] It appears that Guzman intends the term in a colloquial rather than behavioral sense: 'The overcommitment to state control over events creates a suffocating status quo bias that does more harm than good' (Guzman 2012: 790).

[27] Seminal on that topic, including the biases mentioned here, see the contributions in Arrow et al. 1995.

foreseeing every possible contingency are impossible to draft and even trying to come close creates high negotiating costs: contracts will be incomplete since they will fail to discriminate between states of the world that optimally call for different obligations.[28] Due to uncertainty,[29] parties cannot easily design contracts that maximize jointly beneficial investments and at the same time respond appropriately to changing conditions *ex post* which are a prevalent characteristic in international law, since most treaties are long-term.[30] Rationalist contract theory distinguishes between uncertainty about the future (unforeseeability), uncertainty about the actions of other players (asymmetrical information), and uncertainty about the meaning and scope of the contractual provisions (i.e. textual ambiguity and legal indeterminateness). Information asymmetries between the contracting parties pose the biggest problem: each party has information about itself (private information) that the other does not have, giving rise to potential opportunism. Contract theory thus analyzes problems of adverse selection, moral hazard, and verification.[31] A trade-off arises between *ex ante* strong commitment devices, on the one hand, and flexibility *ex post* in order to uphold the efficiency of the contract, on the other hand (Scott and Stephan 2006: 77). Anticipating this, the parties would want to incorporate flexibility to adjust the investment whenever future circumstances render the investment no longer profitable (for either side) (Masten and Saussier 2002: 286). To sum up, under RC assumptions, flexible contracts often are preferable to rigid ones (Fehr et al. 2011: 493).

Behavioral economics suggests a more differentiated view, although the behavioral economics literature on incomplete contracts is still relatively small (Koszegi 2013: 52). Hart and Moore propose an alternative and complementary view, arguing 'that a contract provides a

[28] This defines an incomplete contract as one that 'does not exhaust the contracting possibilities envisioned in the complete contract' (Tirole 1994: 743; and see Scott and Stephan 2006: 76).

[29] For a thorough treatment of uncertainty in international relations, see Downs and Rocke 1995, and for uncertainty in contracts as applied to public international law, see Scott and Stephan 2006.

[30] But see for structural flexibility mechanisms of renegotiation and duration of treaties Koremenos 2001; for flexibility mechanism generally, see Helfer 2013.

[31] Contract theorists distinguish between observable and verifiable information. The former can be observed by the two parties but it may still be that the information is not verifiable in the sense that the observing party is unable to establish the fact sufficiently to convince a neutral third party at reasonable cost, e.g., the investment tribunal. For details see Scott and Stephan 2006: 71–2.

reference point for the parties' relationship: more precisely for their feelings of entitlement' (Hart and Moore 2008: 2). A flexible contract is good in that parties can adjust to the state of nature (the rationalist argument for flexibility), but bad in that there can be a lot of aggrievement and shading[32] (the behavioral economics argument for rigidity). Flexible contracts permit so-called shading in *ex post* performance, while under rigid contracts much less shading can occur. Shading will occur if parties to the contract interpret 'their' reference point with a self-serving bias or deem contracts unfair. Although parties do not feel entitled to outcomes outside the contract, they may feel entitled to different outcomes within the contract.[33] If a party is aggrieved and shades, deadweight losses are caused. This has been confirmed in experiments: grievance and shading occur mainly within a given contract, not outside one (Fehr et al. 2011). Thus, whereas flexible contracts dominate rigid ones under RC assumptions, this is not necessarily the case with behavioral assumptions. Textual ambiguity can thus be problematic from a behavioral perspective, since ambiguity creates space for self-serving biases and other bounded rational behavior. It would call for avoiding textual ambiguity as an informal flexibility mechanism as far as possible and instead introduce flexibility explicitly.[34]

One of those flexibility mechanisms are reservations allowing states to exclude some norms of treaties which they do not like (for whatever reason). Rationalist approaches have been analyzing reservations from a game theoretic point of view, using article 21(1) of the Vienna Convention on the Law of Treaties 1969 (VCLT) as an explanation for why and why not states reserve (Parisi and Ševcenko 2003).[35] This rationalist frame was recently enriched by a remarkable study by Jean Galbraith

---

[32] Ibid.: 3 define shading as follows: 'Perfunctory performance occurs within the letter of the contract and consummate performance within the spirit of the contract. They suppose that a party is happy to provide consummate performance if he feels that he is getting what he is entitled to, but will withhold some part of consummate performance if he is shortchanged: "shading".'

[33] This is especially relevant for renegotiations. Psychologically, this means that a party is not aggrieved if the terms of the initial contract are bad, but is aggrieved if the terms of the renegotiated transaction are bad. See also Herweg and Schmidt 2014.

[34] For other explicit flexibility mechanisms see Helfer 2013.

[35] A reservation precludes the operation, as between the reserving and other states, of the provision reserved; and an objection thereto leads to the reservation being in operation as between the reserving and objecting state to the extent that it has not been objected to.

using behavioral insights in order to analyze treaty reservations (Galbraith 2013). She uses the insights of Sunstein and Thaler on 'choice architecture' (Thaler and Sunstein 2008), especially framing and default options. Drawing on a treaty database, she reveals an impressive correlation between framing and state consent: where states have the implied authority to reserve out of the jurisdiction of the International Court of Justice (ICJ), 95 percent continue to accept it; and where states have the explicit right to opt out of ICJ jurisdiction, 80 percent continue to accept it. In contrast, where states can explicitly opt in to ICJ jurisdiction, only a mere 5 percent of state parties do so on average (Galbraith 2013: 314).

Similar explanations for objections are possible. Not objecting to a reservation can be seen as the default option: states can either explicitly accept a reservation or implicitly consent to it by not issuing an objection within twelve months,[36] explaining the few reservations existing. Behavioral approaches suggest additional design options to treaty-makers. Now, states either allow reservations on all norms, prohibit reservations on all norms, or allow them for some and not for others in one treaty (cf. article 19(a) and (b) VCLT).[37] But a more fine-grained approach would use objections as a decentralized consent-oriented approach. For example, states could change the current default option of interpreting the omission of an objection as an implicit consent to another default rule where the omission is interpreted as an objection (opt-out rule). This would respect the consent of states while taking into account their biases and it would help in solving the problem of article 19(c) VCLT, which permits de facto (self-serving) auto-interpretation if there is no court available deciding on the question of whether a reservation is incompatible with the object and purpose of the treaty. The decentralized solution of article 19(c) VCLT can thus be used in the reverse: if a certain percentage of states does not explicitly accept the reservation, it might be deemed incompatible. This is especially interesting for human rights treaties and some international trade and investment contexts (such as opt-in/opt-out choice architecture in trade in services agreements (Broude and Moses 2016)).

---

[36] Vienna Convention on the Law of Treaties, art. 20(5), May 23, 1969, 1155 U.N.T.S. 331.

[37] See e.g., the total prohibition in the Rome Statute of the International Criminal Court, art.120, July 1, 2002, 2187 U.N.T.S. 90.

V. CONCLUSIONS

This contribution is but a start for outlining where research in international law using behavioral economics might go and where it might encounter difficulties. The goal is not to 'disprove' rational choice (or game theory) and their application to international law, but to use its improvements to inspire new theories and empirical research about international law (including in the lab). To use a coin minted by Einstein: 'Everything should be as simple as it can be, but not simpler.' And sometimes too simple can overlook important insights. In order to understand international law, RC might sometimes be too simple. Behavioral approaches are, we submit, able to generate more and better insights into the functioning of international law. They do not necessarily contradict classical RC hypotheses but may confirm or reject and refine the argument.

IR and international law scholars could use the systematic arguments made by behavioral economists and psychologists in order to understand the 'choice architecture' in international law, the norms and their effect in international relations. It might also help to understand internal processes and the behavior of non-state actors. Predictive power of behavioral approaches depend on what biases states (or elite decision-makers) are subject to and under what circumstances and aggregations mechanisms. The latter can be institution-specific or circumstance-specific.

Every good theory should be testable. Problems surely arise for methodological reasons but surely also due to lack of data. Being aware of the problems does not imply not trying to solve them: by experimental research, by qualitative case studies or large-n studies. This has to be done step by step, analyzing different fields of general and special international law. Only this way can the research be convincing. After all, it will be the empirics that will validate (or not) the research hypotheses advanced by any theory.

REFERENCES

Aaken, Anne van. 2016. 'Towards a Psychological Concept of Law', in Stephan Kirste and Michael Anderheideneds. Eds. *Interdisziplinarität der Rechtswissenschaften*. Berlin: Duncker&Humblot.

Aaken, Anne van. 2014. 'Behavioral International Law and Economics,' 55(2) *Harvard International Law Journal* 421–81.

Aaken, Anne van. 2012. 'International Law: Rational Choice', in: *Oxford Bibliographies Online*. Oxford University Press. Available at: http://oxfordindex.oup.com/view/10.1093/obo/9780199796953-0051.

Aaken, Anne van. 2009. 'International Investment Law Between Commitment and Flexibility: A Contract Theory Analysis,' 12(2) *Journal of International Economic Law*, 507–38.

Aaken, Anne van and Tomer Broude. 2018 (forthcoming). *Behavioral Economics and International Law*. Oxford: Oxford University Press.

Abbott, Kenneth W. 1989. 'Modern International Relations Theory: A Prospectus for International Lawyers,' 14 *Yale Journal of International Law* 335.

Adler, Emanuel. 2002. 'Constructivism and International Relations,' in Walter Carlsnaes, Thomas Risse and Beth Simmons. eds. *Handbook of International Relations*. SAGE Publications.

Arrow, K. J., R. H. Mnookin, L. Ross, A. Tversky and R. Wilson. eds. 1995. *Barriers to Conflict Resolution*. New York, NY: W.W. Norton.

Becker, Gary S. 1976. *The Economic Approach to Human Behavior*. Chicago, IL: University of Chicago Press.

Bendor, Jonathan. 2010. *Bounded Rationality and Politics*. Berkeley, CA: University of California Press.

Berinsky, Adam J. and Jeffrey B. Lewis. 2007. 'An Estimate of Risk Aversion in the U.S. Electorate,' 22(2) *Quarterly Journal of Political Science* 139.

Broude, Tomer. 2015. 'Behavioral International Law,' 163 *University of Pennsylvania Law Review* 1099.

Broude, Tomer and Shai Moses. 2016 (forthcoming). 'The Behavioral Dynamics of Positive and Negative Listing in Services Trade Liberalization: A Look at the Trade in Services Agreement (TiSA) Negotiations', in Martin Roy and Pierre Sauvé. eds., *Research Handbook on Trade in Services*. London: Edward Elgar.

Busch, Marc L. and Krzysztof Pelc. 2011. 'Ruling Not to Rule: The Use of Judicial Economy at the WTO,' in Tomer Broude, Marc L. Busch and Amelia Porges. eds. *The Politics of International Economic Law*. Cambridge: Cambridge University Press.

Chilton, Adam S. and Dustin H. Tingley. 2013. 'Why the Study of International Law Needs Experiments,' 52 *Columbia Journal of Transnational Law* 173.

Coase, Ronald H. 1960. 'The Problem of Social Cost,' 3 *Journal of Law and Economics* 1.

Colin, Camerer. 1999. 'Behavioral Economics: Reunifying Psychology and Economics,' 96(19) *Proceedings of the National Academy of Sciences* 10575–7.

Cooter, Robert D. 1998. 'Expressive Law and Economics,' 27 *Journal of Legal Studies* 585–608.

Crawford, James. 2002. *The International Law Commission's Articles on State Responsibility: Introduction, Text and Commentaries*. Cambridge: Cambridge University Press.

Dixon, Martin. 2004. *Textbook on International Law*. Oxford: Oxford University Press. ch. 1.

Downs, George W. and David M. Rocke. 1995. *Optimal Imperfection? Domestic Uncertainty and Institutions in International Relations*. Princeton, NJ: Princeton University Press.

Dunoff, Jeffrey L. and Mark A. Pollack. 2013. 'International Law and International Relations: Introducing an Interdisciplinary Dialogue,' in Jeffrey L.

Dunoff and Mark A. Pollock. eds. *Interdisciplinary Perspectives on International Law and International Relations: The State of the Art*. New York, NY: Cambridge University Press.

Elms, Deborah Kay. 2004. 'Large Costs, Small Benefits: Explaining Trade Dispute Outcomes,' 25 *Political Psychology* 241–70.

Engel, Christopher and Michael Kurschilgen. 2013. 'The Coevolution of Behavior and Normative Expectations: An Experiment,' 15 *American Law and Economic Review* 578–609.

Fehr, Ernst, Oliver Hart and Christian Zehnder. 2011. 'Contracts as Reference Points – Experimental Evidence,' 101 *American Economic Review* 493–525.

Fehr, Ernst and Klaus M. Schmidt. 1999. 'A Theory of Fairness, Competition, and Cooperation,' 114 *Quarterly Journal of Economics* 817–68.

Fischhoff, Baruch. 1975. 'Hindsight is Not Equal to Foresight: The Effect of Outcome Knowledge on Judgment under Uncertainty,' 1 *Journal of Experimental Psychology Human: Perception and Performance* 288.

Franck, Susan D. 2008. 'Empiricism and International Law: Insights for Investment Treaty Dispute Resolution,' 48(4) *Virginia Journal of International Law* 767.

Galbraith, Jean. 2013. 'Treaty Options: Towards a Behavioral Understanding of Treaty Design,' 53 *Virginia Journal of International Law* 309.

Goldgeier, James and Philip Tetlock. 2008. 'Psychological Approaches,' in C. Reus-Smit and D. Snidal. eds. *Oxford Handbook of International Relations*. Oxford: Oxford University Press.

Goldgeier, James and Philip Tetlock. 2001. 'Psychology and International Relations Theory,' 4 *Annual Review of Political Science* 67.

Goldsmith, Jack L. and Eric A. Posner. 2005. *The Limits of International Law*. Oxford: Oxford University Press.

Green, Donald P. and Ian Shapiro. 1994. *Pathologies of Rational Choice Theory*. New Haven, CT: Yale University Press.

Gross Stein, Janice. 2002. 'Psychological Explanations of International Conflict,' in Walter Carlsnaes et al. eds. *Handbook of International Relations*. SAGE Publications.

Guttel, Ehud and Alon Harel. 2005. 'Matching Probabilities: The Behavioral Law and Economics of Repeated Behavior,' 72 *University of Chicago Law Review* 1197.

Guzman, Andrew T. 2012. 'Against Consent,' 52 *Virginia Journal of International Law* 747–90.

Guzman, Andrew T. 2008. *How International Law Works: A Rational Choice Theory*. Oxford: Oxford University Press.

Guzman, Andrew T. 2005. 'The Design of International Agreements,' 16 *European Journal of International Law* 579.

Hafner-Burton, Emilie M., David G. Victor and Yonatan Lupu. 2011. 'Political Science Research on International Law: The State of the Field,' 106 *American Journal of International Law* 47.

Hart, Oliver and John Moore. 2008. 'Contracts as Reference Points,' 123(1) *Quarterly Journal of Economics* 1–48.

Hart, Paul T. 1990. *Groupthink in Government: A Study of Small Groups and Policy Failure*. Baltimore, MD: Johns Hopkins University Press.

Hathaway, Oona A. 2007. 'Why Do Nations Join Human Rights Treaties?' 51(4) *Journal of Conflict Resolution* 588.

Helfer, Larry R. 2013. 'Flexibility in International Agreements,' in Jeffery L. Dunoff and Mark A. Pollack. eds. *Interdisciplinary Perspectives on International Law and International Relations: The State of the Art*. Cambridge: Cambridge University Press.

Henkin, Louis. 1979. *How Nations Behave: Law and Foreign Policy*. New York, NY: Columbia University Press.

Henrich, Joseph, Peyton Young, Robert Boyd, Kevin McCabe, Wulf Albers, Axel Ockenfels and Gerd Gigerenzer. 2001. 'Group Report: What is the Role of Culture in Bounded Rationality?' in Gerd Gigerenzer and Reinhard Selten. eds. *Bounded Rationality: The Adaptive Toolbox*. Boston, MA: The MIT Press.

Herweg, Fabian and Klaus M. Schmidt. 2014. 'Loss Aversion and Ex Post Inefficient Renegotiation,' *Review of Economic Studies* 1, 1–38. Available at www.restud.com/wp-content/uploads/2014/08/MS17501manuscript.pdf

Janis, Irving L. 1982. *Groupthink: Psychological Studies of Policy Decisions and Fiascoes*. Boston, MA: Houghton Mifflin Company.

Jervis, Robert. 1976. *Perception and Misperception in International Politics*. Princeton, NJ: Princeton University Press.

Jones, Bryan D. 2003. 'Bounded Rationality and Political Science: Lessons from Public Administration and Public Policy,' 13(4) *Journal of Public Research and Theory* 395.

Kahneman, Daniel and Amos Tversky. 1979. 'Prospect Theory: An Analysis of Decision under Risk,' 47(2) *Econometrica* 263–91.

Kahneman, Daniel, Jack L. Knetsch and Richard H. Thaler. 1990. 'Experimental Tests of the Endowment Effect and the Coase Theorem,' 98 *Journal of Political Economy* 1325.

Koremenos, Barbara. 2001. 'Loosening the Ties that Bind: A Learning Model of Agreement Flexibility,' 55(2) *International Organization* 289–325.

Korobkin, Russell. 2000. 'Behavioral Economics, Contract Formation, and Contract Law,' in Cass Sunstein. ed. *Behavioral Law and Economics*. Cambridge: Cambridge University Press.

Korobkin, Russell. 1998. 'The Status Quo Bias and Contract Default Rules', 83 *Cornell Law Review* 608.

Korobkin, Russell, and Chris Guthrie. 2004. 'Heuristics and Biases at the Bargaining Table,' 87 *Marquette Law Review* 795–808.

Koszegi, Botond. 2013. 'Behavioral Contract Theory,' working paper. Available at: www. personal.ceu.hu/ staff/Botond_Koszegi/JEL_Behavioral_Contract_Theory.pdf.

Kuran, Timur, and Cass R. Sunstein. 1999. 'Availability Cascades and Risk Regulation,' 51 *Stanford Law Review* 683.

Levy, Jack S. 1996. 'Loss Aversion, Framing, and Bargaining: The Implications of Prospect Theory for International Conflict,' 17 *International Political Science Review* 178.

Levy, Jack S. 1992. 'Prospect Theory and International Relations: Theoretical Applications and Analytical Problems,' 13 *Political Psychology* 283.

Masten, Scott E. and Stephane Saussier. 2002. 'Econometrics of Contracts: An Assessment of Developments in the Empirical Literature on Contracting,' in E.

Brousseau and J. M. Glachant. eds. *The Economics of Contracts, Theory and Applications*. Cambridge: Cambridge University Press.
McAdams, Richard H. 2000. 'A Focal Point Theory of Expressive Law,' 86 *Virginia Law Review* 1649–1729.
McDermott, Rose. 2004. *Political Psychology in International Relations*. Ann Arbor: University of Michigan Press.
McDermott, Rose. 1998. *Risk-Taking in International Politics: Prospect Theory in American Foreign Policy*. Ann Arbor: University of Michigan Press.
McDermott, Rose. 1992. 'Prospect Theory in International Relations: The Iranian Hostage Rescue Mission,' 13 *Political Psychology* 237–63. Available at www.jstor.org/stable/3791680.
Mellers, Barbara A., et al. 2001. 'Group Report: Effects of Emotions and Social Processes on Bounded Rationality,' in Gerd Gigerenzer and Reinhard Selten. eds. *Bounded Rationality: The Adaptive Toolbox*. Boston, MA: The MIT Press.
Mercer, Jonathan. 2005. 'Rationality and Psychology in International Politics,' 59 *International Organization* 77–106.
Mintz, Alex. 2007. 'Behavioral IR as a Subfield of International Relations,' 9 *International Studies Review* 157.
Morgenthau, Hans J. 1948. *Politics Among Nations: The Struggle for Power and Peace*. McGraw-Hill.
Morrow, James. 1994. 'Modeling the Forms of International Cooperation: Distribution versus Information,' 48 *Interest Organization* 387.
Ostrom, Eleonor. 1998. 'A Behavioral Approach to the Rational Choice Theory of Collective Action – Presidential Address of the American Political Science Association 1997,' 92 *American Political Science Review* 1.
Ostrom, Eleonor. 1990. *Governing the Commons: The Evolution of Institutions for Collective Action*. Cambridge: Cambridge University Press.
Parisi, Francesco and Catherine Ševcenko. 2003. 'Treaty Reservations and the Economics of Article 21(1) of the Vienna Convention,' 21(1) *Berkeley Journal of International law* 1-26.
Pelc, Krzysztof. 2013. 'Googling the WTO: What Search Engine Data Tell Us about the Political Economy of Institutions,' 67(3) *International Organization* 629.
Posner, Eric A. and Alan O. Sykes. 2013. *Economic Foundations of International Law*. Cambridge, MA: Belknap Press.
Poulsen, Lauge N. and Emma Aisbett 2013. 'When the Claim Hits: Bilateral Investment Treaties and Bounded Rational Learning,' 65 *World Politics* 273–313.
Rabin, Matthew. 2002. 'A Perspective on Psychology and Economics,' 45 *European Economic Review* 657.
Rabin, Matthew. 1998. 'Psychology and Economics,' 36 *Journal of Economic Literature* 11.
Samuelson, William and Richard Zeckhauser. 1988. 'Status Quo Bias in Decision Making', 1 *Journal of Risk and Uncertainty* 7.
Schropp, Simon. 2009. *Trade Policy Flexibility and Enforcement in the WTO. A Law and Economics Analysis*. Cambridge: Cambridge University Press.
Scott, Robert E. 2006. 'The Law and Economics of Incomplete Contracts,' 2 *Annual Review of Law and Social Science* 279–97.

Scott, Robert E. and Paul B. Stephan. 2006. *The Limits of Leviathan. Contract Theory and the Enforcement of International Law*. Cambridge: Cambridge University Press.
Shaffer, Gregory and Tom Ginsburg. 2012. 'The Empirical Turn in International Legal Scholarship,' 106 *The American Journal of International Law* 1–4.
Shafir, Eldar. 1992. 'Prospect Theory and Political Analysis: A Psychological Perspective,' 13 *Political Psychology* 311.
Shavell, Steven. 1980. 'Damage Measures for Breach of Contract,' 11(2) *Bell Journal of Economics* 466–90.
Shereshevsky, Yahli and Tom Noah. 2016. 'How does Exposure to Preparatory Work Affect Treaty Interpretation: A Behavioral Study' (mimeo on file with authors).
Simon, Herbert A. 1985. 'Human Nature in Politics: The Dialogue of Psychology with Political Science,' 79 *American Political Science Review* 293.
Slaughter, Anne-Marie. 1993. 'International Law and International Relations Theory: A Dual Agenda,' 87 *American Journal of International Law* 205.
Slaughter, Anne-Marie, Andrew S. Tulumelloh and Stepan Wood. 1998. 'International Law and International Relations: A New Generation of Interdisciplinary Scholarship,' 92 *American Journal of International Law* 367.
Slovic, Paul, David Zionts, Andrew K. Woods, Ryan Goodman and Derek Jinks. 2011. 'Psychic Numbing and Mass Atrocity,' in E. Shafir. ed. *The Behavioral Foundations of Public Policy*. Princeton NJ: Princeton University Press.
Snidal, Duncan. 1985a. 'Coordination versus Prisoners' Dilemma: Implications for International Cooperation,' 79 *American Political Science Review* 923.
Snidal, Duncan. 1985b. 'The Game Theory of International Politics,' 38(1) *World Politics* 25–57.
Sunstein, Cass R. 2000. *Behavioral Law and Economics*. Cambridge: Cambridge University Press.
Sykes, Alan O. 2007. 'International Law,' in Mitchell A. Polinsky and Steven Shavell. eds. *Handbook of Law and Economics*, Boston, MA: North Holland.
Thaler, Richard H. and Cass R. Sunstein. 2008. *Nudge: Improving Decisions about Health, Wealth, and Happiness*. New Haven CT: Yale University Press.
Tirole, Jean. 1994. 'Incomplete Contracts: Where Do We Stand?' 67 *Econometrica* 741.
Tor, Avishalom. 2008. 'The Methodology of the Behavioral Analysis of Law,' 4 *Haifa Law Review* 237.
Trachtman, Joel P. 2008. *The Economic Structure of International Law*. Cambridge MA: Harvard University Press.
Tversky, Amos and Daniel Kahneman. 1986. 'Rational Choice and the Framing of Decisions,' 59(4) *Journal of Business* 5251.
Tversky, Amos and Daniel Kahneman. 1981. 'The Framing of Decisions and the Psychology of Choice,' 211 *Science* 453.
Udehn, Lars. 2001. *Methodological Individualism: Background and Meaning*. London: Routledge.
Ulen, Thomas S. 2005. 'Human Fallibility and the Forms of the Law: The Case of Traffic Safety,' in Francesco Parisi and Vernon Smith. eds. *The Law and Economics of Irrational Behavior*. Stanford, CA: Stanford University Press.

Ulen, Thomas S. and Russell B. Korobkin. 2000. 'Law and Behavioral Science: Removing the Rationality Assumption from Law and Economics,' 88(4) *California Law Review* 1051.

Wendt, Alexander. 1995. 'Constructing International Politics,' 20 *Interest Securities* 71–81.

West, Richard F. and Keith E. Stanovich. 2003. 'Is Probability Matching Smart? Associations between Probabilistic Choices and Cognitive Ability,' 31(2) *Memory and Cognition* 243.

Whyte, Glen. 1998. 'Recasting Janis's Groupthink Model: The Key Role of Collective Efficacy in Decision Fiascoes,' 73 *Organizational Behavior and Human Decision Process* 185.

Zamir, Eyal. 2012. 'Loss Aversion and the Law,' 65(3) *Vanderbilt Law Review* 829.

Zamir, Eyal and Doron Teichman. 2014. 'Judicial Decision making: A Behavioral Perspective,' in Eyal Zamir and Doron Teichman. eds. *The Oxford Handbook of Behavioral Economics and the Law*. Oxford: Oxford University Press.

Index